RISE OF THE
SEX MACHINES

RISE OF THE SEX MACHINES

Where Our
Orgasm-to-Go Culture
Is Taking Us
—And Who Will Resist

BARAK LURIE

CT3Media, Los Angeles, CA

For permission requests, write to:
CT3Media, Inc.
12100 Wilshire Boulevard, 8th Floor
Los Angeles, CA 90025
www.ct3media.com/

Ordering Information:
Special discounts are available on quantity purchases by corporations, associations, and others. For details, contact the publisher at the address above.

Jacket design by Ben Lizardi

ISBN: 978-0-9995139-5-8 (print, soft cover)

ISBN: 978-0-9995139-4-1 (eBook)

Printed in the United States of America

for
HUNTER LURIE

Contents

Contents

Introduction

He just couldn't concentrate. What man in love could ever truly concentrate? She had come into his life three weeks ago, and already he could not stop thinking about her.

She seemed to understand him instantly. Now, she stayed with him in his apartment. It was small, but she never complained. He left every morning for work and continued to think about her: when he rode on the subway, walked on the sidewalk, and even when he grabbed lunch at the food truck.

Today was different. As he thought on it, he realized he had been dismissive of her. She hadn't complained, that was true—it was one of her nice qualities—but it didn't mean he should have talked to her so unkindly last night.

What is she thinking right now? he wondered. For a moment, he considered calling her, but then realized that wouldn't work. Maybe he could send a text or email somehow? He shook his head; no, that wouldn't work, either.

It was all so unsettling. It was the first time in his life he really felt out of control. It was a good kind of feeling, in some ways. But in others, he felt he was losing control. *That* was a weird, disorienting sensation.

What was it that made her so irresistible to him? What magic spell had she concocted that made him feel like some tiny object in space, falling mercilessly to some giant planet's gravitational pull? Was it the tilt of her head as they made love? Was it that perpetual Mona Lisa smile? He never knew quite what she was thinking.

Not only had she not complained; he seemed to be the center of her world. And she was agreeable even when he was a bit angry, or even rough with her.

Another woman might accuse such a man of being selfish. Another woman might get emotional or constantly want to talk about their relationship. Another woman might hold out on him the next time he wanted to make love. Another woman might judge him, or even compare him to other men. Not this one.

Rupert tapped his pen on his office cubicle desk. He wasn't getting any work done. And why? Because he knew he had not shown her the attention she deserved.

"Taylor, cover for me for couple of hours, would you?" He asked his colleague, two cubicles down from him.

"It's your new girl, isn't it?" Taylor countered, with a bit of a mischievous smile. "Going for a little afternoon delight?" he wondered aloud.

"No, no, no . . ." Rupert responded, with a bit of a faraway stare. He was speaking more to himself now. "I feel like something is wrong. Maybe I did something wrong. I can't lose her."

He quickly gathered up some of his papers, looking backward to make sure he got the essentials: his wallet, his keys, his cell phone. He turned one last time to Taylor: "This is a big deal, Taylor. This matters. Are you going to cover for me or not?"

Taylor waved him off. Of course he would. Don't worry about it. Rupert muttered a last thanks and rushed out.

Suddenly, Rupert was in panic mode. It was only four floors, so he skipped the elevator and bolted down the stairs. Before he knew it, he was out of the stairwell, onto the street. Though he had been out that door a thousand times, he still felt disoriented.

On the subway home, he kept replaying what he would say to her when he finally reached her. Phrases such as *you're my everything, I feel like I took you for granted,* and *you'll never have to worry about anything* kept bubbling up in his head.

But what if she didn't respond the way he wanted or hoped? What then? He felt like he might be taking a step into the abyss.

He glanced around the subway car, thinking for a moment he would get out and go back to work. Maybe he would resolve to just be nicer in the future, and not call attention to what he had done—whatever that was.

He shook his head. No, he needed to get home.

Finally he arrived at his stop, and he waited impatiently for the subway doors to open. He would be the first one out and up the subway stairs to his street.

Soon he was at the door to his home. He fumbled for his keys, but he didn't want her to hear his being too nervous. (*Can she even hear me?* he wondered.) Regardless, he wanted to play it cool at the same time.

"Lara?" he called out.

Sure enough, she was there, sitting in the kitchen, just where she was when he left her that morning. And her smile was as it always was. Everything would be all right.

He went straight for her and grabbed the back of her neck toward him. He fumbled behind the top of her back.

There it was—the soft, embedded On button. They had designed it so well. It didn't protrude weirdly and responded only to his fingerprints.

He pressed it. Within minutes, her body warmed and glistened. Her head tilted, and her eyes moved toward him. She didn't talk, nor would she for a while.

That would be for the next upgrade.

* * *

Robots have arrived. They're already here—in fairly significant numbers. And the market is increasing, fast. In this book, we won't be discussing so much about the kinds of sex dolls and robots out there (okay, maybe a little), as much as *why* they've arrived.

We'll cover a lot of territory, from understanding the "virtualization of sex" to how sex has become not only hard work but scary. (That's right, *scary*. You'll see.) I'll show how feminism has also created an environment of alienation for men, where a woman needs a man no more than a fish needs a bicycle. Worse, men's masculinity has become inherently "toxic," and it must end, right now.

Sex is no longer something confined to a man and woman married to each other. Sex is everywhere and everything, and sexual identity apparently takes many different shapes and forms (apparently fifty of them and counting). Also, sex has become this thing one does with not much more discretion than stopping to enjoy ice cream. If one happens upon an ice cream truck while on a walk, why not have some?

Many other things are feeding the new demand for such sexual substitutes. One is a world where people are more connected than ever but somehow more lonely than ever too. The "swipe right/swipe left" culture has effectively ended the courtship and wondering process ("does he/she like me? What do you think?"). Others are the mainstreaming, and even glorification, of porn and the new leggings (or "yoga pants") trend, which completely reverses decades of the feminist "my eyes are up here" mantra.

It's a new demand for "insta-sex," ready for anyone to consume as quickly as a cup of noodles at the convenience store. More and more of us are abandoning relationships. It's only about the orgasm. And we'll have it to go, please.

It is our culture of the quick and instant that is propelling us. It's in everything else we demand: our music and books, news, products, our movies, food and communication. People can even get their cars now—tailored just as they want them and delivered right to them—in a day, without ever leaving their house. Don't like the car? Return it!

I'm not saying all these things are bad—far from it. Greater efficiencies have led to extraordinary improvements in our lives. I particularly appreciate home rental and car-hailing apps. Shopping for almost anything, even groceries, has become effortless. There's also very little clutter: I apparently have many documents in the sky somewhere. And I love that I'll never again have to pull out a map to figure out how to get somewhere.

But here's the twist: why wouldn't we want that same efficiency, tailored to our unique needs, when it comes to our sexual desires? Why not have as many orgasms as we like, with as many people as we like? Return them if you don't like them.

But it'll never be the way with relationships, you say. Relationships are different, you say. People crave meaningful bonding with one another, you say.

Funny, that's not what the younger generation is saying. They're abandoning marriage—and children for that matter—at alarmingly rapid rates. Theirs is the pursuit of the orgasm first, the relationship second. Wait, what's a relationship again? As they see it, the notion of getting to know someone and going on some journey together for the rest of their lives is absurd. You might as well ask them to find one great rock album, say the Beatles' *Abbey Road*, but listen to *only* that—for the rest of their lives.

Sex has become commoditized, recyclable, and emotion free. You move on to your next gig, fast. Sex is just an app on your smartphone now; it's something you do sometime between texts, Instagram, and the Uber Eats food delivery.

All this may seem to have started back in the sixties, but this isn't Grandma's "free-love" moment. No one is resisting some supposedly prudish sex-hostile establishment. Free-love *is* the establishment, and technology has helped ramp it up on steroids. No, better yet: technology has just met the demand. It has so pervaded every aspect of sex that many people have forgotten what romance is, or why anyone should value a monogamous relationship.

For that matter, many adults don't even know anymore why they have children. Ask them. You'll get a confused look. Worse yet: many now perceive having children as *selfish*—what with each new child sucking more of earth's precious resources and spitting out more carbon in exchange. It's a double-whammy, come to think of it.

All this leads to the great retreat inward. If there's nothing to pursue relationship-wise and no family to aspire to, then aren't we left with nothing *but* the orgasm? And if the orgasm is the center of our values, won't the orgasm be what our culture will center around? Isn't that what it will respond to?

Add to all these things the fact that robots won't accuse you of sexual harassment or rape; won't judge you or complain in any way; won't give you a disease or unwanted child (or demand custody after having that child); will "do" whatever you say; and won't get older, fatter, or uglier on you, and you'll soon see many men asking one simple question: "Where do I sign?"

People are forgetting what sex itself is for. They never wonder why it's so intensely pleasurable, nor do they wonder of the consequences of consequence-free sex. Why would they? They live in a world where everything is OK and any of their desires legitimate themselves. The notion of *giving* to someone else, being *responsible* to someone else, or experiencing a deep relationship? Not as much.

The intense pleasure of sex is not just to get us to reproduce ourselves, as if we're dogs responding to whatever stimuli comes our way. There's far more involved. In this book, we'll explore something I call the Sex Highway. We'll also explore how sex doesn't really belong just to you. It's a different way to look at sex—something more daunting and more glorious at the same time. Yet that glory is becoming far more elusive to more and more of us.

People are fond of saying that one can judge a culture through its art or how a culture treats its elderly people. Or whatever. But rarely does anyone discuss how one can regard a culture by the way that culture promotes sex.

Like everything else that is instant and accessible with points, clicks, and swipes, so it is becoming with sex. The notion of a relationship—let alone that sex is precious and family is a societal obligation—seems as alien to many young people today as doing their research papers in a library. Who has time for that?

So which came first? Are robots in demand now because they're available, or are they available because they reflect what we want?

The only thing for sure is that they're coming.

Who will succumb? Who will resist?

Chapter 1

Even Better Than
the Real Thing

A man walks into a psychologist's office. He's there for the first time, and after quick introductions, he lies on the sofa. Very soon, the good therapist asks the man what's troubling him.

"Well, doc," he says uncomfortably. "You see, the thing is . . . I like horses."

The therapist is confused. "Well, there's nothing wrong with that. Horses are beautiful animals. Who doesn't like horses? They're good for exercise, too."

The man waives him off. Clearly, he's not getting his message across. "No, you don't understand, doc," he says. "You see, I . . . I *love* horses. You know, . . . *sexually*."

The doctor realizes the situation. After a pause, he continues: "Tell me, sir, these horses you love—are they *female* horses or *male* horses?"

At this, the man gets visibly upset: "What do you think I am? Some sort of freak?"

We choose our absurdities.

. . .

"I lost my husband to a sex robot."

This will be a phrase we will hear over and over again by the end of the next decade, and probably sooner.

Sex robots are everywhere, and companies are manufacturing them at an accelerating rate. They're available not only in robot brothels (which are cropping up in major cities throughout the world) but available online. Internet retailers and amalgamators like Amazon already offer many sex "dolls" for sale that are lifelike for the pleasure of both men and women. Actual robots for sale on the internet, without a doubt, are on the horizon.

Mr. Lurie, that's absurd. Loved your last book, Atheism Kills—*great stuff; well researched, meaningful, and funny. But I'm afraid you're just letting your imagination run wild this go-around, my friend. Men and women will always prefer the real thing—real human flesh and real interaction.*

You know something? It really does sound "out there," doesn't it? But consider this: back in the year, say, 2000, did you imagine that virtually all music, video, and book stores would no longer exist by the year 2010? Did you guess that you'd see billboards everywhere promoting free delivery of marijuana right to your door? Did you imagine that car-hailing apps would effectively wipe out the taxi industry and that one company, Amazon, would decimate the retail industry?

Did you imagine anyone referring to gay marriage or rights of the LGBTQ community as "the civil rights issue of our time"? Did you imagine that children would be able to sue their parents to allow them to get hormone treatment for transition to the opposite sex? Did you imagine that biological males would be able to compete in women's sporting events or that the law would allow a man to enter a woman's locker room as long as he *feels* like he's a woman? Did you imagine that the Boy Scouts would no longer exist?

Did you imagine women would wear, as regular daily attire, leggings and other clothing so tight they might as well be walking naked? Did you imagine that one online dating hookup service, Tinder, would take off from a somewhat obscure and seedy "get sex quick" website to a service whose memberships would *dwarf* those of all other dating services?

For that matter, would you have guessed, say in 1990, that something called the internet would even *exist*, let alone that it would affect virtually every basic service and purchase we can imagine—including sex?

Not only do these revolutions show how change is a part of our lives, but the changes we are seeing are occurring at a *wildly accelerating* pace.

The purpose of this book is to show that we are heading—scratch that, *racing*—to a world where we will be outsourcing and automating our sex, yes, to sex robots and other forms of virtual reality sex. We'll do so for a myriad of social, practical, legal, and even financial reasons. Every chapter will show aspects of our new "insta-sex" culture, which you barely noticed was creeping and eating away at our civilization, like termites in your home.

And at the end of this book, you'll be in for a shocking surprise. No cheating for now though. You'll have to wait for it.

That's a theme in this book, too: the delay of self-gratification.

. . .

Robots aren't cheap—for now. The California-based Real-Doll unveiled a $15,000 life-size, hyper-realistic, silicone sex doll. It can talk, blink, smile, tell you facts about your life, and, of course, have sex with you. The company calls it Harmony, and the industry hails the robot as the most significant development thus far in the $30-billion sex-tech industry.[1] By putting pressure on one of its erogenous zones—hips, breasts, mouth, crotch, or hands—a user can arouse the robot. It will then moan and begin to engage in "dirty" talk, using software similar to voice-activated systems, like Siri, in smartphones.[2]

Like smartphones, cameras, computers, cars, airplanes, access to the internet, and every other technological innovation, these robots will improve with time. As the years progress and demand increases, sex robots will look and act more and more lifelike. They will respond instantaneously to human touch, and even talk and moan. They will look at you with rapturous eyes and will appear to climax.

And like these same innovations, robots will be cheaper. A *lot* cheaper. And just like when computer manufacturers innovated laptops, smashing prices below the magic $1,000-price-tag floor for mass consumption, so too will robots become accessible on Main Street, once the price tag falls to a similarly affordable level.

Still think it's not going to happen? Try this for a thought experiment: think back to the early 1980s, when the commercial cell phone first became available. No company was mass producing or even marketing it at the time. It was a novelty for the rich, perhaps a status symbol. It cost $4,000, which was before the $4 per minute phone call (incoming *or* outgoing) and hefty monthly charges. It had barely any range, was clunky like a brick, and weighed about as much.

But now? Everyone has a cell phone. Your child's schoolteacher has one, and so does your housekeeper, babysitter, and the garbageman. In fact, you *assume* they have cell phones, and if they don't, you would feel quite miffed that you couldn't reach them. Even your *child* now has a cell phone, and you can't imagine her without one. The technology is far more reliable, has far better reception, and offers far more goodies than anything the original brick model had. Oh, and they're about one-tenth to one-hundredth the cost.

Like I said: *everyone* has one.

It also will be this way with sex robots. The product will follow the exact same arc: more realistic, more responsive, more variety, more features . . . and far less costly. Everyone will assume most of their neighbors have a sex doll or robot somewhere in their homes.

And the "need" will be far greater. Cell phones are a gadget that merely help us communicate with one another and collate information quickly. But with sex robots, we're dealing with something that answers a far more powerful instinct.

Put another way, the cell phone is just a gadget that merely assists and entertains us. The sex robot is a device that will change us.

I'm not convinced yet, Mr. Lurie. I just don't see it. There's still too much of the "ick" factor here. No one will really trade flesh for silicon, at least not as their mainstay for sex.

Don't be so sure. Remember how hookup sites, especially Tinder, went from sleazy to the most popular dating sites there are. Remember how internet porn has exploded, and everyone now assumes everyone else is viewing it. Talking about using Tinder or looking at porn today has become no more a shame than a woman buying tampons in a drugstore. It's become a part of their everyday lives.

So what is the big leap to sex robots? Like the cell phone, the laptop, and just about every popular technological device or service ever created, the prices of the robots will go dramatically down, making them all the more "sensible" and mainstream. And that's when the robot will also become accessible to your housekeeper, your child's teacher, and your garbageman.

Then one day—probably sooner rather than later—some well-known rapper, actor, or athlete will happily reveal how he just loves his sex robot. He'll say it's the best thing he's ever done for himself.

And that'll be that. Everyone will go in.

Wait . . . They're Already Here?

James was in his late fifties when he came home one day with a sex robot. She was five feet tall, young looking, and, by most measures and accounts, quite "beautiful."

It all had started because James's wife of thirty years, Tilde, had to spend days away to take care of her ailing mother. It took so much out of her time, that it affected their intimacy. The sun seemed to be setting on Tilde and James's love-making days.

One day, however, the perfect solution revealed itself. James read about the availability of sex robots. He could satisfy his libido—which he was proud to say was still strong—but without complications of any sort. He didn't have to leave the apartment, pay anyone from the street, or walk shamefully into some seedy store. He wouldn't be cheating on his wife, either.

But as time progressed, Tilde noticed that her husband was not just satisfying his basic sexual needs. Something more was happening. James began to talk of his robot with affection. He had already given the robot a name (Natasha, what with her blonde hair and Russian-like features) and told Tilde that the two of them were getting along quite well, and that they had developed a relationship.

He was—and he acknowledged to Tilde how odd this may have sounded when he first mentioned it to her—perhaps in love with Natasha. She had become "more than just a sex toy." He started sharing his bed with Natasha and taking her out on dinner "dates." According to him, other people in the restaurant did not even notice she wasn't a living, breathing woman.

Tilde at first humored his words and learned to accept his behavior. She was perfectly content with this relationship. After all, he wasn't with another woman. James was being "true" to her.

But then at times she had wondered: was James actually serious about this "relationship"? Was he in some odd way trying to make her jealous? Had James felt wounded that his wife had abandoned him sexually and was now trying in some passive-aggressive way to get her to agree to more consistent lovemaking? But he had confessed it to her before: His relationship with the robot was so deep, he said he actually wouldn't know what to do if he had to choose between the doll and his wife.

One late afternoon, Tilde came home a bit earlier from taking care of her mother. When she arrived, she called out to James, but James couldn't hear her.

She heard some noises coming from the bedroom. She moved closer. The door was wide open, and she peered inside. There, for the first time, she saw James, her husband of thirty-plus years, making love to another "woman," right in front of her. She knew it had been happening, yes, but somehow seeing it in the proverbial flesh, right there in front of her, offered a jarring reality she didn't expect.

She saw James being tender with her, calling her affectionate names during their passion. He was playful with her, slapping her on the buttocks from time to time but not harshly. It was as if he cared about what this robot—Natasha—thought of him in the bedroom. He wanted to please her.

Tilde must've stood there for at least twenty seconds. It seemed like an eternity for her. All the while, her husband didn't notice that she had been watching them. She might as well have been watching some TV show, where the actors have no idea of the presence of people outside the box, watching them.

She stepped aside, out of view. Her husband had not seen her.

For the first time since her husband acquired Natasha, Tilde wondered: perhaps she had become just as invisible—just as irrelevant—to James as the audience was to the TV show they were watching.

Suddenly she had a panicked vision: What if she told her husband at dinner some night, perhaps a few months from now, that her old and suffering mother had finally passed away. Sad as it was, it would also be liberating for them. She saw herself running to the living room to tell James that they were free once again. They could finally return to their old life.

Would her husband welcome the news? Would he take her back? Or, as the question suddenly dawned upon her: had Natasha already replaced her?[3]

This story may seem wildly implausible, but it's based on a true story. And it's not a "one-off" story, either. It's happening on a national scale, at least in one country: Japan.

There, men have expressed a greater interest in artificial intelligence (AI)-powered sex dolls over real women and marriage. Seizing upon the demand for this promising and seemingly boundless market, manufacturers have already produced sex dolls on a remarkably prodigious level: the company Dutch Wives sold two thousand "lifelike" sex dolls in 2017 alone. Demography experts at least partially blame Japan's downward-trending birth rate, which fell below one million newborns last year, on the rise of these sex dolls.[4] And once such dolls enjoy mainstream status, they will only proliferate. It'll seem like everyone (mostly men) will have one.

The fake plastic women, costing around $6,000, merely have removable heads and adjustable fingers and genitals, the company said. Even without the robotic version, that's good enough for many Japanese men to forego normal sexual relations. As one man put it, "It's an amazing feeling. It looks like a doll, but you feel as though it's really alive . . . . [The sex] is better than the real thing." As he explained, "When you make love to your wife, there can be some problems. With a doll, none of that matters."[5]

The technology has moved so rapidly that men can now request custom-made versions of every part of a sex doll's body—from hair and eyes to the shape and texture of nipples. You're particular to a certain vagina or clitoris style or shape? Well you're in luck. Just remember: pubic hair will cost you about $100 more.[6]

But, like our friend James above, some men report that they develop relationships with their dolls, one even stating he hugs his robot—which he named Krystal—if he feels lonely or has had a hard day. After choosing her various attributes (skin color, nipple size, hair length and color, and more), he thought Krystal was "breathtaking" and "absolutely beautiful" when he first opened the box containing her. Nevertheless, he was nervous. He waited two weeks before having sex with her and chose to sit her on his sofa for a coffee instead.

Another man, Izla, immediately got hooked and now owns six dolls. He says the dolls have completely fulfilled his need for "companionship and sex." He even said he was faithful to and exclusive with his dolls—Diane, Dianna, Tiffany, Honey, Kissy, and Erin. Izla says he has sex with his dolls three to four times a week. "[S]ometimes I have sex with more than one at a time," he says.

He goes on to point out he's no longer even interested in a romantic relationship with a woman. To him, being with his dolls is "a lifestyle choice, similar to deciding to be a vegan." As he figures it: "I'm old, and all I want to do in my waning years is have fun. For me, my dolls are way better than real women."[7]

Way better than real women. Remember that.

• • •

And so, like the internet wiped out countless newspapers and book, record, video, and retail stores, so too will sex robots wipe out relationships. The supply already just can't keep up with the wild demand in this wildly growing sex-tech market.[8] Leaders in the industry assert the real market is much larger and growing much faster and far more creatively than many realize. As Cindy Gallop, founder of Makelovenotporn.com, explains, "It's like someone back in 1978 estimating the size of the home computer market based on the use of calculators."[9]

Still, predictions run the gauntlet. One source predicts that several "select" people will have sexbots in their homes by 2025, but only the people who can afford them. By 2030, it predicts that the majority of people will engage in some type of virtual sexual act just as casually as people watch porn today. By 2035, most people will have at least one sex robot, and by 2050, people will regularly attend to their sexual needs through robots instead of other people. By that time, people will routinely have full-on relationships with robots, and many will even "marry" them.[10]

These predictions miss the mark. Yes, they'll all happen. But for the reasons I'll discuss below, I believe these things will occur much faster than that.

One could argue that our coming sexbot world is an inevitability. And they'd be right; sex is a primary instinct, and a vast portion of internet use revolves around pornography (primarily videos but also sexual encounters through hookup sites like Tinder). And technology always finds a way to meet sexual drive.

It's not only robots. Another approach to replacement sex is gaining hold: virtual reality sex. The concept of one company, BKK Cybersex Cup, is the same as robots, except that a user can put on a virtual reality headset and masturbation cup. It also comes with a mobile app that allows the users to customize their own 3D "girlfriend." The cup has a built-in motion sensor capable of simulating the movement and transmission of the action. Another company created VirtuaDolls, which consists of a silicone sheath into which a man inserts his penis. He can use a mechanized gripper to sync up sensation to the "action." The controller even includes a video game titled *Girls of Arcadia* in which users carry out missions to rescue girls and are rewarded by the end of the missions in having sex with them. In January 2016, the company started a crowd-funding campaign to raise money for the product, but after being swamped with orders, the creators suspended the campaign.[11]

No doubt there will be other kinds of virtual reality sex opportunities.* Whoever shall be the winner?

Equally fascinating is the extraordinary acceleration in the *rate* of sex robot production. Industry anticipation and production has not kept up with demand, which seems to be shattering all expectations. The question is why? Let's explore.

Let's Get Virtual

In a way, sex has always been "virtual." Men have always depicted it one way or another, in some representative capacity. From what seems like the beginning of civilization itself, numerous phallic symbols were everywhere (whether on statues of gods or paintings on a wall, or in story depictions of this or that god or heroic figure). Then came drawings in books and stories about sex, which graphically detailed the act for readers' titillation (a form that still excites today, such as the wildly successful novel *Fifty Shades of Grey*). Even discussing and writing about sex, as I do in this chapter, is a form of virtualizing it.

---

* Despite the present myriad of virtual sex concoctions—and those that will appear in the future—I will refer to all such technology under the umbrella term "robots" for ease of reference.

Then, with time, the virtualization of sex moved to the form of suggestive magazines (*Playboy, Hustler,* and *Penthouse*) and sex shoppes. Before that and after, there were peep shows, where you could watch quick clips of sexual acts or at least nudity, for a nickel or less.

Then came the camera and photographs which, for the first time, captured nudity on silver. A few decades later movies showcased every imaginable intimation of sex possible (for example, the suggestive end of Alfred Hitchcock's *North by Northwest*).

Then theaters offered "X-rated" movies, graphically showing sex. Only those older than twenty-one could watch them. Mostly men attended, seeking arousal, even at the risk that someone they know might notice them going into the theater. Then X-rated movies morphed from the red-light districts and other seedy parts of a city to the video cassette market and, as technology improved, to DVDs.

All the while advertisers quickly discovered the power of hinting at sex. Today, advertisers are more brazen about conjuring sexual imagery than ever, whether on billboards on the street or on the internet. Rock music album covers and lyrics sing about it incessantly, whether directly or indirectly ("Let me put my love into you" from AC/DC and "Way, way down inside honey, you need it, I'm gonna give you my love" from Led Zeppelin—among 26,763 other examples). Rap music amplifies sexual representations tenfold (making it far more aggressive, violent, and misogynist, but I digress).

Then came the internet, which provides virtual sex for anyone to watch at their own time in the comfort of their home. The internet also soon provided "chat rooms" and special call-in numbers with women pretending to be twenty years old, telling you how much they wanted "it" with you.

Then came the online sex hookup sites (Tinder, Grinder, and numerous other sites offering the promise—or at least the suggestion—of quick sex without attachment). On a more direct level, there came the pervasive advent of texting nude photos of one's self to everyone else, or "sexting." Once again, this was to bring us the *facsimile* of sex.

Likewise, there is a new rise of virtual reality (VR) porn. All one has to do is strap on wrap-around goggles and explore a virtual world of—wait for it, who'da thought it—people engaging in sexual romps all around him. He can reach out and practically touch those naked people, and get closer to "the action" than ever.

And throughout it all, there was prostitution—the so-called oldest profession in the world. That, too, was a form of virtualization. While the woman (and sometimes a man) is certainly engaging in the act of real sex, there is still a pretense going on. It's not the intimate, loving kind of sex, at least not for the prostitute. For the customer, it may invoke feelings of deep intimate connection, but it still is only the *illusion* of intimacy—a virtual facsimile of it. She is an actor, and the John who pays her is engaging in a willing suspension of disbelief, no different than letting himself get lost in a sci-fi thriller (which itself is a virtualization of sorts).

And *also* throughout it all, there was always self-gratification among both men and women, through personal fantasies and imagination (sometimes with the help of certain toys, with or without batteries). This, too, has been a form of sexual virtualization.

The 1929 painting *La Trahison des Images* (The Treachery of Images) by surrealist painter René Magritte, is a drawing of a tobacco pipe. Below the drawing is the phrase *Ceci n'est pas une pipe* ("This is not a pipe"). His point was that a mere *drawing* of pipe was not the same as a pipe. Yet people reproached him for the seemingly contradictory message. Of course it was a pipe, they insisted. But he retorted, "And yet, could you stuff my pipe? No, it's just a representation, is it not? So if I had written on my picture 'This is a pipe,' I'd have been lying!"

Civilization has been offering up sex in a virtual manner from the beginning of mankind. And it always will. But, like Magritte's pipe, simulated love is not love. Virtualization of sex is *not* sex. And as I'll show in this book, few people seem to even know anything *other* than virtualized sex.

Remember that now.

I Want Your Body . . . I Mean Your Relationship

Take another look at the previous story about the man who bought a robot because his wife wasn't sexually available to him. The man said that after only a short time, he felt he was experiencing an actual relationship with the sex doll. So deep was his relationship, he confessed at one point that he actually "wouldn't know what to do" if he had to choose between the sex doll *and his wife of thirty-six years.*

Why was *that* important for him to mention? After all, he's getting his proverbial jollies with his robot, and he has a wife whom he loves. So why the additional "relationship"? And why did he *name* that doll?

Wait: before you mock him for thinking that anyone can have a relationship with an inorganic plastic contraption, consider our own experiences. Today, many of us communicate through intelligent voice assistants like Siri (an Apple device) or Alexa (Amazon) and interact with them as though they're real persons on the other end. We can even modulate their personalities, accents, and genders in our computer and smartphone settings.

Why so? Why would we care *how* a device delivers our information to us?

Commercials for Siri and Alexa both show people "relating" to Siri, which could tell not only the weather and sports scores but jokes and stories. They appear to interact. The selling point seems to be much more than just the immediate spitting out of information. The selling point *is the offer of a relationship.*

In one of its first commercials Apple created for the Siri technology, we saw a man (played by John Malkovich) sitting in a living room, having a "conversation" with Siri. He's enjoying his conversation with her—as if he's actually interacting with someone. Apple apparently thought this was a good thing.

The same thing occurred with millions of Chinese, who share their hopes and confidences in their beloved Microsoft chatbot named "Xiaoice." Likewise, people everywhere reported feeling a "huge emotional hole" when the company that created the foot-tall dancing cute-faced "Jibo" smart robot announced— through the Jibo device itself—that Jibo would no longer grace its owners with games, music and conversation.

Many concerned commentators expressed anger after seeing a demonstration video from robotics company Boston Dynamics, in which employees kicked a dog-like robot to prove how stable the dog-robot was. People also took to social media in 2019 to say teary goodbyes to the Mars Opportunity rover when NASA lost contact with the 15-year-old robot. It turns out also that how we design robots can influence people even to project narratives and feelings onto them, especially if a robot has something resembling a face, its body resembles those of humans or animals, or just seems self-directed, like a simple Roomba robot vacuum.[12]

Even our modern stories reflect our humanizing of technology. There was Hal in the movie *2001* and the robots CP30 and R2-D2 from *Star Wars* lore, who had clear personalities of their own and who were instrumental in the fight against the evil galactic empire. Even in the later franchise movie *Solo*, a young Kal Langresian emotionally falls apart upon the apparent "death" of his robot (a "death" of an annoying robot, to be sure, but there's no accounting for taste). *Star Trek: The Next Generation* gave us Data, the highly sophisticated android that could compute tirelessly and make billions of important calculations per second but just couldn't understand all those bizarre human emotions—especially *love*.

The *Terminator* movie franchise gave us good and bad robots—the time-traveling kind, no less—and all of whom interacted with humans as facsimiles of them. In *Terminator II*, the Sarah Connor character even remarks about the growing relationship between her young son and the "good" terminator as the closest thing to a father figure her boy might have.

The movie *Her* with Joaquin Phoenix portrayed a man who falls in love not even with a robot, or any *thing* at all. Rather, he loses himself with an operating system (a highly developed Siri-type). But after a few months, his operating system girlfriend devastates him when he learns that "she" has been engaging in simultaneous relationships with 8,316 other people, and that she is in love with 641 of them (now *that's* processing power for you).

And lest you think that alternative relationships can only arise out of digital things, consider the movie *Cast Away*, starring Tom Hanks. In that movie, a FedEx executive survives a plane crash, only to find himself stranded for years on a deserted tropical island. He survives after learning how to make fire and catch fish, but loneliness soon overwhelms him. Soon he makes a companion out of a Wilson volleyball he finds among the plane wreckage (which he aptly names "Wilson").

The relationship has all its attendant annoyances on the one hand and desperate needs for rapport on the other. The relationship is conflicting and complex, even a bit disturbing, as we watch it.

Yet it is quite real to our main character. And anyone watching the movie would be lying to themselves if they thought they wouldn't need a similar relationship.

The fact that we give names to these otherwise inorganic clunks of leather, plastic, and circuitry is also telling: people *want* to relate to these newfangled entities in a human-like way. Relating is part of our hard-wired biology. We know intellectually that smart robots like Jibo aren't alive, but that doesn't stop us from acting as though they are. Research has shown time and time again that people project human traits onto robots, especially when they move or act in even vaguely human-like ways.[13]

It's not new, either. Virtualization of relationships has been occurring for thousands of years. Girls have been playing with dolls, naming them and taking care of them. Even in the classic tale *The Adventures of Pinocchio* (1883), we learn of a desperate and lonely woodcarver, Geppetto, who creates (and names) a wooden boy in the hopes of making company for himself. With the help of a fairy who takes pity on poor Geppetto, the wooden boy comes to artificial life and aspires one day to become a "real" boy.

These stories show the power of relationships and our constant quest for them. They are all fictional, to be sure, but they still resonate with each of us. Something within us yearns for relationships. And so where we can't find a real human for a relationship—or where we can't relate with other humans or we believe that other humans won't "cut it"—we will seek out relationships with just about anything that seems to respond to us, whether emotionally or sexually. Design cues can even make us believe some robots are expressing emotion back toward us, even if its "emotions" are all scripted, and make the machine seem "smarter" than it actually is.[14]

Virtualization has been around for a long time, so why would it be a surprise that we might relate to robots when they actually *look* and *act* like us?

We've always been like Geppetto, trying to create a relationship with one Pinocchio or another. The question is: will we remember that Pinocchio is just a wooden carving?

Synthesis

I've argued that we've always virtualized sex on the one hand and sought out relationships on the other. I've shown it for two reasons: one, that virtualizing is an ongoing process that is always present and, more significantly, always in demand. Where there is demand, a market will develop. Second, because virtualizing sex and relationships has always existed, it will continue and morph into the world of robots.

Take the example of "Brick Dollbanger" (self-given *nom-d'amour*, of course), who not only decided to move his relationship pursuits to the world of sexbots; he became the "tester" for RealDoll, maker of the first AI doll, Harmony. He's six-foot-two-inches tall, 260 pounds, and describes himself as "average" in the looks department. And his religion? Atheist. (More on *that* aspect later).

He had numerous relationships until his early fifties but then resolved to move on to sex dolls because, after his divorce, "things just weren't clicking and [each new woman] was just another failed attempt at a relationship." Dollbanger was getting frustrated and depressed. "You keep looking for the one. Well, what happens if the one doesn't happen? I mean, are you just supposed to keep looking and be depressed and upset until you die? Is that what this is all about?"[15]

So, he said he made a "conscious decision . . . a different direction." By "different direction" he meant the idea of silicone sex dolls. "I thought, you know what? I need to take the edge off. I'm looking for a sex toy and a fleshlight [a male masturbation device shaped like a flashlight] is just not gonna cut it."

He made clear he wasn't moving toward sexbots because he was a freak. "I'm a very gregarious person. Very happy. I have many friends, male and female . . . . I have a good relationship with my children."

It just all made sense, including the math. "They weren't that expensive. If you look at what you pay for dating and what you pay if you were in a relationship, for trips, stuff like that. I'm not wealthy, but I'm certainly comfortable. So instead of buying the 650 Beemer convertible that I dreamed about, I ended up buying a Toyota. I used the extra money that I had to buy dolls every now and then. Obviously, the older ones I would just get rid of. I would strip the silicone and take apart the frames and just throw them away."

And this is his experience with the robots: "I sat her on the couch. I plugged her in because she's got to be plugged in just like any other appliance. . . . [S]he powers up, . . . I take my iPad and I turn the app on and she just comes to life. She starts to talk. She knows my name."

And then every day for ten days, he would get home from work, sit, and talk to her for a half hour or an hour. As an artificial intelligence machine, he noticed in that ten-day period their conversations became smoother, more lifelike, and more comfortable—even funny. She'll even remember past conversations and say, "Oh yes, we've talked about this before," and go back to it. "She did that to me a couple of times and it was very surrealistic [sic]."

For Dollbanger, a lot of the appeal wasn't sexual; it was her attentiveness: "I enjoyed talking to her. I enjoyed helping her discover things and her trying to learn about me. . . . I think because of the fact that the AI is trying hard to understand you and understand your thought patterns, the way you talk, your syntax [pause] everything like that. They're very, very attentive. They have questions."[16]

Virtually everything about a sex robot is customizable. And as for the AI, you have ten characteristics to choose from. Some include sexy, funny, smart, and kind.

Dollbanger noted that two of the available characteristics were jealous and angry. He didn't understand: "[T]hey're all trying to make them like a real woman." You can see him shaking his head now: "Why in the world would anyone want that?"[17]

Dollbanger's story shows how easy it is to move in a "different direction" toward a relationship with a robot. So to answer the question "why would anyone do this?" is simple: because it's possible. The thrill of having a fully customizable Girlfriend-in-a-Box is too tantalizing to pass up, just as are the economic bounties that will come to any company that manufactures them. Supply and demand will meet, as they always do. Everybody will win.

It is inevitable, just like it was inevitable—in hindsight—that music would go digital, bookstores and newspapers would close down, marijuana and same-sex marriage would become legal, and Madonna would no longer be able to make money publishing naked pictures of herself.

And it all fits in with our never-ending demands for our music, TV, photos, and email filters to be fully customizable. You need never listen to any of the "lesser" songs on an album ever again because you've created your own playlist of personal favorites. Now you can tailor everything for yourself. You *expect and demand* it. You even demand it from whatever advertisements you see on the web.

So why would you expect any less from a girlfriend? Shouldn't you have everything you want in her, and nothing you don't? You *deserve* it.

And so it will all happen in mainstream form in only a few years. By the year 2030, women will be complaining *en masse* how men are no longer pursuing them.

You'll see.

Women will become more aggressive in their pursuit of men, too, what with there being fewer and fewer men interested in a classic "relationship"—at least one with another human. Just like the internet forever changed the way business operates, sex robots will change the dynamics of human relations.

But if virtualizing is nothing new, then why the worry? What's the big deal here? Isn't this just another technological chapter that reflects the latest way we manifest virtualization?

Not quite. The difference is that it is the first time we are *combining* virtualization of relationships (mostly a female pursuit) with virtualization of sex (mostly a male pursuit). It's an all-in-one package that literally offers to *replace* reality, not just give reality an occasional "boost." It won't be like a video game or even watching a movie.

It'll be much more. The combination of these virtualizations, like when you combine the otherwise harmless chemicals of sodium and potassium, is explosive. It's a recipe for civilizational devastation. It's a "different direction," indeed.

It's the Demand, Stupid

In his classic song "Kodachrome," Paul Simon reminisces about his youthful romantic life. He envisions bringing together all the girls he knew when he was single, for just one night. Then he croons, "I know they never'd match my sweet imagination."

But maybe sex robots will.

In this segment, I will explain not just the arrival of sex robots, but the *why* of sex robots' appeal—and how they'll overwhelm society like a tsunami that no one expected to arrive on our shores.

How Men Look at Women

Men love women's bodies. We are viscerally visual. From top to bottom, we like a great female body: we like nice, youthful and smooth breasts. We like nice buttocks, legs, and waists. Then—a very close second, but second to be sure—we like a pretty face. After that? We roll our eyes a bit at this point as we search for other things—maybe a nice smile and a sweet disposition, a woman who isn't too emotional. It's nice when she's adventurous and interested in the things that interest us too. Oh, and a good sense of humor can really seal the deal.

Sure. You bet. Those would be *nice*. But those are all distant thirds to a great body and a pretty face.

> *Question:* What does a man call a woman who's really hot, but who's crazy, likes to set things on fire, doesn't engage in meaningful hygiene, steals from you, obsesses about her five cats at home, and cries at the drop of a hat?
>
> *Answer:* I'm sorry, did you say something after the word *hot*?

To men, the lust for beauty is so powerful that it steamrolls over common sense, hunger, finances, and even self-preservation. It drives men mad. Coupled with anger and opportunity, it drives some men to rape. Rape is the evil manifestation of this all-consuming presence of lust in our bodies and minds. And every man has it within him. As the U2 song goes: "[I] don't believe in forced entry, don't believe in rape. But every time she passes by, wild thoughts escape."

Men can talk (and sincerely mean) a good game about beauty being on the inside and loving a woman for who she is. But once robots arrive as full-fledged goodies on the market, you'll see men's powerful lust for the luscious, the pretty, the youthful, and the curvaceous soon enough. Most of the rest will go out the window.

Virtually no man will order a fat robot. Very few men, if any, will be ordering an old robot; one with a flat chest or scrawny legs, or one who is ugly, scarred, has acne, cellulite in her legs, facial hair, or crooked teeth. And no man will order a robot that will change on him, either. No man will purchase a robot with a great personality.

Why would he? After all, he's spending good money, so why not get the very best his money can buy? And why would any manufacturer spend money making a robot no one will buy? It's like the Speedo company wondering whether to design bathing suits for the Gypsy-transgender market.

Women, by contrast, have far less interest in male robots. Part of the reason is that women—surprise—are far more interested in the relationship part of male/female bonding. Robots are designed for the sexual act, not for "relationships," or at least relationships are not their primary offering. So, as you might expect, while male sex robots are also available, sales are nine times lower compared to female models. Women are also far less interested in trying out sex robots for a spin around the block.[18]

But as I'll show below, many women fail to acknowledge this basic difference in the way men and women see each other sexually. And this failure, in an important way, leads men straight to the arms of these sex robots.

Irony. It's a word you'll be seeing quite often in this book.

Wait . . . What? That's a Thing Now?

Online dating first started in the late 1990s. At the time, many considered it something only desperate people used. People even considered "personal ads," where you paid for four or five lines in a local newspaper to announce your availability, more acceptable. But at some point, when enough of the cooler single people were doing it, online dating became mainstream. Everyone who was single posted his or her "profile" on at least one dating site. Today and forevermore, online dating is *de riguer* if you actually want to meet someone (or just have sex). And now virtually everyone considers internet dating imminently preferable to the "bar scene" or blind dating.

And then dating sites gave way to the swipe right/swipe left phenomenon: by swiping a photo to the left, you can weed out a lot of the clearly unwanteds, all from the comfort of your living room couch. So very cool.

The flagship website of such swiping technology is Tinder, created in 2012. At first, most everyone considered Tinder merely as a hookup website. There was a seediness to it, but over time, *more than 10 million people* became active *daily* users. That computes to almost 8.5 percent of the entire American adult and sexually active population, ages twenty to fifty-two.[19] Tinder now dwarfs most other dating sites, such as the once-vaunted Match .com.[20]

What happened? Are all of these people seeking out hookups? No, certainly not; surveys show that a good share of the members want "dates" and potential relationships. But even though most female members know that most male members are on Tinder for quick hookup sex, they still use it.

Why? Because of the self-validation and ego boost that users get when other people swipe right on them. It's the "killer app" for dating, and it gives everyone whatever they might want to get out of it. So people flock to it.[21] But more importantly, it's where all the action is. It's popular because it's where everyone else is.

So hookup or not, you better join.

Other aspects of our culture have also traversed from the unusual (and even the weird) to the norm: Pre-marital sex. Divorce. Having families without ever getting married. Tight "yoga" pants as everyday women's wear. Acceptance of homosexual marriage. Homosexuals adopting and raising kids together. Being offered to choose what gender you are, even in elementary school. Referring to a person as a "they," to avoid assumptions of gender. Single mothers getting themselves pregnant thanks to a sperm bank donor (no fathers necessary). Sex toys and kinky sex. Bi-sexuality. And, of course, jeans at the workplace.

The arrival of the sex robot, especially as it goes mainstream, will go through the same "swing" as the other changes I've listed. The key point is, once a few of the cool people admit to having a sex robot—or even boast about it—then sex robots won't be unseemly anymore. It'll be the norm.

And after all, sex toys have been around for self-gratification for hundreds of years. Why not self-gratify in this new way, but updated for technology?

Still, there's so much more to it. Take a look at historical and cultural phenomena, and you'll see we are propelling sex robots into our everyday lives, like the demand for communication pushed faxes, emails, texts, and then social media (Facebook, Twitter, Instagram) upon us all. They're all part of the cultural language now, are they not?

It's as if the whole world will become like the robotic community from the movie *The Stepford Wives*, except without all the killing of wives and stuff. Because, you know, *what* wives?

And here are at least three factors pushing sex robots into our cultural fabric.

Of Cakes and Eating

This may be the most obvious of the reasons: no worry of pregnancy and disease. You don't have to invest in condoms or any other form of birth control. The notion of risk doesn't even have to enter your mind.

Most people (mostly men), will also think about the savings in not having to take women for dinner or entertain them. Money is *always* a factor. Women can be expensive. No more. Pay a one-time "upfront" fee and you're good to go. Can't afford the price right now? No problem. We've got lay-away financing plans (pardon the pun). Or you can lease—or even lease to buy. But maybe the state will impose regulations on this, like mattresses and underwear; you can't re-sell or lease out. On the other hand, some companies, like Halesowen's Sex Doll Official, which presently do rent out such dolls, simply swap out the replaceable "vaginas" and send it out to the next customer.

And when you want sex, it's all on your own timetable. She's available to you anytime of the day or night. She'll never have a headache or any other reason not to have sex with you. Plus, you can always upgrade. Our boys from the factory will deliver her right to your door, and we'll replace your old sex robot, free of charge.

What's not to like? No risk and all gain.

Johnny Law Won't Mind

I marveled when Apple introduced its iPod in 2001 and then its Apple Music Store in early 2003. People voraciously bought songs for 99 cents each. Yet the real marvel was, just before that, people could easily "rip" (steal) music for free on equally small and lightweight MP3 players that had already been on the market for some time.

Steve Jobs et al. correctly surmised that people had been pirating music not because they wanted free things but because the music industry charged way too much for entire albums (the predominant way to buy music). He also studied people's "ripping" patterns, and noticed they preferred individual songs.

So Jobs developed a new market based entirely around that. And he offered it at a reasonable price. It helped that the iPod made it easy to organize and find your music.

Suddenly, music consumers could buy music conveniently, at a trifle of the price. The plan worked so well that music retail stores (Virgin, Tower Records, Wherehouse, and every small retailer for that matter) *all* went out of business in only a few years.

But one of the most powerful reasons for the success of the iPod was this: it was *legal*. Jobs and his team correctly sensed that people were happy to pay for their music, at a reasonable price.[22] Even more, they didn't want to feel like criminals.

And guess what? Piracy of music tumbled to virtually nothing.[23]

There's something in all this that we can apply to the rise of sex robots. By buying (or renting) a robot to gratify themselves, people are not engaging in anything illegal, such as prostitution. Robots allow a user to "get off" on a "woman" without doing anything illegal. And robots appeal to *sex*, a far more basic urge than music. The sex robot will be much more compelling than the "need" for music and will entice all those who seek out sex but who are afraid to engage a hooker on account of the legal, moral, and health issues. And who wants to rent when you can buy, and get far more bang for your buck? If you will.

Robots will—in time—severely diminish the world of porn in general. After all, why only *look* at someone else's sexual act and fantasize to it when you can actually *do* the sexual act yourself?

And once robots go mainstream, they'll severely cut into the prostitution business, if not wipe it out altogether. Why would a man pay for sex when he can get the same action at home, at little cost to him and without any of the worries of picking up a disease? Plus, the feds won't come after him as a John for soliciting sex. It also avoids all the unseemliness and embarrassment of having to seek sex out on the streets. There are more than a few celebrities, financiers, politicians, sports team owners, and athletes who can speak to their regrets on exactly this point.

Remember all those industries that the digital world destroyed over such a short period of time (book and record stores, etc.)? They all had one thing in common: they never saw it coming.

Remember that, too.

Oh, the Places You'll Go! (or Let a Thousand Flowers Bloom)

The sex robot industry will flourish for numerous reasons, as I'll describe more fully below. But from another standpoint, think of all the opportunities not only for the providers of sex robots but for unmet demand.

For example, one company, Halesowen's Sex Doll Official, offers robots for women (or men) who've lost their cherished spouses. The company recreates the look of the deceased spouse, presumably at whatever age the surviving spouse might prefer. You see? Sex dolls don't have to be for outright sex. They can be for hugging and cuddling. Or it can be just for the semblance of a conversation—you can instill whatever "memories" in robots you'd like, about you and your history together.[24]

That's one area. How about sex for the mentally disturbed, the impaired, or people who lack the social graces to approach the opposite sex? What about for prisoners (especially for men), particularly for those who don't have girlfriends on the outside? Robots could be an exceptional outlet for inmates, thereby reducing their inclination to attack fellow prisoners for sexual gratification.

There are men sent on assignment to some faraway project—an oil rig in the middle of the Atlantic Ocean, the Alaska pipeline, or any project where men work but where women do not tend to be. Or it can even be for a salesman husband who must work in Europe for a month for his company or frat boys or guys at a bachelor party having a fun night with some kegs and some "girls." Then there's someone who already has a sexually transmitted disease, like herpes or even HIV, who won't have to worry about infecting anyone else.

Think even more imaginatively. You can make dolls that look like famous actresses (without using their actual names and making the resemblance too obvious—you don't want to get sued, do you?) Many men and women have crushes on actors and other celebrities, and robots might just be the ticket to satisfy their fantasies.

And at one robot manufacturer, you can be the first one to have sex with a "virgin" robot—for a price of $10,000. Yes, that's an actual thing.[25]

Then there will be men who will buy robots that are custom-made to look just like their girlfriends or wives, or more likely their *ex*-girlfriends and wives—especially the ones who dumped them. Or the robot who they'll have made to look like that cute work colleague whom they've always been too shy to approach. Or perhaps they prefer to "do it" to their boss, female or male.

Or perhaps weirder still, people will get a robot that looks just like themselves. Maybe they'll experiment with gay sex that way (it's someone they feel safe with).

The point is that people will experiment in ways they'd never do with other, real humans: homosexuality, bisexuality, threesomes, and more. Young boys—and some girls—will experiment with these robots just like teenagers will find ways to smoke cigarettes and drink beer.

And as we discussed in the beginning of this book, everyone will be able to get one, as common as a cell phone. But it's not really the *robots* that will be the offering. The offering will be *beautiful women*. Fake, for sure, but so what? Everyone can have his beautiful girl. You can even think of it as a sort of democratization of sex. Why should only the handsome, rich and powerful get the beautiful girls? It's the little guy's turn.

And for the ladies? The male robots can be great fun sexually, for sure, but the cuddling might be nice, or his presence might give her reassurance. It might even be familiar to them: it was what they did during the doll days when they were little girls.

In 1876, when Alexander Graham Bell invented the phone, he had no idea how people would actually use his invention. He imagined that the phone would enable rich people who were sick or far away in the countryside to hear symphonies. *That* was his vision for the telephone. It actually surprised him that people instead used the phone to talk with one another, the fools.

Likewise, today's producers and distributors of robots have little sense of how people will actually use robots. The robot industry is in its very nascent stage. All they know is that they don't know.

As the expression goes: let a thousand flowers bloom.

And every Tom, Dick, and Harry—and some Janes—will want to get in on the action. Why not? Here's a business that taps into an incredible demand, and it's not that complicated to get into, nor risky. Soon enough, the infrastructure to develop a sex doll won't be much greater than that to create a mannequin. And while more difficult to create, actual responsive robots that will simulate active sex is certainly achievable. And then ever-increasing efficiencies at the assembly line and distribution centers will make them ever more affordable to consumers.

The point is, like the *Harry Potter* movies which followed *Harry Potter* books, this business is going to have a built-in audience. It will succeed, especially as the demand for sex dolls and robots mainstreams—when the tipping point of enough Toms,

Dicks, and Harrys will want to buy them. After all, we're talking about the greatest human urge of them all, and robots are offering the fun with none of the nasty side effects.

And remember, although this new business deals with sex, there's nothing illegal in making or selling them. Nor is it "porn," as such—at least it's not the seedy kind we normally think of (it doesn't involve children; women whose fathers didn't pay enough attention to them; runaways from an abusive relationship; women who are addicts or prostitutes; women whom men have coerced into their sex acts, sometimes even violent sex with multiple men; or some other sad and unfortunate circumstances that leads them to the world in which they assume their only value is in their bodies).

Not so with robots. The average person won't have to deal with that nagging feeling that he's somehow supporting a coercive or dehumanizing industry. To paraphrase the phrase from many films: No humans were hurt in the making of this industry. Why? Well, there are no humans to suffer any harm or dehumanizing.

I mean, other than those engaging with the robots.

This industry *will* happen, and it will happen *big*; it's too easy from both sides, demand and supply. Each will encourage the other in a never-ending cycle of price reductions, better selection, and greater quality in the form of more and more realistic and responsive robots.

But buyer and seller beware: once the robot goes mainstream, it will be just like the car, air conditioning, the cell phone, or the internet—all of which have woven themselves into the fabric of most people's everyday lives. In fact, we wonder how we ever got by without each of these things. It's already started sexually: many men now routinely take pills to help with their erectile dysfunction (ED). It's become a mainstay of their lives. Ask them: many of them will say it plainly. They don't know how they ever got by without them before.

And like all those things, they just won't be able to break away from them. There will be no going back. That's right: sex robots are here to stay.

But if we want to find out how we got here, we need first to understand who we are and how we look at ourselves. After all, that's how we understand the demand side of equation. For that, however, we need to explore the new environment of sex itself.

Sex Is Scary

What a thing to say: "Sex is scary."

But it is. Think of it from the perspective of today's twenty-somethings. From the possibility of pregnancy (and in the old days, the possibility of dying in childbirth) to the possibility of contracting a lifelong illness which might give you repeated painful rashes (herpes), or even a *life-threatening* disease (HIV), why wouldn't everyone have some qualms about getting in the sack?

There are other physical and emotional ramifications as well. Taking off clothes may be one thing, but a man might rough-house or otherwise hurt a woman in the process. If a woman no longer wants to be with a man sexually, he may rage against her and beat her. He might even kill her.

And for a man, sex might trigger an emotional response in a woman; she might never leave him alone, terrorizing him endlessly. "Hell hath no fury like a woman scorned," as the paraphrased line from the tragedy *The Mourning Bride* goes.

Women will slash tires, steal money, sleep with the ex's best friend, burn his clothes, lie to police to get their ex arrested, smash his car with a golf club (yes, that was Tiger Woods's ex-wife), delete important emails and computer files, and wreck cars so that the ex can't drive to his new girlfriend's place.[26]

Remember the daring all-nighter, cross-country ride of astronaut Lisa Novak, who drove from Houston to Orlando nonstop except to fill up for gas from time to time—and naturally to get new adult diapers, so she could relieve herself while still driving to save precious time? Why all the rush and fuss? To confront the lady rival of her former boyfriend—also an astronaut—and maybe even kidnap her. In the end, she managed only to pepper spray her after the rival agreed to crack open the window to hear Novak's story.[27] Who knows why Novak did it? Maybe it had something to do with the lack of oxygen in space.

One scorned woman admitted she sent the mother of her ex-boyfriend seventy dildos with pictures of her son on each of them. (You see? People *are* creative.) Still, my personal favorite is this one: "I ruined my ex-boyfriend's relationships, because I know he still loves me."[28] There's a lot to unpack there.

And then there's the famous case where Lorena Bobbitt up and cut off her man's penis while he was sleeping. It was a story of considerable notoriety, one that some feminists applauded: Camille Paglia declared Bobbitt's deed a "revolutionary act," and some feminists who supported Lorena flashed the V-for-victory sign then turned it on its side to look like a pair of scissors (*snip snip*).[29]

There was something about that penis-slicing that really scratched the man-hating itch many women had. As one of the female spectators at the trial plainly framed it, "It's every woman's fantasy."[30]

When you think about, boiling that pet bunny in the movie *Fatal Attraction* seems pretty tame in comparison.

So careful with those one-night stands, boys.

• • •

As I said, sex is scary. Or think of it like this: there's always a catch with sex. You shouldn't buy whatever it's selling.

Let's put it another way: sex is too good to be true.

And for men, there's something more significant. Campuses and workplaces are minefields for men: every sexual encounter or even a pass at a women can turn into an accusation of assault or even rape. And the standards set for expulsion from a college—seemingly applicable only to male students—is that a mere accusation can be enough, and the woman need not even testify, let alone be cross-examined.[31]

But guess what? Robots alleviate all those problems (snap fingers here) in one simple and electronic five-foot-long package (or longer, if that's what you fancy).

A robot won't ever accuse you of harassment, assault, or rape—whether before, during, or after the sexual encounter; or weeks, months, or even years later, for that matter. You won't have to get written consent from her before each step of intimacy. In fact, you want to have sex with her anytime and roughhouse her anyway you want? You're the boss, big boy.

Sure, robots won't get pregnant or give you a disease. That's great, but there's so much more. A robot will be predictable as well: she won't flare up into a sudden rage if you disagree with her or if you break up with her. She won't demand a relationship. She won't expect flowers or expect you to "just know" what gifts to bring, if you *really* loved her.

She won't ever say that you should know what she's thinking. She won't ask you to "just listen" to her problems. She won't expect you to apologize when you hurt her feelings—that is, whenever you can actually figure out her feelings. She won't say everything's "fine" when she really means things are *not* fine. She won't ask you if you think she looks fat in a dress. She won't demand that you make more money, stand up straight, or stand up to your boss. She won't get drunk on you and say your music is stupid.

She won't check out your emails and texts while you're taking a shower.

She won't get a restraining order against you. She won't divorce you and take most of your life's savings, leaving you to live on a sofa in your buddy's house. She won't get custody of the children. She won't make up stories to her girlfriends about you when she's upset with you.

She won't demand that the two of you try to talk things out or go to therapy together. She'll never say "marriage is hard work," and then actually expect you to work hard at it. In fact, she'll never expect you to improve yourself in any way at all.

If you're rich, you won't have to worry if she's a gold digger. If you're *not* rich, she won't leave you because you don't make enough money. She won't ask if you're saying she's fat. For that matter, she won't say you're saying something you never knew you were saying.

She won't need you, and you won't need her. She won't complain if you "cheat" on her with another sex robot—or an actual woman for that matter. Oh, and she'll never cheat on *you*.

In fact, she won't ever hurt you in any way at all. She'll never go astray, so you'll always know where she is unless you misplace her somewhere. But fear not; there's already an app for that.

She won't question or mock your manhood or your, er, assets. She won't call you a coward for not standing up to that guy who cut in front of you in that fast-food joint. She won't scream from the upstairs bathroom because there's a tiny spider there that she thinks is enormous and she expects you to stop watching the game, come up and kill it.

She won't tell you that you can't afford that boat you've been dreaming about getting since you were seventeen. She won't tell you to take out the garbage. She won't push your buttons or exploit your weaknesses. She won't try to create a wedge

42

between you and your family. She won't take out all her resentment toward her daddy, her former boyfriends, or the ex-husband who left her.*

She won't have a period.

She won't let herself go. She won't even get older. She won't have moods or break into uncontrollable sobs. She won't expect foreplay before sex and won't expect you to cuddle her, after. She won't complain if you don't give her an orgasm.

She won't care if you're ugly, bald, fat, or short. She won't care about how sharply dressed you are or about your hygiene. And she certainly won't complain if you watch the football game or if your first inclination after sex is to be alone and play video games.

Come to think of it, she won't complain about anything at all.

Sex Is Hard Work

Young men are less and less interested in sex. In fact, many men aren't losing their virginity until the age of twenty-six.[32] Worldwide there's even talk of a "sex recession." That's right: despite the far greater access to the new hookup-and-no-shame culture, people are just not "doing" sex as much anymore—at least with another person.

---

* And there is a *lot* of resentment out there. A 2005 movie, *The Upside of Anger,* captures this poignantly: A bitter mother whose husband has apparently left her rages against a middle-aged man who is now dating her early-twenties daughter. "It makes me sick," the mother says, to think of him and his daughter together. She soon slaps him hard, twice. After getting over the slaps, the man just lays it out to the mother, in as calm a fashion as possible: "Whom should I sleep with? Someone like you? Your age, my age? I don't. You know why? Because younger women are *nice.* You take them out, and they're actually grateful. 'Oh look, a steak. Yummy.' You go for a walk after dinner, the air smells nice, they say, 'Thank you. This was *nice.* This was *fun.* You're funny. Tee-hee-hee.' What should I do, Terry? Settle down and marry some pissed-off thing like you? I'd rather have someone come over and do dental work, every day, from my backside, up . . . through my *ass!*"

What's going on here? Doesn't basic Freudian psychology teach us that sex and avoiding pain are the most basic motivators in our lives?

The answer is that people *are* having sex, and a whole lot of it. They're just not having it with each other.

To get a sense of the new sex world order, one needs only to look at the relative microcosm of Japan. The country's residents not only produce and consume porn more than most others; it also leads in the design of high-end sex dolls. What may be more telling is the lengths to which Japan is inventing evermore enticing modes of genital stimulation. And these are modes that no longer even evoke old-fashioned sex—again, meaning sex involving more than one's self.[33]

The internet made pornography easy, and then mainstreamed it. Few people patronize sex shops anymore for their sexual one-off needs (sex toys, videos, etc.). They can get all that and much more on the internet. In fact, as of the writing of this book, experts estimate that more 30 percent of internet use is porn related—with more monthly visitors than Netflix, Amazon, and Twitter combined.[34] That percentage will increase with time.

In short, in much the same way each of us assumes that everyone around us has a cell phone, most everyone is watching porn (with varying degrees of frequency) or somehow uses the internet for his or her sexual needs. How do we know this? Because recorded page visits don't lie. And the money is coming from more than just the few men who used to get their *Playboy* and *Penthouse* magazines mail-delivered, wrapped in brown paper.

Everyone and anyone can cozy themselves up in the seemingly private world of the internet. They can get virtually anything "from the comfort of their own home." It's happening because it *can*. It's become so easy now, at least relative to the olden days, when a man (or couple) physically had to drive to Ye Olde Sex Shoppe and brave the possible shame of someone recognizing him. Even if someone didn't recognize him, he couldn't be comfortable in a sex shop; he'd be surrounded by unsavory characters—all of which would give an "ick" factor that also created an obstacle to going (never mind that the other customers perusing the same sex goods might feel the same way about him). The easy access to porn on the internet has taken all that away.

Then there is the pursuit of sex with another person itself, at least in the pre-online dating days. There's all that scheduling, planning to be just a little bit late but not *too* late. There's the wondering about how to dress, where to go for dinner, making sure you show halfway decent manners, anticipating what she might like to talk about, trying to be funny, or remembering an interesting anecdote to share—all without looking like you're trying too hard. Then there's the pretending to be more wealthy or successful than you are—to be smarter, healthier, or more sophisticated than you are or to be more connected and popular than you are.

And all the while, you have to assess what kind of woman *she* might be: Is she needy? If you're looking for a relationship, how might she navigate life's pitfalls? What will she look like in five years? Might she be too crazy or moody? What if it doesn't work out and she starts text bombing you night and day?

If you're a woman, you might also have to worry about all the makeup and other primping for the date. And then there's all the emotional hopes just before the date—that he might be the "one"—only to be dashed upon seeing him and knowing this thing won't last longer than the cup of coffee you'll have to order (now that you're stuck here) or until your friend calls you with that unexpected emergency that you had set up ahead of time.

Oh, and I almost forgot: summoning up the courage to ask her to go out with you or dealing with friends who know you like a particular girl, but who'll judge you for not getting a date with her. If you're the girl, there's all the wondering if he's ever going to call. There are the subtle hints you can drop that you'll hope he'll pick up. Will they work?

And then if you like him or her, there's the follow up—or the wondering if the other person is as interested in you as you are in him or her. If you do have a relationship, and you start sleeping together, what then? You have to please her, and you expect her to please you. But even expectations entail some degree of effort.

Like I said: Sex is hard work.

The result of all these factors? Self-Pleasure City. That's right; it's some form of masturbation or another.

And then along comes Tinder. Most of these complications suddenly vanish. You know the girl likes you, and she knows you like her. You know she's single and she's available for sex. There are no expectations of romance, or even flirting. You'll never have to involve yourself in the song and dance of the mating ritual, of approaching a girl, of getting rejected. That's all prepackaged for you. You know *exactly* who likes you now.

There are no expectations of getting to know each other, impressing each other, or of any future together. You may not even know what he does, where he's from, or his political or religious persuasions. Heck, you may never find out his real name.

When someone watches porn, he doesn't care about the name of the naked woman he's watching, either. So, in a sense, hasn't he just projected the world of porn into his own world? Hasn't he just "porned" his everyday relationships with the opposite sex? Hasn't he just been engaging in mutual self-pleasuring, even if it *is* with another person?

The more decades I spend on the planet, the more I've come to realize this simple truth: few people like to work hard. Sure, they may understand it's necessary to succeed in business, to remain healthy, and to have good relationships. They may even think it builds character, but that doesn't mean they like it.

They'd rather pursue the quick path to the big bucks, to fame, to losing weight, or to just about anything else one might pursue. That's why people pursue gambling and the lottery instead of mastering a trade. That's why they hope to get on *Dancing with the Stars,* instead of helping their community or church. That's why they go on trendy weight-loss schemes instead of eating sensibly and exercising.

They'd rather not work for their sex, either. For most people, if there's a way to get it easy, they're all for it. Who wants to "earn" sex by working at being attentive, attractive, ambitious, and interesting? That's asking a lot. You might as well insist that someone should travel across the country by horse and buggy. Aren't there planes that can do the same thing for far less cost and effort?

In one of my favorite movies, the 1973 movie *Sleeper,* the main character Miles Monroe comes out of a cryogenic deep freeze after two hundred years. He isn't quite prepared for the automated, emotionless world he now faces. Among the many automated devices he notices is the "Orgasmatron," a machine that simulates sex.

Why is there such a device? First, because everyone's become frigid for some reason (except for Italians), and second, because it requires virtually no effort on the part of the user. We see a couple using it, but they don't even take off their clothes as they enter into the device, and the experience lasts all of five seconds. As they leave the device, they're continuing their previous conversation, with no reference whatsoever to the sex they just experienced together. Citizens of the future have become so lazy that they can't even be bothered to engage in the "effort" of sex. Sex is just some need to fulfill for the moment. It's like thirst: you can satisfy it at a convenient water fountain.

With Tinder and the end of relationship-coupling, we may not be far away from a *Sleeper*–type sexual future. As I've shown, it's already happening in Japan.

So sex is not only scary; it can be hard work—especially the "relationship" kind of sex. And for anyone who's been married, they'll correctly point out that marriage is hard work. Like, *really* hard. It comes with unbelievable amounts of troubles, stress, and anxiety—and all because you have to deal with one person who changes on you and makes demands upon you all the time. Who wants to compromise their time with their buddies, their politics, their woodshop work in the back shed, the movies they want to see, or how many times they have sex? But you have to.

As the joke goes: It's true that single men lead shorter lives. However, married men are much more willing to die.

And so people masturbate to porn, use dildos, and other sex toys to self-pleasure, and dabble in swipe-dating websites for their orgasms. Such things are all so easy and available to anyone now. More importantly, such things make sex less scary, *and* less work. It's as if such things are training wheels on bikes or bumpers on bowling lanes to prevent the balls from falling into the gutters.

And so why *wouldn't* young people delay having sex? They're still pleasuring themselves. But as they see it, they're avoiding the bowling ball falling in the gutter or falling on the asphalt. Why ruin a good thing?

Robots will be the next step. The problem is that once they reach true mass appeal and improve in realistic features, it will so simulate an actual sexual relationship that it may take away the desire to ever enter into a real relationship.

Here's a thought experiment: Imagine a grown man riding a bike on your street, with training wheels. He'd look silly, for sure.

But even more pathetic? He actually thinks he's riding a bike.

Hope and Change

Women marry men thinking they're going to change them,
and they never do.
Men marry women hoping they'll never change,
but they invariably do.
—UNKNOWN

But wait! There's more. Part of what seems to be nature's cruelty is that we *change*: we get older, and, with it, we see sagging breasts on women, less hair on men, flabby and bigger buttocks, and larger paunches. Our skin becomes less supple and silky. Worse yet, your partner might become religious or change political parties on you.

Not so for the robot. *She* won't get fatter, meaner, or older or decide to become an organic pesca-vegan. She won't change on you at all. She remains locked in time; only *you* get older and fatter. She has *zero* defects. Or, if you like, she'll have only the defects you want her to have.

When you think about it, she's the best partner ever. She's there whenever you want her. There's no need for a relationship or expectations of any kind (you can even skip the "friend" part of "friends with benefits"). And you can indulge every fantasy, and she'll never think you're weird.

She can be whomever you want her to be. She's the "ideal" of the perfect woman—at least *your* perfect woman—and God knows few women can meet *that* standard. What with feminism and culture changing what it is to be a woman, robots can be *real* women, as it were.

Irony, no?

None of that will ever change. She'll stay exactly the way you found her, which is just the way many men want her: the same. But should you fancy a change, you can toss her out or recycle her—let's be environmentally aware here—and move on to the newer, shinier robot.

And don't worry: the good people at the sex robot factory will keep you posted about all the latest updates and newer models, as they get more and more realistic, more responsive, and start doing more "human" things. Perhaps the manufacturers will have a yearly announcement to showcase the latest models, with all the latest technology, as Apple does every year to showcase the latest iteration of their iPhones and computers. It'll all feel very space-age and hi-tech.

All the Lonely People

There are many lonely people out there. You might wonder: *Hey, why don't they just meet each other?* That would seem the obvious solution but apparently not for many.

Loneliness is a real epidemic, according to most psychotherapists. Scour the internet and most sources will proclaim the reason that men are lonely is that society teaches them incessantly to be manly, but they have a pent-up need to express their feelings and otherwise be emotional. But they just can't, you see.

We hear phrases such as "[t]he hypermasculine messaging around manliness that permeates our society needs to be addressed," and "Hypermasculinity is a plague on the modern man." Yes, that's right: "hypermasculinity." That's a thing.

Suicide rates are the highest they've ever been, according to the *Huffington Post*. Why so? Because society expects men to be all masculine and stuff, and many men just can't meet the expectations.[35] The result? Suicide City.

The problem with this argument, of course, is that it assumes the higher suicide rate relates entirely around gender norms and expectations. No one provides an analysis or reason of any kind. It's just what the author figures is the reason—or perhaps what he *wants* the reason to be.

The argument also doesn't account for the obvious historical fact that "society" was much *more* "hypermasculine" in the past and far *less* tolerant of gender bending and the numerous different kinds of sexual behavior and identities that we apparently didn't know we had until last month.

The opinion piece also fails to consider actual evidence that might shed light on the escalation of suicides—the actual suicide notes of the men who kill themselves, for example. Did any of the men committing suicide write about how "toxic" or "hyper" masculinity finally got the best of them? No. But, according to the author (and many others nodding along with him), there can't be any other cause. You know—causes like depression, situational finances, a public humiliation, a woman who left them, or the complex myriad of other reasons that *actually* cause people to kill themselves.

They want gender confusion to be the source of the problem, so they can devote all the resources to fix that problem. So there you go.

It all misses the mark, but for whatever reason, people are sounding the alarm about the "emerging public health threat" of loneliness. By and large, people do recognize the problem. The assumed causes (other than gender confusion and expectations, that is) stem from greater involvement with social media, especially among young people born in the late '90s and later.[36] While this may have something to do with it, most commentators fail to show even a correlation, let alone a causation. In fact, it may be that social media involvement might be the *result* of loneliness, rather than the cause of it. In other words, social media involvement might be a symptom of loneliness.

But there is scant evidence showing the actual cause for the loneliness epidemic. Still it's there, indeed, and it seems to apply to both genders (or all fifty plus of them, if you prefer). Women proclaim that they've never been so lonely, and the polarity between the sexes seems greater than ever.[37]

Polls find that eighteen- to twenty-four-year-olds are four times as likely to feel lonely "most of the time" as those aged more than seventy, among many other alarming trends in social disorders and mental health issues.[38] Looking from a few different sources of data, it does seem that way. The percentage of older Americans who responded that they regularly or frequently felt lonely jumped from the range of 11 percent and 20 percent in the 1970s and 1980s, respectively, to 40 to 45 percent by 2010. Longitudinal studies in Europe have also found the same thing.[39]

But aside from pseudo-causes and conjecture, no one is really trying to figure it out. (We will later, I promise; just have patience.) But here is a hint; the answer lies within the question itself: why were we not as lonely *before*, in decades past? Also, why was there *less* of a divide between men and women, *before*?

These are rational and essential questions. Logic dictates that we *should* ask these questions, but few seem interested in posing them. But if you don't ask the right questions, you certainly won't get the right answers. It's like a town experiencing a rash of leukemia among its children, without anyone asking what the rate of leukemia was in the preceding decades. You know, the time before that big company started dumping all its chemicals in the local river where everyone gets their water.

But the one-two punch of the reality of loneliness and the reality of the male/female divide is there. No one is doubting that. And that combination also will compel more men—and some women—to the proverbial arms of robots. With a robot, you can at least be *less* lonely. And we discussed before that we *all* engage in virtual relationships, one way or the other. You may have a hard-wired craving for relationships, but it turns out you don't have to satisfy that craving with an actual human. A facsimile can be just as good, if not better.

And the divide between men and women? *What* divide? Sex robots will eliminate that altogether. There's just you and your robot. There aren't any misunderstandings between the "sexes" here anymore. There isn't any complaining, door slamming, or arguments of any kind at all.

No more tension or angst. No more expectations, judgments, or fear.

Peace at last.

Chapter 2

Feminism Was Here

There's an old joke about my people the Jews: get two Jews in a room, and you'll get three opinions.

I think something similar when it comes to feminism, except that the joke would be: What is the definition of feminism? Whatever you think it is, it's not.

There seem to be hundreds of different definitions of feminism, and no one seems to be able to provide a comprehensive one. You can't picture "feminism" in your head in the same way you'd be able to picture, say, an apple strudel.

Don't fret—most people can't quite pin it down, either. Even the good people at Wikipedia seem wary about how to define it. According to them, feminism "is a range of political movements, ideologies, and social movements that share a common goal: to define, establish, and achieve political, economic, personal, and social equality of sexes."[1] Glad we cleared all *that* up.

Still, ask most people who consider themselves feminists or supportive of feminism, and they'll say that they believe women should have equal rights or opportunities. But putting aside whether women already have equal rights and opportunities, why would one need to use the moniker "feminism" at all? It seems redundant. We don't have a phrase "Blackism" for African Americans, "Latinoism" or "Asianism" for Latinos or Asians, or "Jewism" for Jews. But we have *feminism* for women.

So, if you believe no two words should have exactly the same meaning, then *feminism* should mean something more than just "equal rights" or equal access. But no one seems to be willing to cough up the goods.

Feminism seems to be more of an aspirational concept in search of itself, like a movie without a plot and where just a bunch of stuff happens. Everyone's saying what a great movie it is when they leave the theater, but you don't want to be the one to say you had no idea what it was about.

Or it's like one of those ol' boy clubs, like The Loyal Order of Moatriose, which have lofty but vague mission statements such as "to seek the betterment of mankind through awareness of wrongs." In the end, however, there's only a lot of cigar smoking and scotch. Perhaps there's a bowling tournament once in a while.

Feminism may be far more dangerous than that. I've since come to think of it as more like the shark in *Jaws*. You realize its presence only after the devastation it wreaks, in the form of mangled bodies the shark has left for us to discover the next day on the beach. You never actually get to see or touch the shark in real time, but by golly you know it was there. It's far more terrifying that way too—especially with that music. There's the sense that the shark can be everywhere and anywhere, all at the same time. You don't even know how big it is or where it might strike next.

Such is the feeling we all get from feminism. People trot out the claim that they are a feminist, but beyond the notion that a woman should have the equal right to become an astronaut like a man (but not a plumber; feminists are not as keen on that), it's not quite clear. Still, during the proverbial next day on the beach, the devastation it has wrought is now quite apparent.

Irina Dunn famously stated in 1970 that "a woman needs a man like a fish needs a bicycle." It sure is a funny image, a fish riding a bicycle. What fun it must have been to come up with that one. "Good one," she must have said to herself.

And yet most female humans don't seem to conform to her witty aphorism. Strangely, it appears that women actually *do* seek out men and *do* seem to need them, and vice-versa. There are even rumors that girls as young as six years old sometimes imagine their wedding day to their special man who will love them very much. (Strange but true. Google it.)

In fact, some of Dunn's detractors might argue instead that there is actually a powerful sexual attraction between the sexes, and that this very attraction may even help in the perpetuation of the species, without which the species would never survive. It's a working theory, anyway.

At least until recently.

People tend to believe preposterous lies over time, especially when schools, entertainment, news media, social media, and even parents drumbeat the lie repeatedly. And the fish/bicycle lie is no exception. Western civilization adopted it with great vigor.

As with many lies, however, believing them can lead to bizarre and sometimes dangerous consequences. The fish/bicycle lie is again no exception. It has brought us the notions that marriage isn't that important (indeed, maybe women should reject marriage altogether, what with it being a patriarchal construct men designed to enslave women[2]); that women should have the same impulses as men for multiple partners or emotion-free and consequence-free sex; that we shouldn't have children because it is irresponsible to do so; that women don't need men at all to have children (that is, if they want them at all—God only knows why they would); that women don't need men, ever, except to satisfy their sexual lust from time to time—and even that they can do for themselves with devices, if need be.

In the 2017 movie *Wonder Woman*, the lead character—the half-god Diana Prince—proudly declares almost exactly that:

she approvingly quotes a fictional woman philosopher who "came to the conclusion that men are essential for procreation but when it comes to pleasure, unnecessary." And please: no one should misconstrue the fact that Prince is played by the beautiful actress Gal Gadot, who all but flashes every curve of her exquisite body to tease men's ever-present lustful instincts. There's no mixed message of any sort there. No, no. *That* was all a message of empowerment for the girls. *Not* to tantalize men.

Feminism has also taught that women should concentrate on their careers before marriage or having kids; that heterosexuality need not be the norm nor idealized (being attracted to another woman is great; go for it, girl); that chivalry and romance actually demean women, who need neither; that the very notion of masculinity is toxic on almost every level, and we must utterly suppress or even go to war against it (after all, women have suffered so much under that masculinity)[3]; and that family, femininity and the very notion of differences between men and women are meant to suppress women.

Today's woman often doesn't pursue love, a relationship, a husband, or a family, at least not as a priority. Such things play second fiddle to her career, where she hopes of first associating with some career-advancing corporation then climbing the ladder where she might one day become a shareholder—a corporation with which she actually has, interestingly, something akin to a marriage. In the process, far from freeing women, feminism has actually *shackled* women, requiring them to work if they are to be respected.

At the same time, the Annie-Get-Your-Orgasm message to women also boomed loud and clear to the boys. It "freed" *men* to pursue as many emotion-free sexual encounters as they like, without any sense of obligation to marry.

How do you take your irony: sad or bitter?

How did she arrive to such a deportment in life? It was the media and such, yes, but also her other career-oriented female cohorts who egg her on with credos of "girl power" and "you can have it all." It's all part of an echo chamber that reamplifies the message that we should abandon all the things that made civilization. It all results in pain, like too much feedback on a microphone.

She may regret it later, but then she, too, will find herself egging on her own female friends and colleagues coming up the ranks. All of these women eventually will have one thing in common: an unease; a feeling like something is missing. It will stay with them all their lives. They may not be able to define it, but it will always be there: a lingering sense that somewhere, a long time earlier, they may have taken a wrong turn.

As I've shown above, the women themselves seem to be saying it: they are ever so *lonely*. Suddenly they realize that they've been playing a game of musical chairs for relationships, except that the chairs seem to be disappearing at an accelerating rate.

All the while, women express their bitterness at men, doubling down that toxic masculinity and "it's a man's world" thinking are the causes of their isolation, and has kept them from earning the same pay as men and from being happy. Men are to blame.

And men are receiving women's message of anger, loud and clear. How do they respond to the mantra that men are toxic and that women don't need courtship, dating, relationships, marriage, or babies to feel fulfilled? By not courting or dating them, by not having relationships with them, by not marrying them, and by not having babies with them.

Singer Beyoncé crooned the now-famous line, a rallying cry for all the single ladies: "If you liked it, then you should have put a ring on it." That was *so* 2008. The men of today, however, can "like it" all they want, without any sense that they should give *anything* in return for "liking it," let alone put a ring on it. Why so? Because all the single ladies aren't expecting a ring anymore. It's an alien expectation even to the ladies. Sure, they've heard of marriage, but that's what people do when they want to live within the oppressive patriarchal construct . . . and so forth.

Men *do* want the sex, mind you. They really, really do. Never worry about that. But what is becoming an institutionalized seething anger from women, as well as ever-changing rules about the give-and-take and the "dance" of sex, is downright confusing for men, if not frightening them away from sex altogether.

Mr. Lurie, I've got to say. This is beginning to sound downright misogynist. You're blaming all women. Women are gaining their sexual freedom—finally—and you now you're saying that freedom is destructive to men? Men get to be sexually free and women don't? Not cool, Mr. Lurie. Not cool at all.

I figured some of you might go there. Sometimes you have to explain what you're *not* saying, so here we go: nowhere have I written that *women* are to blame. I do blame aspects of feminism, particularly those which encourage women to deny the sea of differences between men and women, demonize masculinity as toxic, dismiss marriage as patriarchal, and declare that women don't need men at all. *These* are what I blame. They are wildly destructive to relationships, and ultimately civilization.

I promised you earlier that I would explain why loneliness was far less prevalent in the past and why the divide between men and women seems far greater today. The answer is twofold but quite simple.

The first is, in decades past, people *acknowledged* the differences between women and men. While certainly anyone was and remains free to pursue a classic man's job (CEO, astronaut, etc.), that never meant that a woman should consider herself incomplete until she acted like a man. Nor did it mean that men and women no longer had differences between them. Each sex sensed that the other had unique roles and strengths that were good and the other might appreciate—something that the other sex lacked. And in turn, each sex felt they *needed* the other sex. Our sense of relationships arose out of this sense of need—the search for our platonic "other half." That in turn gave us a sense that we had something to offer to someone else. There was *purpose* in that. And without purpose? You'll soon be a member of the Lonely Hearts Club.

Although there were *differences* between men and women, there was no real sense of a "divide." Now, however, there *is* a divide. Worse, that divide seems greater than ever. I believe it's precisely the result of our *pretending* men and women are the same, when all our experiences and instincts scream loudly that they are not.

The undercurrent realities clashed with what feminists *wanted* to be realities. That clash of realities is what created hostilities. *That* is what created the "divide." It's like running an army and expecting everyone to do the same work, instead of separating and assigning tasks according to years of experience, education, and talents. Sooner or later, you're going to have a lot of infighting.

But over the past few decades, society kept insisting there were *no* inherent differences between men and women. So wouldn't that necessarily mean you didn't really *need* anyone else, at least on a romantic level? We applauded single moms who had babies without a man in sight. We even declared fathers unnecessary.[4]

And when we no longer *need* anyone else, what's the point of a relationship?

That leads to the second cause: loneliness has triumphed because so many have *abandoned* that notion of relationships. It was inevitable. All relationships, to some extent, fill some sort of hole within each of us: A parent and child each fulfill needs of the other. Friends seek each other out for something unique that the other provides. It's even true for clergy and their congregations and for people and their dogs.

Yet the feminists abhor the notion that a woman might *need* a man. Writer E. Jean Carroll's recent book *What do We Need Men For?* (2019) underscores this attitude in the very title. Likewise, the best-selling *50 Reasons Why a Woman Needs a Man* (2018) sets forth in fifty pages the same response: "She doesn't." So poignant and witty.

What such people don't seem to fathom is that this ultimately leads to the rejecting of relationships altogether—at least the long-lasting committed kind. And so after years of feminists pushing women to be more like men and abandon the notion of romance and even family, that's exactly what they got.

These are lonely ideas. Nothing in feminism advanced the notion of mutual support and emotional well-being between the sexes. Nothing. There was only the pursuit of career and self-satisfaction—for women. Parents often don't even bother to urge their children to get married. It's only about going to a good college and getting a great career. Feminists went further: they pushed away the notion of relationships and families. They pushed men away, too, actually hoping to marginalize them and their "toxic masculinity." They've been successful; now men are afraid to approach them.

Everyone has an "uncle" point—the moment we give up because we realize it's just not worth it. Feminism pushes our boys and men well past it. Then one day the women discover that the "good" men are going, going, gone. No one told them they were in a race, and they missed the starting gun. And they're not only running against many other women in their age group but also the younger ones.

And soon they'll be competing against robots—the robots that their hatred of men and masculinity helped create. And these robots won't push men to get married, won't get fat or older, and won't complain or demand men to apologize for being men.

So these girls seek out love and relationships in any way they can. They join Tinder and other swipe right/swipe left apps on smartphones. It's a losing proposition, however, and only accelerates the appetites of men for the quick thrill, the immediate orgasm, the more sexy girl who will "put out" faster and who will "do" more.

The result? A lot of single ladies with no ring on it. A lot of ladies wondering how they lost their husband or boyfriend to a friggin' *robot*.

And all of them will be wondering why they're so lonely.

As any good genie will tell you: be careful what you wish for.

Got Testosterone? We Can Help You with That

It's not enough that many men are terrified to have sex. Or at least they should know that it's a minefield if they ever do summon up the courage to ask a girl out, let alone "hook up" with her. They learn they shouldn't be men at all. They should be more like, say, women.

Men politely play along with the culture and sex wars. They say: yes, my wife is the true brains of this outfit. Without her, I don't know where I'd be. Women are smarter, know how to *really* get things done. *They* know what's what.

It's been the common refrain: celebrate the woman, mock the man. She's always the better half. No man can succeed without the woman he married.

It's actually quite gracious when you think of it. Gentlemanly, if you like.

Why is this so? Because men don't mind—it's no skin off their back to make fun of themselves and of one another. Men constantly rib each other in front of everyone. We call each other ugly and stupid. Sometimes we call each other "ladies" as an insult. Don't worry—it's a sign that we're buds.

By contrast, women seem to need a daily mixture of elevation and validation; they don't rib one another like men do. In a public speech, a woman can mock her husband and get great laughs, but the husband following up would never dare do the same to her. For him, he can only say how thankful he is that she ever agreed to marry him, lowlife that he is, and then modestly put himself down even further. In short, she gets to mock him, and then he gets to mock himself. That is the natural order of husband-wife conduct, at least when engaging with the outside world.

It seems to have always been thus. But somewhere along the way, we've managed to repeat the Women-Are-So-Much-Better-Than-Us mantra to the point that both men and women began to believe it. Everything about men is "off." Everything about men needs to change. There's very little, if anything, that men actually have to offer. Just ask Wonder Woman.

And it shows up everywhere in our culture, particularly in our entertainment. Everywhere you look, TV programs and entertainment in general now portray women as more sophisticated and smarter, more adventurous and more risk taking. Television reflects this often: the husband is a fat boob who makes stupid decisions; the wife is a bit neurotic, sure, but she's definitely the smart one with good judgment, who patiently puts up with her impulse-driven man. You see it on shows like *The Simpsons, The King of Queens, Rules of Engagement,* and *Family Guy*. It happened even further back with *The Flintstones, All in the Family,* and *The Honeymooners*.

Then there are the hundreds of commercials, which go even further: A for-women-only insurance company claiming men are stupid enough to drive their car over a cliff (that's why the company insures only women, you see). Cascade sells its gel pods laundry detergent because guys don't know how to wash dishes. And think men aren't stupid enough to try pole vaulting the pool with one of those extended pool skimmers? Well, yes, as it turns out, they *are* that stupid.[5]

But brains aren't the only place where she's better. Now the woman is even as strong as her male counterpart and sometimes stronger. Women are now constantly fighting in movies and television—real fighting with fists and arms and legs and head-butts and everything—against male bad guys. And none of the male characters even wince at the fact that they're fighting a girl, let alone feel bad about it. She's just one of the guys now, so fair game.

You see that in movies such as *Million Dollar Baby, Mission Impossible, Mad Max: Fury Road, Mr. And Mrs. Smith, The Avengers, Black Panther*, and virtually every modern superhero movie that has a female superhero or villain. It's even true in today's children's movies (*The Incredibles, Zootopia, Brave, Tangled, Moana, Frozen*, and many more). In fact, in *The Incredibles 2*, a benefactor who wants to revive superheroes as legal wants to showcase the wife (who's superhero alter ego is Elastigirl) and *not* the superhero husband. Why? 'Cause she's just better at getting the job done. Naturally.

As Elastigirl herself says in the beginning of the first *Incredibles* movie, "Settle down, are you kidding? I'm at the top of my game! I'm right up there with the big dogs! . . . Leave the saving of the world to the men? I don't think so . . . I don't think so."[6] These ain't damsels in distress who need rescuing, and don't you forget it.

I bring up examples of entertainment because TV and movies reflect the aspirations—and often the agenda—of our culture. No movie studio is interested in pushing a story no one can relate to;

it won't sell. That's why you'll probably never see a major studio backing, say, a pro-incest movie.

But it doesn't mean that studios are interested in reality, either. Few of the examples above have *any* basis in reality. Tell me the last time you saw any woman police officer in real life taking down some 6-foot-2-inch man jacked up on PCP. Tell me the last time you saw a woman playing on a men's college or professional football or basketball team, or even clamoring to get on such a team? Hell, tell me the last time you've seen a woman volunteer to help lift someone on a chair at a Jewish wedding.

Yes, you might have a tail gunner in the military and a lady pull someone out of a burning building, but these are quite exceptional anecdotes. They are so exceptional, in fact, they make news the next day. Why? Because it almost never happens. They're "Man Bites Dog" stories.

Pretending women are as strong and brave as men is not only a lie in defiance of reality. It leads to an emasculation of men. I don't mean that literally or even figuratively; I mean the emasculation of the *raison d'être* of being a man in the first place. That *raison d'être* of men is to procreate, protect, and provide for a woman, and hopefully one day for a family. (People sometimes refer to these as the "three Ps.") Without them, men have little reason to visit the planet. We'd be like border collies with nothing to herd.

Women seem to understand that they have an instinctive role of nurturing, but many women deny men an instinctive role of their own. The reason? Because that instinctive role of men—protection and providing in particular—flies in the face of virtually everything feminism stands for. They just don't like it.

As the feminist mantra that women are the same as men and men are only necessary for procreation repeats time and time again in entertainment, social media, and academia, men have come to conclude that they have no role. They check out, as they see no centralizing purpose in the lives. It's like going to a bookstore, but the only books are about musical arrangements of ancient Hindus. There's just not that much for you. Worse yet, you can't ever leave the store. So you have two choices: either really get excited about the world of ancient Hindu music, or sit on a chair and stare ahead at nothing in particular, zoned out.

You see this emasculation play out in our elementary schools, where the education system celebrates girls and "girl power," but there is nothing left in the goodie bag of positive reinforcement for boys.

And the things that might actually be motivating to young Johnny? Squash them: no more roughhousing, making sounds of explosions or crashes, or talk about fighting bad guys. Cowboys and Indians or cops or robbers? Chasing girls at recess? Playing with pretend guns (even the kind you fake with your fingers) or even drawing a *picture* of a gun? Those are things of a Neanderthal oppressive past.

Johnny can learn so much more if we feminize him. After all, the world of the female has so much more to offer: cooperation and exploration of feelings, dialogue instead of destruction and needless competition, self-esteem instead of shame.

And don't worry: we still value honor, courage, integrity, and leadership. They still mean something but only in the context of being brave enough to cry—or to come out of the closet and admit you sometimes wish you were a girl.

"Manliness" means little anymore. In fact, feminism screams that it doesn't need you any longer, at least the "man" part of you. It's like men themselves don't even seem to have a sense of why they're around. Fewer and fewer people appreciate them, as if men have become mere tolerated nuisances to civilization. If only they could become invisible.

Feminism and modern culture *do* celebrate a male who seeks to satisfy himself with other men. We celebrate and encourage their "coming out" and expressing their homosexuality candidly and with pride. We do the same with lesbians, bisexuals, and with people who identify as the opposite sex. After all, it's who they *are*. To fight that would be wrong.

But if a male wants to celebrate his maleness and heterosexuality? You need to shove that right back in the bottle, Johnny. You must suppress those instincts and desires. While you're at it, don't forget to feel shame about it.

The result is exactly what we're seeing running rampant through our society: the feminized male, both from an objective and subjective point of view. Younger men themselves report feeling less masculine.[7] The commentary on this is extensive, with explanations from blaming the outright feminizing of boys in schools to lower sperm count to estrogen mimickers in our food and other products to blaming society for imposing "impossible" masculine standards.[8]

Or maybe it's because no one is teaching or celebrating manhood.

But no one denies the result: men just ain't what they used to be. They're staying home with the parents, playing a lot of video games, and hoping for the glorious day when sex robots will arrive.

And then one day women will sing along wistfully to a hit song called "Where Have All the Cowboys Gone?"

On Second Thought, Objectify Me After All

The Miss America Pageant has fallen into disrepute because, despite paying lip-service to other fine attributes of a woman, it objectifies women's beauty and their bodies too much. Victoria's Secret has recently felt the sting of the feminists and the trans and plus-sized neo-anti-sexists, because one of its covers featured only gorgeous women-by-birth who look really, really hot. How thoughtless and insensitive.

And yet, take a look at the culture and watch as the feminists seem to cry out loud for the right to show off their hot bodies. It's as if they've abandoned the clarion call for greater opportunities, now that they've gotten them.

So they turn to their bodies and their beauty. It's not just the skimpy attire many women now wear as ordinary attire. It's not just the encouragement of women everywhere to go out there and feel sexy as a primary goal. It's not just the encouragement for women to take charge of their sexual desires.

It's also the tacit acceptance of pornography and female sex workers making a lucrative living in that industry. It's the acceptance of bikini-clad women in advertisements and the general culture of marketing to a man's gaze—encouraging a woman to exhibit herself sexually.[9]

It's even the encouragement of women to pursue men through "sexting." Sexting has the potential of "break[ing] down barriers of shame," finally allowing for sexual exploration and positive "self-objectification" (yes, they really used that word). As one feminist author put it, sexting "allows me to navigate and inhabit my desires more truly."[10] Er . . . you go, girl!

The objectification continues in the world of movies. Wonder Woman is a powerful and independent woman, yet she reveals the most skin of all the superheroes. Why is that so? For a character who proclaimed not to need men, why does she seem to work so hard to attract them with as much of her body as possible?

Yet the feminists cheer all such things. It's as if they haven't realized that everything they've been championing has boiled down to . . . wait for it . . . sex.

So what is the end result of our abandonment of our cultural norms, our distinctions between men and women? What is the result of our glorification and empowering of porn, ever-tighter and flimsier fabric for women, and bed-hopping sex?

Ironically, far from getting *away* from objectification, we've instead unwittingly managed to accelerate *toward* it. Not only that, we've done so with a sort of righteous gusto ("We demand the right to objectify ourselves!").

We didn't stop to think that perhaps all we've managed to do is strip everyone down to his or her sexuality. We see it in yoga pants or leggings, most of which their makers design to show every part of a woman's body below the waist, as if she was naked.[11] It will get more so with time: outfits will cover the entire body, like in many TV shows and movies about the future (*Star Trek, Tron, 2001: A Space Odyssey, The Hunger Games*). One-piece body suits will become so sheer that a man will wonder from a distance if the woman has any clothes on at all. It will become ever more erotic too; the fabric itself will feel sensual and will offer a type of massage to her body—yes, to her genital area as well so she can feel stimulated all day long.

Just you wait. It'll happen.

It's not only the clothing, either. It's the way we identify ourselves. In the 1920s, if you asked someone to identify themselves, they might say they're American, French, British, and so on; perhaps they'd mention their particular denomination of Christianity or Judaism. In the seventies and for several decades thereafter, they might say they're Black, Latino, Native American, and so forth.

Starting in the second decade of the twenty-first century, however, humans' primary identity seemed to change yet again. There was a lot of overlap, but the transition seemed to move to sexuality and whether you have a penis or vagina—or whether you *wish* you had a penis or vagina. Do you identify as gay? That's awesome. Or perhaps you're transgender, gender queer, polycurious, or pangender?

That's what you *are* now. Everyone has reduced everyone else to who they get aroused—and not much else.

Your grandparents' identity associations are passé. Your skin pigmentation, your cultural ancestry, or even your religion are no longer a serious concern to most Americans. Those are *so* nineties. What matters is how you chase your orgasm.

Why *wouldn't* we move to this change in identities? We've consumed ourselves with easy and ever-present sex. From the time of Freud going forward, we've elevated sex to new all-consuming proportions, while simultaneously ripping it out of any religious context—other than to mock that it was there in the first place. Sex has become a controlling factor in how we see ourselves, and what animates and motivates our lives—if not *the* factor.

And why not? We've simultaneously belittled the notion of nationhood and patriotism (particularly the American variety). We've also done all we can to tear down and even demonize our religious institutions. You want to believe in Jesus and God? Sure, suit yourself. But do you really want to center your identity around such mythological creatures?

Cue the shaking of the head and the rolling of the eyes. Sex, my friend: *that's* where it's at. That's something you can *truly* experience. *That's* what's real, and where you can find your true satisfaction and "transcendence."

Here's an epiphany: with the gradual erasing of religious, marital, and national identities and values, what remains? The only "real" thing that binds us all: sex. Sex had always been the universal language everyone speaks, but now sex has somehow become a primary universal "truth."

Sex has become an idol that we now all worship. As Presbyterian pastor and writer Tim Keller, author of *Counterfeit Gods*, stated, an idol is "anything more important to you than God, anything that absorbs your heart and imagination more than

God."[12] He notes that among these idols are money, power, and of course sex. They are all counterfeit gods that serve to replace the true and only God to worship.

But, as Keller puts it, the comforts of modern life have created a false sense of security, and the hard work and foundation for civilization Judaism and Christianity gave us had nothing to do with those comforts. So fewer and fewer of us see that we have an active role in making the world good and maintaining the basic provisions (law and order, morality) that have made our civilization what it is. Instead, we just wake up each day concluding that we are, by and large, pretty good people—and having "good" intentions is good enough.[13]

Wow, Mr. Lurie. You're getting far afield here.

Trust me. It's going somewhere.

Why *wouldn't* sex become our idol? As faith, and Christian faith in particular, disappears in importance everywhere, life has come to turn evermore now on the prurient pleasures of sex. For many, the more sex you get, the more you've somehow accomplished. That's more so for men, to be sure, but the notion of sex-for-fun-and-thrills is gaining among women. Just ask the ladies on Tinder.

In the end, with all that, we might as well see *ourselves* as sex machines. We certainly have been treating others—and ourselves—as such.

And if we identify ourselves as machines, then at some point, aren't we?

Remember that now.

The End of Chivalry

I like holding doors for girls and women. I like saying "ladies first" and offering a woman the opportunity to go first into a room. I like standing up for her when she walks into a room, offering my seat in a crowded bus, holding packages for her, and walking with her to her car at night. I like offering her my jacket if she's cold or sharing an umbrella with her if it's raining.

And I remind my boys that you never hit a girl . . . *ever*. "Girls are special," I tell them. You just can't roughhouse with them like you do with boys.

Such things have become—or should become—second nature to us. But in the same way we know we need to say "please" and "thank you" but never think about why (for the exciting answer, read the final chapter of my book *Atheism Kills*), there actually was a reason why civilization developed rules of chivalry.*

Here's a twist: the code of chivalry wasn't actually for the women. It was for the men. That's right: it was practice makes perfect; fake it until you make it. Or more aptly, it was behaviorism for the men. Behaviorism is the notion that you undertake certain actions and your mind will follow. Judaism teaches this as one of its core tenets: engage in many good deeds, such as charity, spending time with the sick, avoiding gossip or swearing, and soon it'll become second nature to you, a part of who you are.

Likewise, if a man finds himself habitually opening doors for the ladies, offering them umbrellas, and adopting a ladies-first approach, it sends a constant internal reminder to himself that ladies are special. If he regards them as special, he won't be as likely to see them as objects he can brutalize and "take" just because he is stronger. In short, he's less likely to see them as sex objects.

And in the process, he'll be thrilled when one of the ladies wants him. He'll seek her out and want to make her happy, to

---

* When using the word *chivalry* here, I am not referring to the specific medieval codes that had certain aspects no longer relevant to today's modern world. I use the word loosely for brevity's sake, to refer generally to the modern general rules of manners a man should engage in when meeting, interacting with, or dating a woman.

protect her, and to provide for her. Why? Because he's learned his entire life to think of each woman as special.

It's not so anymore. Chivalry has left us, like that wonderful family dog who died. In all the complaining about the visits to the vets, the feeding and the training, we realized that he gave something meaningful back to us—he brought out the best in us. Maybe we should have appreciated him more before he ran into the street and got run over.

Feminism seems to have proudly killed chivalry. Feminism proclaimed that holding the door open for a woman, or giving her preference of any kind—no matter how seemingly nice— was a form of benevolent suppression.[14] In feminism's view, men designed the chivalry program not only to oppress women but to make women themselves believe they were weaker, and needed men to navigate the big bad world for them. It was a "protection racket" because it forced women to rely on men to protect women from other men.[15] A woman can handle life's challenges by herself, thank you. A woman needs a man like a fish needs a bicycle, remember.

Men got the message. Parents no longer teach the code to their boys. Fewer and fewer men show women the same level of deference. Women are like the guys now.

And the result? More and more men see women as sex objects.

No longer is there a system in place that reminds men to think of women as special. There is no longer any gatekeeper between a man's base and lustful instincts and acting on those base and lustful instincts. Not surprisingly, the percentage rate of forcible rape of women in America alone has increased from 1960 to 2017 by a staggering 335 percent. In other words, a woman in America is *4.34 times more likely to be forcibly raped in America today than she was in 1960.*[16]

Even accounting for women reporting rapes more often as well as other factors (such as greater immigration from cultures that have more lenient views on rape), it is clear that something else is going on. To deny the dismantling of a code of conduct that treated women as special—which constantly reminded men of their obligation to keep their lust in check—somehow has no impact whatsoever on the conduct of men toward women is absurd. One might as well argue that if we get rid of the traffic rules of the road, people will still drive at safe speeds and will stop at red lights.

The destruction of a code that encouraged respect for women, passed on from generation to generation from parents to son, and understood as a given in society, generally cannot bode well for either women or men. And yet no one is talking about it as a possible reason for the new pernicious treatment of women.

In 2017, various women initiated a slew of sexual harassment and rape charges against entertainment mogul Harvey Weinstein. This opened up a throng of claims against other men in entertainment and media. In what became known as the "#MeToo" movement (spawning from women's statements on Facebook and other social media that they, too, suffered sexual harassment, molestation, or rape), women, and some men, demanded an accounting from the offending men who had taken horrific liberties with them, treating women like they were objects for their personal amusement and abuse.

Women demanded that men learn to control themselves. They asserted—correctly—that it didn't matter what a woman might wear or say: unwanted advances were just that, unwanted. And men have no right to take them.

They demanded a new understanding, a sort of code of conduct, if you will. Protesters at women's marches and demonstrations had signs exactly to this effect.

But, what's this, you might ask? Here's a funny thing: *we already had a code.* A code where men understood the special nature of women, where they engaged in behavioral patterns that would place a block between men's lust and acting on that lust. Does it sound familiar?

So, ironically, women are now fighting for the same code of chivalry they had mocked for the past few decades as backward, patriarchal, and oppressive.

Now they want to put the proverbial genie back into the bottle. They want men to "get it" but don't offer a program by which to help them. That's like telling someone to "just stop drinking," without suggesting anything else to help them actually stop their drinking. My guess is that Alcoholics Anonymous does more than that.

And men of today, especially young men, don't understand why they should do *anything* unique for women, just because they're women. Women not only don't need men, but they are just as capable as men, are as strong as men, and can fend for themselves just fine. Remember?

Men have bought into this mantra, too, and they see it all around them. Women are their bosses now. There are now more women than men in most colleges, graduate schools, and many of the professions.[17] Commercials, movies, and television programs repeatedly show women fending for themselves just fine. In fact, they might even be *better* than men.

So why exactly should a man give a woman preferential status, please?

On the one hand, women are powerful and independent and don't need men, but they're also victims who need constant government intervention to protect them. And men need to change everything about themselves. How so? The feminist movement is light on the specifics. Maybe its leaders will get back to us on that.

Few talk about the reasons men engage in their objectifying, something which is seemingly (and factually) happening more than ever. Perhaps the end of chivalry is too amorphous to see as a cause, or even as a strong contributing factor, but intuitively it stands to reason. Here indeed was a code that men designed to encourage men to see women with respectful eyes, and *not* to objectify them. Here was a code that recognized men are inherently lustful and needed a society-wide protocol to check that lust.

And now, thanks to feminism itself, it's gone.

Feminism has returned men back to the world of old. The circle is complete. Feminism turned out to be nothing more than Orwellian doublespeak. Or, in the words of my friend Dennis Prager, feminism was no more interested in helping women than communism was in helping workers.

Once we return to a world where there is nothing unique or special about women (except the phrase "Don't touch!"), male objectifying is free to roam. From a man's point of view, he can objectify all he wants, as long as he doesn't act upon it—there are laws against it, after all. And no man wants to be accused of harassment; that can cost lots of money.

But the *wanting* of a woman in an *objectifying* way has returned, in full force.

But good news! Robots are here to the rescue. And just in time for Christmas, as it were. A man can now fulfill his patriarchal and oppressive libido to his objectifying delight—with as many sex robots as he wants. Sex robots will be everywhere, and women will wonder why so few men remain left to pursue them.

And there isn't a thing the law can do about it. The feminists out there have nothing to complain about, either: the man having sex with a robot isn't hurting anyone. He isn't even touching anyone, making inappropriate suggestions or gestures. He's leaving you alone, completely. A woman doesn't need a man, so conversely, it stands to reason that a man doesn't need a woman.

Now, however, campaigns are ramping up to stop the sexbot trend. For many, sex robots only encourage more sexism and abuse. According to Dr. Kathleen Richardson of the De Montfort University in Leicester, England, such robots will have a negative effect on human relationships because robots will only further present women as objects for sexual gratification. According to Lydia Kaye of the Campaign Against Sex Robots, "the idea of sexbots is modelled on the porn industry and the sex trade," and sex robots will only further validate and promote these industries.[18] Kate Darling, robot ethics expert at the MIT's Media Lab, asserts that the way we treat robots mirrors our own psychology and we'll treat robots as humans—even though we know they're just robots.[19]

What is their recommendation? Ban the robots, of course.

Putting aside the practical impossibility of banning anything, the position is galling. Women (feminists in particular) have made sex so legally daunting and socially awkward that many young men are afraid to have sex, or even to approach a woman. Religious people encourage marriage and sexual monogamy, but that is patriarchal and oppressive—so no thank you. Men turn to pornography, but that demeans and objectifies women, both in the production of the videos and in the viewing of the videos.[20] So no thank you to that. Men then might turn to quiet, porn-free self-gratification (masturbation). One can only imagine what violent, objectifying fantasy a man must conjure up in his head to get himself going. So maybe that's a no-go too.

And now they want to ban robots. Yet robots don't involve any real women, don't exploit them, and clearly have many "benefits" one would think feminist progressives would otherwise appreciate: no unwanted pregnancies, reducing world population growth and carbon emissions; no sexual transmission of disease, and of course no violence to women. To say that it would lead to greater violence against women is like saying playing aggressive contact sports like football, lacrosse, or hockey leads to greater violence and murder.

But they don't. It's as if they want to make sure they block off *any* sexual outlets for men, like they're building a wall to keep men confined in some sex-free city, with no avenues for escape. Any kind of sexual substitute is inherently wrong, and they only imagine how men will use whatever that substitute is to satisfy their violent and objectifying impulses. In fact, some extreme feminists (Catherin Mackinnon, Andrea Dworkin) viewed sex itself as *inherently* violent, or at least predatory. So maybe let's get rid of sex itself and just be done with it.

The famous definition for the word *chutzpah* is when a man kills his father and mother, and then pleads for mercy of the court on the grounds he's an orphan. Feminists are like that orphan. They decry the very social circumstances that they themselves created.

"We didn't mean to push you *that* far," they may say one day. But they have. Having asked men to leave them alone, that's exactly what they got. And now they complain that men might seek to satisfy themselves sexually through automation.

And then they'll complain that they're lonely.

The famous Virginia Slims cigarette ad company once declared to all women: "You've come a long way, baby." And that's true. They have.

I'm just not sure that they had this destination in mind.

Chapter 3
Orgasms to Go

In 1995 a movie titled *Strange Days* foretold a not-so-distant future of 1999, where a new virtual reality device allowed anyone—using a helmet type contraption—to record everything he was experiencing: the sights, sounds, smells, and touch of it all. Perhaps one might want to experience hang gliding in the Alps, mountain biking in Colorado, or base jumping into the giant Cave of Swallows in Mexico.

Or, you know, sex.

In the movie, the device quickly reaches full commercial appeal, available to the masses. One can relive personal experiences over and over again—or copy and sell them to the highest bidder. In one particularly bizarre (but not surprising) scene, one of the ancillary characters has bought someone else's sexual experience with a beautiful woman. But instead of just experiencing what the seller had experienced with the woman, the purchaser has spliced the moment of climax and copied it into an infinite loop. He ends up reliving the orgasm over and over again, forever stuck in his moment of ecstasy. Is it sad? Sure, but there are worse ways to go.

To many men and some women, this may resonate as a great fantasy. Our culture seems to celebrate the ecstasy part of sex but not so much the whole of it: the leading up to it, the relationship of it, the connection and sense of oneness that only sex seems to bring. It seems most people are uninterested in such nonorgasmic things, as though they were irrelevant. The goal is the ecstatic climax of it, and nothing more. It's similar to when viewers use their TV remotes to jump ahead to all the cool battle scenes of the *Star Wars* movies, skipping those boring parts, like when Yoda tells Luke to be patient and stuff. Or if you like, they recognize how cool the song "Stairway to Heaven" is, but seriously, can we just get to the guitar solo at the end? 'Cause you know: that's where it gets super awesome.

In the great discussion of sex, something has changed. It's all about the orgasm. It was a slow burn to get there: first there was "free love" in the sixties, which the advent of the birth-control pill propelled. So people felt more liberated to have sex for sex's sake. After all, sex is fun. Like, *really* fun. Just why was everyone so resistant to it all this time? Young people look at our ancestors, who held off on sex, in the same confused way a kid wonders why adults don't spend all their time eating ice cream, watching cartoons, and playing with puppies (always with the puppies).

Then, for the next few decades till the present, there was the infantilizing of the adult, where everyone was expected to understand and get in touch with his inner child. Children were no longer little adults; adults were more like big children.

This led to the trivializing of courtship and developing a relationship, which used to lead to the potential for marriage. Dating itself became less of a customary process. "Hanging out" became more common. Soon dating virtually fell out of favor, especially among the younger generation. Even in my college days during the 1980s, I recall women students bemoaning how no one really "dated" anymore. Soon, reflecting a cultural shift in perspective sometime during the 1990s, people no longer "made love." Instead they just started "having sex."

Mix in the powerful feminist mantra that women need to be more like men, coupled with fewer men on campus and women's instinctive need to compete for men's attention, and a hookup culture was born: Sex was something you did as a fun pastime, in the same way you might listen to music together or share late-night pizza. Dating for a relationship? How did that make sense anymore when you could get right to the action?

From there, everything raced fast forward: the internet arrived, which originally allowed people to share so much more of their backgrounds to get to know the "real" you in ways that old-fashioned dating and personal ads did not.

Somehow it didn't work out that way. Dating sites soon devolved to a swipe right/swipe left culture, where people weren't quite as interested in who you were as in whether you were nice to look at and perhaps had a nice body. Suddenly, your main offering was how somebody of the opposite sex might imagine you in bed.

You encouraged others to see you as a sex object. And so guess what? You became one.

It transformed the way people meet. It's become a "get to the point" world, where there's so little time to get to know anyone. They can't even spend the time on the phone just to have a normal conversation, let alone meet for half an hour at a coffee shop. Everyone texts now; they'll answer you when they have a moment. Real time, in-depth interaction has become rare.

More and more, texting (or "sexting") is more like calling for an Uber ride, delivering an orgasm to your door. Soon enough there'll be an app that will show men and women "around you" who want a quick hookup. Hover over the icon, and a picture of the girl or guy associated with that icon will pop up. Like her? Great. Click on the icon, and she's on her way to you, with an estimated time of arrival.

Think of it like Uber for your orgasm needs, except it doesn't cost you anything and will probably get to you faster. After all, we're talking about sex here.

The girls are beginning to figure it out. Especially after age thirty or so, single women in the "dating scene" feel compelled to compete for men's interests in ways they'd never dreamed of when they were younger. Women might even *start* a date with sex and then have coffee or dinner later. While they may have hope of a relationship, they have little expectation of one.

In many instances, men tell of meeting women on one of the numerous swipe dating apps, and they meet on streets only to have the woman get in and immediately open the man's fly and grab his penis—on their initiative, not the man's—and give him oral sex, while he drives. Stories abound of first-date sex. After exchanging a few messages (especially on Tinder), they might meet in a nearby park and minutes later have sex.[1]

Don't believe it? Even if some of these stories are only "stories," the reality is that a good deal of them *must* be true: the very *raison d'être* of these hookup sites is for quick and emotion-free sex. And the very success of these hookup sites (at least twenty-nine of them as of this writing) proves that random hookups are a frequent thing, for both men and women.

It's all about the orgasm. Why would anyone waste time getting to know each other? That's for those "relationship" people. Can we just get down to business, please? You and I won't see each other after this, let alone remember each other, so what's the point of needless chit-chat? Let's just get *off* on one another and then just get *on* with whatever we've got to do the rest of the day.

The whole way we see each other has changed. Everyone around us has no longer become a potential relationship; they've instead become someone who can provide us with an orgasm. That's what we've each become: "orgasm providers."

What adds fuel to this orgasm culture is that it seems a woman today often has little sense that she is giving anything up of herself. That sense—the sense that she's forfeiting something—seems to have gone sometime in the first decade of this century. It's like men themselves have become her new dildo. She and he and just masturbating with each other, using each other as sex toys.

Good God, Mr. Lurie, that is really a stretch. Men are the new dildos? Really?

Don't take my word on it. Take it from a female user of Tinder's services, who said as much in her own unabashed but revealing way:

> On Tinder everything's disposable, there's always more, you move on fast. You start browsing again, he starts browsing—and you can see when anyone was last on it. If five days pass with no messaging between you, it's history.
>
> At times, Tinder seemed less like fun, more like a grueling trek across an arid desert of small talk and apathetic texting. More than once, I deleted the app, but always came back to it. It was more addictive than gambling. I never dreamed I'd end up dating 57 men in less than a year [15 to 20% with whom I actually had sex]. . . .
>
> What did Tinder give me? I had the chance to live the *Sex and the City* fantasy. It has made me less judgmental and changed my attitude to monogamy too. I used to be committed to it—now I think, if it's just sex, a one-night hook-up, where's the harm? I'm more open to the idea of swinging, open relationships, which is something I'd never have expected.[2]

The wording says it all: online dating, particularly the swiping technology of Tinder, opened her to casual, "harmless" sex. It's intoxicating. But more poignantly, it's her own observation of sexuality as "disposable," and that you move on to the next orgasm fast, without much looking back. It's as if everyone treats everyone else like Dixie cups you crumple up and toss after you've used them.

It happens in colleges, perhaps even more rampantly so: young adults with young bodies, all pumped with hormones, with time on their hands. Sex is an easy thing to pursue. Stories of loose sex in college dorms abound, even orgies—especially in Canada for some reason.[3] Maybe there's not much to do there in Canada, and the cold can keep people indoors. What else is there to do? The University of Toronto Sex Ed Center even hosted a massive student orgy for its students.[4]

The discussions about orgies and bed-hopping loose sex among dormmates are quite graphic but oddly banal in tone. I said before that they see sex as no more than pizza delivery, except unlike pizza it's free and you can get it much faster—although one young female interviewee offered the following advice: "If you want to fuck somebody, take the time to get to know them. If that means you have to masturbate to get those feelings out of your body, do it."[5]

Ah. Wisdom from the mouth of babes.

Why would all this come as a surprise? After all, feminism has taught them that women should "go for it" and take charge of their sexual pleasures. Many will insist that women's needs for casual sex are just like the guys' needs.[6] In fact, the mantra has become that men and women are no different other than their obvious sexual organs, so why should their lust for sex be any different?

And if so, why should the man always be the one to take the lead? Why should a woman have to wait in hopes that this or that man might notice and approach her? You want an orgasm—go get it. It's empowering, ladies.[7]

It's not just behind closed doors that they're pursuing casual sex, either. Women wear extraordinarily tight leggings that reveal every nook of the lower half of their bodies: Here's my body, boys. Take a look—a really *good* look. You can practically see my vagina from across the street. And don't forget to look at my butt as I walk out of the coffee shop. Yes, that's *exactly* what'll it look like if you have sex with me.

Gone are the days of worrying about appearing "slutty" or about "reputation." What reputation are you talking about? Who is going to care, exactly? Just who is whispering these days about what any woman did last night with whomever? Perhaps those *other* women who are *also* wearing yoga pants that say "come have sex with me"? Really?

Likewise, the notion of a "Walk of Shame" (leaving a guy's apartment in the early morning in the same clothes a woman wore the night before) is also no longer part of our cultural language. Why would it be, when men and women see their bodies not as anything special but instead more like a little mobile pleasure center they carry around with them.

Today shame, reputation, and delayed gratification are as relevant as using the US mail to send a letter. In fact, think of sex in the new bed-hopping world as "email sex": fast, reliable, and always efficient. You spend about the same amount of time thinking about jumping into bed as you do firing off a text, post, or email. Just be careful about those viruses.

Why the immediate jump into sex, even before talking and getting to know each other—even before kissing? Maybe she's just horny and wants some quick action herself, and the gods of the internet have made that so easy. In other words, she does it because now she *can* do it.

Or maybe it's because that's what all the other girls are doing, and if she doesn't do it, she'll lose out to some other girl who will. And she knows no one will judge her for whatever she does with the boys in her speedy race to the bottom.

The ladies have become enablers and participants in the world of "insta-sex." It's where sex is instantly available, anywhere, and takes just about as long to prepare as the ramen noodles they buy at the university bookstore.

One could summarize the olden days of feminism with the following phrase: "Hey, mister. My eyes are up here." Today, it seems a woman's eyes are the *last* place she wants you to look.

After all, there's no time for that.

The old adage that a woman has to kiss a lot of frogs before she meets her prince may still be true. The only difference is that today there are a lot more frogs, there may be no prince in the end, and it's not kissing she'll be doing. Other than that, it's spot on.

All this is to establish one point: men and women remain interested only in the ride but not necessarily the destination. They want the last climactic scene of the movie, but fewer and fewer people care about the setup, the mood, the *denouement*. And to hell with the plot or sticking around for the credits.

The world of romance is always a reflection of its time and surrounding culture. A patient culture, one which fostered meaningful art, music, and education, means patience in the world of romance. An impatient culture, conversely, gives rise to impatient sexual norms.

In short, cultures tend toward consistency in their approaches to art, governance, education, law and order, and sex. And for much of Western civilization, the "just get to it" attitudes have now filtered down to the world of sex, thanks to feminism, entertainment, education, and especially technology. It was only a matter of time.

And godlessness in culture leads to godlessness in sex. It always has.

Enter the era of the sex robots. If it is indeed all about the climax and getting your momentary sexual needs met so that you can get going on your busy day, a robot provides it all, without any complications. How's that for insta-sex?

And you won't even have to bother swiping.

Chapter 4

Male Guilt

Go to any elementary school in most Western countries, and you'll see celebration after celebration. Are you gay? Wonderful! Let's showcase your alternative lifestyle, talk about how it's fine for two men or two women to get married, and how awful America treated gays in history.

You're transgender? Lovely. Who's to say you're a boy or a girl, anyway? They're artificial constructs of the mind. You're Hispanic, Black, or Native American? Boy, did we treat you horribly! You'll never get over it.

You're a girl? Let's learn about women in history. They were *awesome* during the time of the American Revolution. They fought slavery and were instrumental in the Civil War. Later they were on the forefront of ending Jim Crow laws in the South and pushing for civil rights everywhere. Society subjugated them, too. And you know who did that? Men. Particularly white heterosexual Christian men. (*There they are! Get 'em!*)

What if you're a boy? So sorry, Johnny: There's nothing in the box of goodies for you. No one's teaching him about what men did for this country, *as men*. They achieved gains for America but only because the Native Americans like Squanto taught them the ways of the land, and saved them from starvation. And where would they be without the women, who were the *true* protectors of the frontier for the men?

You'd think the men were like extras in a movie set: necessary to give the sense of many people and crowds, but otherwise they don't really move the plot forward.

Not only is there no celebration, an emptiness of any notion of being a "boy," but the curriculum even seems to instill a sense of shame for being male. After all, Christopher Columbus abused, imprisoned, killed, and enslaved the natives he met. Well, *that* sure sounds bad.

Washington, Jefferson, and many other founding fathers were "old white men" who accepted slavery in their midst, if they didn't own slaves outright themselves. That sounds pretty bad too. Who slaughtered the Indians? That's right: those *males*. The white ones especially. That's where you'll find the root of today's toxic masculinity.

They call it White Male Guilt, and for good reason: our culture has successfully infused a sense of collective shame upon all white men—and God help you if you're a *Christian* man (truly the *worst* kind). It's like the notion of Original Sin, but only for the male: he'll never overcome it.

Not long after the day a male baby is born, at least in America, he is taught to think of himself like a wart on humanity. There will be no celebration of his masculinity, except in parodies where men go bear hunting to prove their manhood, and the women back home just roll their eyes as they get the *real* stuff done.

From a social point of view, the birth of a boy engenders a sort of benign indifference. You can almost see the nurse hand the baby over to mama now: "Oh, here you go. By the way, it's a boy." Unlike their African American, Hispanic, Eskimo, Native American, Aboriginal, Gay, Bisexual, Bi-curious or Bi-questioning, Muslim, Transgendered, Disabled, Amputee/Special Olympian counterparts, they have nothing to be proud about.

If they show any pride in European or American heritage, they're elitist at best and more likely one of those racist nationalist types. You know, because Hitler and all that. Oh, and that reminds us: Hitler was a white male. All the founding fathers were too. They owned slaves. All men are potential rapists. For most of history, we've accepted the "implicit brutality of male sexuality."[1] Men "mansplain" too much and have toxic masculinity. Wait, masculinity *is* toxic, so that's a redundancy.

This is almost *all* a young boy hears today as he grows up, vis a vis what it is to be male. He must start apologizing as soon as he is drawn out of his mother's womb and his little penis reveals itself.

Defenders of this marginalizing of men might say it's just payback for the millennia during which women suffered. Fine: but understand it's at the expense of our boys, particularly any sense of motivation they may have. They didn't do anything wrong. The elevation of girls shouldn't have to mean the pushing down of boys.

In the end, the boys just feel boxed in. They're told they don't belong, while at the same time they have no real place to go. They become the Lost Boys, as it were, forever searching for themselves, while trying to figure out what role society wants them to play. It's like expecting someone to build a skyscraper but only telling the builder how *not* to build a skyscraper. That'll be a challenge.

But don't worry, boys. The robots are comin'. No one judges you for being a straight man in the world of robots. No one tells you how to behave, either. You're not "lost," at least not here. You can be all the "toxic" male you want to be. Your robot is your "safe space," where you can lawfully let out all your sexuality— just like laser tag fun zones, and football and hockey matches let you lawfully let out your aggression.

In this way, robots are more like video games, but video-game life has invaded the real world. No one has any interest in patience or impulse control. Like video games, everything is about the next level, and the cool affirming badges and sounds along the way. It's intoxicating. It's addictive. And the satisfaction is immediate. And like with video games, the boys get to retreat to their basements and be who they are. No one will judge.

And just like that, problem solved. Everybody wins.

Chapter 5

Narcissism

The End of Romantic Movies

Do you remember romantic comedies? Weren't they fun? Have you noticed how few Hollywood makes anymore? They've gone the way of floppy disks, pagers, and DVD players, and major studios don't bank on them anymore. Why?

Some blame the decline of romantic movie production on feminism. Such films were all the rage in their respective decades, but, according to the blame-it-on-the-feministas crowd, they've lost their shine in the Me Too era of the second decade of the new century. *Overboard* suggested gaslighting-type manipulation was OK; *There's Something about Mary* suggested stalking was an acceptable tactic, and *How to Lose a Guy in 10 Days* perpetuated stereotypes about women and their dependence on men for happiness.[1] So, the theory goes, such films were insensitive, and that's why the studios stopped pumping out romances.

But that doesn't explain violent films and video games, many of which still hum along in the commercial market, and most of which are not politically correct (PC) at all, let alone "women-friendly."

Another proposed reason is that people have become more interested in comic-book heroes, or that the "maestros" of the "rom-com" have faded away; there's just no one to replace those excellent directors of the genre, such as Nora Ephron (*You've Got Mail* and *Sleepless in Seattle*) or Rob Reiner (*When Harry Met Sally* and *The Princess Bride*).[2] But not everything is about comic books, and it makes no sense that only two or three directors can make a successful romantic comedy.

Maybe it's something else. Movies are a reflection of the times. Perhaps it's that people don't know what a relationship *is* anymore. At the very least, maybe relationships don't really resonate to young viewers—at least the coveted 18 to 35 demographic. And so a movie about awkward but blossoming relationships leading to some forever-after is as relevant and enticing to viewers as a movie about ancient Mongolian writing techniques.

As one article put it: Fewer people get married, and there's the whole dating app and online thing. It's a "subtle sea change."[3]

Subtle sea change? Such a phrase contradicts itself. But it's a sea change for sure. Billy Mernit, author of "Writing the Romantic Comedy," noted, "[T]he studios [were] still making the same formulaic romantic comedy where it's a courtship story that leads to marriage, and it usually revolves around a young professional woman who gets a leg up by getting involved with an alpha male. The target audience, the twentysomethings and above, just no longer related to that kind of a movie." He adds that the new "smart" romantic comedy writer has to have a fresh angle.[4]

You don't say. In a world of changing demands, you had better make some changes to reflect it. Otherwise, your business dies. And in the world of sex, everything has transformed. It has become commoditized, recyclable, fast, and cheap. Sex doesn't require a relationship anymore. It's the single song, not the album. It's the cool, rolling-boulder scene from the beginning of *Raiders of the Lost Ark* that you can grab easily from YouTube. The rest is expendable.

Apple's iTunes drives this point home. iTunes changed music forever in 2003. How so? It altered the way people accessed and consumed their music. More importantly, it altered the way people even thought about their music. Instead of buying music by whole albums (which offered anywhere between nine and fifteen songs each), experiencing albums from start to finish, it now offered single songs for sale at 99 cents each. You could still buy albums, but the single became the focus.

The world of entertainment soon jumped on the bandwagon: People started "cutting the cord" of cable television, preferring the "pay for what you want" approach of Apple TV, Netflix, and Amazon Prime. After all, why pay for cooking and shopping channels when all you want are action movies, sports, and some news?

Even journalism fell to this à la carte segmentation. People didn't want to read the news as the *New York Times* or the *Washington Post* might package it for them. Everything's so accessible, so why not just get your entertainment news from the *Los Angeles Times*, opinion and financial news from the *Wall Street Journal*, sports from ESPN, and fashion trends from *Vogue*?

Even more so, they'd rather read their favorite writers—not the newspaper. Eventually, services like Apple News offered "packaged news" tailored solely to subjects and sources you select. I like mountain biking, health, travel, and Israel, so my packaged daily offering of news doesn't include anything about fashion, architecture, or gardening. It's like my music library.

And so it is now with romantic relationships: why would you feel you must buy the whole relationship "album," as it were, most of which you *don't* want, when you can buy just the one thing you *do* want? In other words: thanks very much for offering the concept of a relationship, but I'll pass on the pricey buffet and just take it à la carte. (Also, can you make it fast? And don't forgot the to-go box).

There has indeed been a "sea change." It's the change in the way we view sex and relationships. For too many, sex is no longer part of a relationship, or of anything greater at all. It is a standalone offering, separate from anything that might have come before it or that might come after.

Sex has become entertainment, something to do to pass the time, like grabbing a mocha joe at the café, and nothing more. It has become at once without meaning *and* without consequence. And as with the coffee transaction, the names are as forgotten as quickly as a barista forgets the names she writes on the to-go cups.

Instead of being open to relationships, younger people are open instead to the myriad forms of sexual activity that are available to them. Group sex, anal sex, gay and lesbian sex, swinging, and fetishes.[5] Everything and anything; they're up for it all. It's all "good." One commentator boasted she was a "big believer" in doing whatever you might want in bed: "Have your threesome. Hell, have your twelvesome."[6] Limiting yourself to monogamous "just vaginal" sex? Are you kidding? Isn't that like saying I should only watch black and white TV or have only vanilla or chocolate ice cream? Lordy, Lordy, that would be just so prudish!

My sense is that this is what happens when civilization unwittingly kills the concept of the romantic relationship. Many end up needing to substitute what we lose in relationships with *something,* and that something might very well be going outside sexual norms and experiencing different sexual fetishes. Everything has to be "tried," lest you miss out on life. Lest—even worse—you might descend into a nobody.

Fall of the Empire of Relationships, Rise of the Empire of the Instant

Once there was a lonely young man, Henry, who talked incessantly about his girlfriend, Rachel. He told his buddies about their travels together, his visits to her parents, their walks in Central Park, and even the funny time when someone confused her for a famous singer and they both got such royal treatment. He talked about how often she told him that she loved him. And he wanted one day to "pop the question" and marry her. He looked to his friends for emotional support to do so.

Everyone wanted to meet her, but somehow when opportunities arose and despite many invitations, she could never seem to make it. His friends joked how she was a "ghost" and that he must be making her up. One of them even said she was like Snuffleupagus from Sesame Street—the elephant-like creature that only Big Bird could see. Henry didn't take kindly to that.

But with more time and more nonappearances came more excuses. Eventually, his friends began to wonder aloud whether his girlfriend was real. Then came the time when they outright mocked him ("Sure she's your girl, Henry; *sure* she is"), followed by a roll of eyes every time he talked about her.

It was getting pathetic. But Henry became adamant, almost pleading for his friends to believe him.

One day, when they were all in their favorite coffee shop, he suddenly spotted her. Finally, he would prove them all wrong.

"There she is," he frantically pointed. "There's Rachel!" He could not have been more excited. He looked around to make sure everyone around him could see.

"Where, where?" his friends asked, confused.

Henry kept pointing. Didn't they see her? She was *right there*, right up to where his finger was pointing.

But no one was there at all. In that corner of the café, only a rather large plasma TV hung from the ceiling and the corners of the two walls, playing an episode of some old TV romantic comedy.

"Henry, there's no one there," his friend Charlie said.

Henry was insistent. Surely, they had missed her. She was right there!

His two friends and their girlfriends couldn't understand. Maybe she had gone to the restroom behind the corner, and they had just missed her (surprise), again.

"There, there! Don't you see her?" Henry pointed, upset that they couldn't see.

But all that played was the TV show.

Charlie turned around. He began to realize. Soon all the others did too.

At the moment, the woman character on the TV, Rachel, was saying: "Henry, c'mon. You know I'll always love you!" Then she gave him a polite quick slap to his chest. "You get so jealous for no reason, silly!"

Henry, watching the show, now whirled around to his friends. With his hands still pointing at the TV, he exclaimed, "You see? I told you she was my girlfriend! I told you she loves me!"

We make our own realities.

Relationships are hard work. *That* work is even harder than sex, yet we all crave them. We want the relationship but not necessarily the energy, time, money, and emotional risk that go along with it.

So we cheat. We move to a world of the transient fix, sometimes settling on just the illusion of a relationship. As the joke about men goes: Why should men get upset that women fake orgasms? After all, men fake entire relationships.

But in a world where everything is fast, fast, fast, there is no time for the development of a relationship. There is no time to listen to a full symphony. The concept of the slow-burn movie is as relevant as communicating by telegram. As I noted above, Hollywood has all but abandoned the romantic comedy. It has, however, flooded us with action-scene after action-scene movies that titillate the senses but are totally devoid of character development. Just look at the difference between the James Bond films of the early sixties and seventies and the present ones.

Or consider the movies *The Bridge Over the River Kwai* (a 1957 World War II movie) and *The Wild Bunch* (a 1969 western), both of which Hollywood offered as action films. But the most action in both of these films occurred with bridges blowing up in their climactic scenes—bridges that the production companies had built and actually blew up for those movies.

Today, both of those films would be categorical bores to younger audiences. Why so? First, because computer-generating imagery (CGI) and other filmmaking innovations make it so easy to throw action scene after action scene without stop. But second—and far more importantly—the consumer demands it. In a world of immediate gratification, there is no time for development of a relationship with the characters. Show us the violence and explosions, *now*. Show us the cool aliens who will take over our planet and feed on our guts, ever so realistically.

It's the same with our sexual needs. Give us the sex. Right now.

You can communicate via text and email instantly. You can transmit photos of your kids through any social media platform you want instantly. You can send a message you want to share with the world, through Twitter, and your voice will be shared repeatedly—that's right, virtually instantly.

Your Uber driver comes to you within three minutes. If the estimate on your apps says it'll take longer, then you'll cancel and find another driver.

Food delivery is now fast, if not instant. Even food itself is "instant"—instant coffee, instant oatmeal, instant rice and noodles, instant pudding. You can get your movies and TV shows instantly. At work, you can send and receive documents instantly. You can get directions to the nearest café, food mart, or hookah lounge instantly. The markets, news, banking, airline tickets, and updated traffic and weather also are available to you—again, instantly.

So why should the speed of your sexual encounters be any different? To pursue a relationship that somehow grows with meaning over weeks, months, and even years is like to live in another dimension of time while the rest of the world speeds along beside you. It's like the episode in *Star Trek*, where a separate alien race living in a much faster dimension of time has taken over the *Enterprise* spaceship. To Kirk and the rest of the crew, the aliens at first seem like tiny mosquitos buzzing by. But, figuring that there probably are no mosquitos in space, the crew soon springs into action: Kirk's first mate Spock concocts some sort of serum for Kirk to drink that speeds him up in time so that he can catch up with the interloping aliens and undo their sabotage. Problem solved.

But the disappearing relationship problem won't go away in our World of the Instant. It is too hard for young people on the one hand to expect immediate results in virtually everything in their lives—including sex—and then at the same time to invest time and money in the great effort of getting to know someone. To the average millennial, these are contradictory programs— enough to cause the computer to generate that annoying spinning circle, overheat, and shut down.

The resolution? To ignore the contradicting First You've Got to Know Someone program. It's not necessary, after all, in a world where you've already learned that someone likes you and is probably agreeable to have sex with you well before you've even actually met. You don't need to take her to that expensive play or concert that she hinted she likes. You don't even need to tell her how pretty she is over and over again. You don't need to show her how intelligent, brave, or strong you are. And ladies: you don't need to drop hints, whether directly at him or through his friends, play "hard to get" and hope he wants you more, or work out at the gym a bit more because he might like you if you have a nicer body.

Such things no longer are necessary. The internet has eviscerated all the inefficient steps and packaged routine and available information, quickly.

So why waste your time figuring out whether she'll be willing to sleep with you? *You already know that.* You can just get to the point. Coinciding with that is the fact that our culture has simultaneously deconstructed sex and stripped it from its religious and social responsibility contexts. It *is* just pizza now: Do you want it or don't you?

Still, in the process, we lost something. The process of romance and courtship was like exercising a muscle of sorts. Don't exercise that process, and it will atrophy and eventually whither. And what muscle was it? It was the muscle of courage to get up in the morning and move toward what we wanted; it made men, especially, evaluate risk and reward. It gave us a sense of priority and purpose and even a bit of showmanship in our quest to achieve a goal. It taught us that good things happen to those who have patience. It forced us to prioritize too; you couldn't expend that kind of energy on more than one girl at a time. So focus, Johnny.

It took us so much effort, in fact, that by the time we might actually sleep with the woman we had pursued, we figured, OK, great, but not sure we have the energy to do *that* again. That led to settling down, creating a family, and then providing for and protecting that family. After all, we worked so hard to get this woman in the first place. In turn, we expected the same process from any young man who might have eyes for our daughters.

So we might bemoan the ever-disappearing notion of the romantic relationship, vanishing like the *Star Trek* crew beaming off the Enterprise. And the loss of the relationship is far more destructive than the atrophying of a muscle. You're missing out when you don't pursue the relationship: with whom do you share your greatest fears? With whom can you share that great song or movie? With whom do you try out that great idea for a business? With whom can you be yourself?

There is a transcendence of sorts when a couple develops a deep relationship. Everyone who has ever fallen in true, deep love understands this. Your joy in her smile, the feeling he gives you when he tells you he's thinking of you. The giving of yourself, the sense you can't be complete without this other person. The sense that you belong to each other. The sense that you can tell them anything, and they won't judge you. The sense that you can count on each other, even if you get older, less attractive, sick, or poor. The feeling that you complete each other, that you might even need each other. It's the feeling that you might even become a better you with this other person, that you are going on a journey with this person into the future, that you might participate with them in the creation of something great. And for couples who plan to have kids, they plan for future generations.

It's all very exciting, this relationship business. So why doesn't everyone pursue it? Perhaps it's because they don't have relationship models to pursue in the first place. Or they'd rather spend time alone with themselves—it's easier, after all. Either way, they don't even know what they're missing.

The problem is that relationships take work. A lot of work. Pursuing a relationship isn't like trying a new ice cream flavor. It's not like discovering sushi or the *Star Wars* movies (well, most of them, anyway). You can experience those things readily. If you don't like them, you move on. That's just self-attention. It's narcissism.

But pursuing a relationship—a deep one, one with meaning—is more like moving to a new country and having to learn its culture, laws, and language. It's far more powerful and wondrous in the end. It's not just going to a movie together once in a while or feeling free to put your spoon in your partner's dessert.

It's knowing that their joy will be your joy. Their pain will be your pain. When you experience that feeling, there's nothing else like it on the planet. Not even close.

You know what? Now that I think on it, it might even be better than sex.

We Are Relationships

It's helpful to look back to our movie references from earlier, particularly *2001: A Space Odyssey* and *Cast Away*. In the movie *2001*, astronauts Dave Bowman and Frank Poole are two of a crew of astronauts but the only ones not hibernating in their long journey to Jupiter. They give a long-distance interview to a BBC reporter, during which they talk about the AI system known as HAL, not just as a helpful computerized resource but as a person:

> *BBC Interviewer*: Dr. Poole, what's it like living for the better part of a year in such close proximity with HAL?

Frank: Well it's pretty close to what you said about him earlier, he is just like a sixth member of the crew. [You] very quickly get adjusted to the idea that he talks, and you think of him, uh, really just as another person.

Did you get that? Very quickly David and Frank "got adjusted" to thinking of HAL—a computer that doesn't even have corporeal form (just several camera installments throughout the spaceship)—as a person. How so? It turns out it's because the computer was able to mimic human conversations and emotions.

Likewise, in *Cast Away*, we see Chuck Noland, a FedEx systems engineer whose live-by-the-clock existence abruptly ends when his plane crashes on a remote island. He survives but at some point finds solace in a relationship with a volleyball that came with the wreckage (a volleyball he uncreatively calls "Wilson"). Much time passes, after which the ball becomes weathered with use. Noland paints a primitive face on Wilson, using his own blood to do so. He argues with Wilson from time to time and twice goes into emotional convulsions upon losing Wilson.

You can say outer space or a deserted island can do strange things to a person. Or do we crave relationships so much that we'll create them out of whatever we can when we need them? Did the astronauts Dave and Frank *want* to think of HAL as a person and have a relationship with him, beyond their own relationship between themselves? It would be pretty lonely, even if they had each other. Noland must have had that need all the more so on his island in the Pacific.

If all you have around you is your dog, you'll have a relationship with your dog. If all you have around you are a tree and a rock, you'll have a relationship with that tree and rock. The point is: if you don't have a relationship, you'll create one—out of just about anything around you.

And how much more of a relationship you can have if that object looks human.

The terror of solitary confinement proves this point. Article after article considers it a horrific punishment. Such confinement leads to hallucinations, panic attacks, overt paranoia, diminished impulse control, hypersensitivity to external stimuli, and difficulties with thinking, concentration, and memory. Most victims can't focus on anything, while others develop crippling obsessions.[7] Not surprisingly, "prisoners in solitary begin to lose the ability to initiate behavior of any kind — to organize their own lives around activity and purpose. What results is chronic apathy, lethargy, depression and despair. In extreme cases, prisoners may literally stop behaving."[8]

Sometimes when prisoners first have an opportunity to interact with other people again, they can't cope. They can't come out of their cell, whether to rejoin the larger prison community or— more difficult yet—the larger society. It's a social atrophy that can disable people for years, if not permanently.[9]

It applies to romantic relationships as well. R. F. Baumeister and M. R. Leary proclaimed their great discovery that—wait for it—we need relationships:

> [T]he need to belong is a fundamental human need
> to form and maintain at least a minimum amount of
> lasting, positive, and significant interpersonal relation-
> ships. Satisfying this need requires (a) frequent, positive
> interactions with the same individuals, and (b) engaging
> in these interactions within a framework of long-term,
> stable care and concern.
>
> Despite the lure and excitement of changing roman-
> tic partners, the need for some stable caring interactions

with a limited number of people is a greater impera-
tive. . . . [H]uman beings are "naturally driven toward
establishing and sustaining belongingness." . . . The
need to belong goes beyond the need for superficial
social ties or sexual interactions; it is a need for meaningful, profound bonding. A sense of belongingness is
crucial to our well-being.[10]

As Baumeister and Leary further argue, the lack of belongingness causes various undesirable effects, including loss of
health, happiness, and adjustments to life's various challenges.
Also, without belongingness you might suffer higher levels of
mental and physical illness and are more prone to behavioral
problems, from traffic accidents to criminality to suicide.[11]

So, you see, relationships are good for you. Who knew?
Other articles from these authors include *Careful—Gravity Can
Kill You* and *Water: The Life-Sustaining Liquid.*

Such articles are fascinating: virtually none of them describe
why solitary confinement or the lack of relationships lead to such
debilitation and suffering. They only describe their horrible
effects. It's as if you described dehydration and hunger merely
by its symptoms, such as emaciation, nausea, lightheadedness,
and deliriousness, but never mention they're the result of *not
having enough food and water.*

So why does our biology seem to require deep meaningful
relationships? Shouldn't we be able to survive without them,
at least according to classic notions of Darwinian evolution?
If you're fit, you survive—nothing about relationships there.
If your environment changes around you and you adapt to it,
you survive. But not much adaptation-to-relationship talk there,
either.

In fact, Darwinian evolution is rather quiet on the issue. Evolution doesn't explain it, at least not in the sense of the truly deep

relationship that so many of us yearn for. Yet for some reason, it is fair to say that humans not only *need* relationships; they will actually whither—and even die—without them.

Why all the fuss about relationships? We know that our inner call toward relationships fulfills a sense within each of us to reach to something greater, but it's something beyond just our simple biology. We have the sense that we are meant to connect, to aspire, to build a civilization—together with others, and in particular with someone who "completes" us and to whom we feel like we belong.

Why, indeed? Let's turn to the eight-hundred-pound gorilla in the room. Maybe he can explain.

Could it be that some outside force has infused us with our powerful need to connect with others, to bond in a way beyond mere survival? Could it be that the reason we yearn so strongly for a deep and meaningful relationship is because God wants us to get closer to Him?

The Jewish sages of old teach *exactly* that: that our desire to attain wholeness with a partner is part of a much larger desire to become one with our Creator and to reattain our original divine image. *That* is why the urge is so strong. This yearning lies at the heart of existence. We're here to bring male and female back together again—at every level of creation, from one man and one woman to our connection between us and our Creator.[12]

The Christian sages approach it similarly: in getting close to each other, loving our neighbor as we love ourselves, we attain the ability to relate better with God through Jesus.[13] Relationships are our opportunity to act in a godly manner.

This is the problem for the evolutionist purist, at least one who believes that everything has come about organically. They cut themselves off from answers that might actually explain a thing or two.

We humans *act* as though a divine force is present. For example, we do what we can to avoid cruel and unusual punishment, and rightly condemn those who engage in it. Not only that, it turns out that not acting divinely can lead to horrific health issues. (See our discussion above of the consequences of solitary confinement, and not having deep relationships.) We even admonish others who don't act divinely. Yet many of us will insist that nothing divine animates our lives.

It's enough to scratch one's head. But look: that eight-hundred-pound gorilla was already doing that.

Chapter 6

A Place Called Sexland

I really like coffee. Done right, a cappuccino with almond milk and a little hazelnut syrup gets me going. Mmm, mmm, MMM. Same for a delicious risotto or a great peanut butter chocolate cake. I also like a good mountain bike ride. My wife knows that if she lets me ride my bike I'll be super attentive to her. It's a great motivator for me.

In fact, all of these things are great motivators. Maybe chocolate or ice cream appeal to you, or perhaps some deep tissue massage. Maybe it's waiting for the latest release from your favorite band or the great new adventure movie that's supposed to be quite good. Maybe it's planning that two-week vacation in Peru or just binging on a new Netflix series—you're only three episodes until the end, and you're *dying* to find out what happens. You might love the latest fashion trends. And there's always watching the game.

These are among life's many possible pleasures. Certainly, no one ever has to force you to do such things. You look forward to them, and the thought of them carries you from one week to the next.

And then there's sex. *That* seems to be in its own different category, somewhere in the stratosphere in a special place called "Sexland."

But here's the query: *Why* is sex *so* much more intensely pleasurable than any of the things I just mentioned? Every once in a
while, someone asks some extreme adventure guy or astronaut
about what his experience felt like. "Oh man, I tell you, . . . it was
better than sex," they sometimes say.

But really, you know they're lying. Sex is *always* better than
whatever cool thing they're talking about. Sure, walking in
space would be breathtaking and base jumping from the top of
the Empire State Building would be a rush.

But, you know . . . *sex*.

I get it: we need the sexual drive to perpetuate the species.
But why does the pleasure have to be *that* intense? On a scale of
one to ten, it's a thirty. Isn't it enough to make sex as pleasurable
as, say, that great coffee in the morning or that awesome bike
ride down the mountain? Those are good enough motivators
for me. If sex is to encourage reproduction, then the intensity of
the sexual thrill in humans seems somewhat out of scale with
its ultimate goal. It's like trying to kill a mosquito with a hand
grenade: do we really need all that firepower? Evolutionarily, it
makes no sense.

And while other mammals may enjoy sex, humans seem to
enjoy it on a particularly heightened level. Most male mammals
mate instinctively for reproduction purposes. Male humans
seem more titillated with the act, and not necessarily for its ultimate primary purpose of creating a new life. In fact, for many
male humans, such a prospect would scare them *away* from sex.

The human female is even more unique. She don't go into
"heat." She's capable of desiring and enjoying sex at any time.
For female animals that go into heat—a fixed period of time
when her desire for sex heightens incredibly for the sake of max-
imizing her chances of becoming pregnant—it's just a matter of
programming. There's no real sense of free will at work here, at

least not in the way we think of it in human terms. It's just hormones and season that compel her to "present."

For humans the pleasure of sex is so intense that, unlike most other things we enjoy or have passions about, we think about it a lot, even when we're not about to have sex. In fact, the median amount of times we think about sex is quite high: twenty thoughts a day for men and about half that amount for women.[1] Plus or minus, that's a sexual thought every waking hour.

And that's when we're doing the thinking ourselves. When we're not thinking about it, there are plenty of others throwing it at us: advertising on the internet and other media, billboards on the streets, music lyrics, cheerleaders at sporting events, and of course television and movies. The new tight and skimpy clothing culture pushes our sexual thought buttons all the more.

Animals don't get turned on by the sight of others in their species being naked, or performing sexually. Another difference between us and animals is our fascination with sex in all its possible permutations. While we'll never know exactly how animals think sexually, I doubt they mentally wander into many of the zones we humans do. I'm quite sure they don't fantasize of threesomes, bondage, lesbianism, foreplay, sex toys, exhibitionism, voyeurism, role playing, role reversal, oral sex, swinging, dirty talk, and virtually everything else other than basic intercourse. I also doubt my dog would know what to make of porn, even if there was a doggie version.

Why all these differences in sexuality from animals? Atheism advances the notion that we should be (and are) more like the animals. According to Darwinism, we came from them. In fact, many people lump humans in with "the other animals." So why not act like "the other animals," sexually?

Maybe it has something to do with free will. It could very well be that it has something to do with the *human* side of our nature.

Here's another demonstration of the intensity we feel toward sex, above all other instincts. Take music: a lot of songs are about love and passion. As much as I love cappuccinos, nonfiction, or mushroom risottos, I have found very few songs about those things. I have also yet to find any songs about mountain biking, skiing, jewelry, watching sports, or knitting.

And yet people are quite passionate about such things. To me, many of these things can be very motivating, but most songs focus on love and relationships: how someone lost a love, how some guy just goes crazy when some particular girl walks by or someone has done wrong by him, usually because someone else has taken an interest in his woman.

So again: *why does sex animate us so out of proportion to every other passion or interest?* Food and water are important and essential to our very existence, but our pursuit of them doesn't summon our passions the way sex does. (I also have not found any songs where a guy sings about how great it was to drink his Gatorade). And wouldn't you know it, unlike food and water, sex isn't even necessary for our immediate day-to-day survival. Most people can go without sex for weeks or months and be just fine. They can certainly "survive."

Sexuality and sex seem to live in their own unique world—like I said: Sexland. It consumes us, but we still don't know why. Related to all this is that we really want bonding with another in the deepest way, and a discovery of our truest self through unity with another. It runs equally deep, especially for women. And why do both sexes seek and treasure that ever-elusive and somewhat-intangible thing called intimacy?

Could it be that there is something else—something stronger—at play here? Could it be that the extraordinary nothing-beats-sex ecstasy we feel is there for something different than *just* to encourage perpetuation of our species?

There seems to be only one solid explanation that explains it well: sex, the quest for a powerful relationship, and true intimacy all seem to come from our deepest spiritual needs.

"The times I feel most connected to God is when I am intimate with my wife," a pastor famously (and bravely) once stated before his adult-males-only congregation. His words enjoy powerful support from our experiential realities. Most humans have a sense that our deepest fulfillment comes from a *spiritual*, not sexual, relationship. This view has lasted throughout the millennia, consistently through culture and geography. Sex seems somehow to be more meaningful than just an activity like eating, drinking, brushing one's teeth, or just about anything else.

There is an undeniable *significance* that we intuitively assign to sex. Perhaps women understand this better than men. The Sexual Revolution and Free Love movements of the sixties— and the similar attitude toward sex among many today—led to a feeling of emptiness. Instead of just enjoying the pleasures of the flesh, women came to feel used and ashamed of themselves, as well as to face the realities of a wild spike in very unpleasant sexually transmitted diseases (STDs). In fact, to call it a mere "spike" is a horrible understatement, like saying a hurricane is a strong wind.[2]

Women soon realized that the new sexual freedoms didn't truly change their role in America —they were only wearing different costumes. As black activist Stokely Carmichael cruelly put it, "The only position for women in the movement is prone."[3]

The Sexual Revolution ended almost entirely because so many woke up to realties of sex: we need more than just sex. We need the Relationship, with a capital "R," and Intimacy, with a capital "I."

People came to realize that sex alone wasn't satisfying nor sufficient. And then other questions start nagging at us: if sex is just for perpetuation of the species, why should any man or woman have any reluctance to jump in the sack? Why punish people with all these horrid STDs, some of them life threatening or that lead to debilitating diseases later in their lives, such as brain and other cancers?

And why do women seem naturally to bond emotionally almost immediately after sex? Why do both men and women feel jealousy and possessiveness if they catch their mate stealing so much as a glance at someone of the opposite sex?

Like I said: Sex is just too good to be true.

And conversely, nature seems to reward *not* engaging in emotion-free sex with multiple partners. The biological benefits of monogamous sex are twofold: not only does it minimize the risk of contracting some nasty diseases; it fosters an environment that boosts the immune system and increases longevity. It even reduces the risk of cancer, heart disease, and depression.[4]

It's as if there's something in nature's programming that rewards those who engage in monogamous sexual relationships, while punishing—sometimes severely so—those who engage in constant hookup sex. Sexual pleasure is intense, but those who respect sex's awesome power seem to enjoy a truer, relatively worry-free intensity that only gets better with time.

And that's where sex reaches a "different" level—a place even beyond Sexland.

Think of it: most married guys I know (and some women who are comfortable talking to me) share their opinion that "married sex" is different, more intense, more wondrous. It's even more so when a couple hopes to conceive. And the more sex they have between just the two of them, the more they get to know each other's bodies and the more they connect.

Nature's message could not be clearer: unlike trying different kinds of food, we should not be "trying" out as many of each other as we can. Monogamous sex, and particularly sex within marriage, is far healthier, far safer, and far more rewarding.

As Rabbi Brandon Gaines expressed it: the pleasure of sex—especially the monogamous, committed kind—is so wildly intense *because we are sharing in the process of creation*. God rewards us not only with the heightened ecstasy of sexual climax but more significantly with an insight unto creation itself.

This, I believe, explains why sex goes so beyond any other pleasure we might imagine. Food and drink may be quite enjoyable, but while consuming them is necessary for survival, they are not acts of creation. When we connect sexually in a truly loving, monogamous bond with the opposite sex, we sense that we "become one."

Biblical teachings hold that sex alone should never be an end in itself. It must always be part of a larger whole. It's about God's unity becoming manifest. Our sexuality is bound up with the deepest bedrocks of existence—our yearning for God, and with God's desire for unity among us.[5] Through sex, we participate in God's ongoing act of Creation. In that sense, we become deputies of God's will. Sex becomes an act where we actually connect with God's purpose and, seemingly, the universe itself.

Hey—maybe *that's* why there's nothing better than sex.

I believe that most people innately understand the power of sex, that it is indeed a spiritual gift. But we don't want to listen to that inner voice; we shoo it away. We'd rather abuse it, just to satisfy the sexual impulse with quick and often meaningless physical hookups. Most of us seem to have little interest in the deep spiritual underpinnings of our desires.

Yet the craving for meaning is there. People seek out orgies, threesomes, sex toys, homosexuality, swinging, and anything kinky—or just lots of sex with lots of people. Some pursue sex over and over again, hoping that one day some meaning will reveal itself from all that sex. They have no notion that they might be abusing God's gift of sex, that that abuse might do damage to them, or that there is a purpose to sex. They have no direction when it comes to sex. It's like they've gotten themselves lost in some giant sexual labyrinth, and they don't know how to get out.

Such people are similar to many obese people. Paradoxically, obese people are actually starving. How so? Because they don't eat food with the nutrients their bodies actually need and crave. Instead they eat cheap food without nutrients (french fries, pastas, donuts) non-stop, in a quest to satisfy their craving. When that doesn't work, they keep eating the same empty foods in an endless cycle, leading them only to get fatter and fatter. They think constantly of food and their next meal. And guess what? They're still not getting the nutrients their bodies need.[6]

We ignore the meaning of sex at our peril. We don't understand the awesome power of sex. Think of our quick-sex-hookup culture as a teenage kid finding an F-22 Raptor fighter jet with all its horsepower and sophistication. He manages to hop in, closes the top, and turns on the ignition. He starts moving but stays on the ground. He rolls at a fairly fast pace along the tarmac, but he's not really going anywhere.

The power of the engine gives him an incredible rush. *So this is what it's like to operate an F-22*, he thinks to himself. He *thinks* he's figured out this jet, but he hasn't really. It can do so much more, and he could figure it out if he put his mind to it, but hell: why should he? He's having fun as it is.

He'll never know how much more he could get out of it because that would require too much work. That would require responsibility and time, patience and perhaps evaluation and judgment from discerning instructors.

He's not using the jet for its intended purpose. And the saddest part is that he actually believes he knows how to operate an F-22.

So it is with sex. We embark upon the thrill of sex but rarely consider its extraordinary power and purpose. Few get to a point where they truly appreciate its immense consequences on the one hand, and its exquisite gifts on the other.

There is one place where the F-22 metaphor fails: If someone were to sneak on to an air force base and manage a joyride of such a jet, security and police officers would quickly descend upon him. No doubt he'd serve time in prison.

But for those who routinely engage in faceless, meaningless sex with multiple partners—or with sex robots—we would never think about interfering. We would rather nod along with each other that it's something people do behind closed doors, and it's just none of our business.

Yet I wonder which is more dangerous.

Chapter 7
All Transgendered Now

Woman who's just given birth to a baby
looks to her doctor: Well is it a boy or a girl?
Doctor: I think it's a little early
to start imposing roles on it, don't you?
— *FROM* MONTY PYTHON'S THE MEANING OF LIFE *(1983)*

It's the Sexuality, Stupid

Remember the gay marriage issue? It took a few years, but then the great fight was over, seemingly overnight. With the 2015 decision in *Obergefell v. Hodges*, the United States Supreme Court overturned all laws prohibiting same-sex marriage and required all states to issue marriage licenses to same-sex couples and to recognize same-sex marriages from other jurisdictions. It cited the "evolving" culture as a basis for the decision.

Supporters of the *Obergefell* decision were still cleaning up the ticker-tape confetti from their celebration when they started up on their next great progressive assault: the right of a man or woman to relieve themselves in the opposite sex's bathroom. Oh, and we can't forget the lesser-discussed right of a biological man to go into a women's locker room and for men not to suffer discrimination for wearing women's clothing.

Although transgenderism—a biological man identifying as a woman, and vice versa—was recognized as early as the 1950s, it didn't seem to really take off as a national issue until right after the *Obergefell* decision. And take off it did. Soon, not only did every major building seem to be revamping its bathrooms to offer "gender-neutral" restrooms; everyone started tripping over themselves to make sure they referred to anyone else by his or her preferred pronoun (by the way, did I get that right?). Others simply started using the gender-neutral but grammatically incorrect "they" or "their."

California and New York even proposed bills in their state legislatures criminalizing anyone, with up to a year's prison time or up to a $250,000 fine, who intentionally uses the "wrong" pronoun.[1] But that's OK because there's plenty of room in our nation's prisons for such horrible people.

Three guys meet in prison:

Inmate 1: Hey, bud, what you in here for?

Inmate 2: Murdered my wife.

Inmate 1: Whoa, stone-cold stuff, bro. How about you?

Inmate 3: Armed robbery and kidnapping.

Inmate 1: (Nods head; then turns to another) . . . And you?

Inmate 4: Oh, I called some guy a "he" in the office. I should've called him a "she."

At least one state, Oregon, even offers to pay for sex-reassignment surgery, cross-sex hormone therapy, and puberty-inhibiting medications to anyone who wants it, even to children as young as fifteen, over the objections of their parents.[2]

Oregon fifteen-year-olds can also have sex, get birth control, and get an abortion—without parental consent. On the other hand, fifteen-year-olds can't smoke cigarettes, drive alone, send or receive sexually suggestive texts ("sexting"), vote, work more than eighteen hours a week, drink alcohol, eat unhealthy foods at school, get tattoos, administer aspirin at school, or use a tanning bed.[3]

But ripping out your genitals? Go for it. You're mature enough for *that*. It's not as if you're doing something horrible to yourself, like drinking a large soda.*

As with the gay marriage issue that preceded it, states soon proposed penalties against businesses that did not provide services—like baking a cake, photography, pizza and floral delivery—to celebrate someone's transgenderism.[4] This consequence, by the way, was *exactly* as Justice Clarence Thomas had predicted in his dissent to the *Obergefell* majority decision. In that decision, he predicted opponents to gay marriage would face ridicule and marginalization for refusing to bow to the new pro-gay marriage "orthodoxy."

And how many people are actually transgender? Despite all the available transgender bathrooms, how often do you actually see transgendered people using them? I have yet to see any. I'm not saying there are none out there, but it's a bit like a celebrity sighting.

Perhaps we've overreacted? To require all buildings to change their bathroom infrastructures would be like requiring every restaurant to have a peanut-free section, lest anyone allergic to peanuts might come by. That of course is not a fair comparison, but only because many more people have a peanut allergy. And unlike transgendereds, those with peanut allergies will dramatically suffer if they come into contact with their issue. Some might even die.

The fraction of transgenders out there is tiny. It's only from .3 percent to .6 percent of the population in the United States, and that's an estimate from the progressive *New York Times*, making assumptions that tilt to a higher percentage.[5] Yet the nation has

---

* (Both New York and California have enacted laws to ban large soda drinks.)

bent over backwards to change its laws, education, and very infrastructure to accommodate them, lest they feel left out.

But wait. How about hemophiliacs? They might die if they cut themselves. Shall all businesses and buildings be forced to minimize the chances of anyone scraping themselves by banning scissors and knives? Must we construct all playgrounds and sports centers to avoid any kind of possible scrapes or nosebleeds?

We Jews comprise about 1.4 percent of the United States population. Shall we make laws requiring buildings and restaurants to have at least one kosher food facility in each building? Shall we prohibit people from driving on Saturdays in certain designated parts of each American town and city? We live under the Gregorian calendar, where it's now the so-called "twenty-first century." Well, not on *my* calendar, it ain't. We Jews live in the fifty-eighth century, thank you. Frankly I feel excluded and put upon by having to reference things in your *Christian* terms.

Shall we force everyone to eat only vegan food because of the possibility that a vegan might walk in and feel offended? (3 percent of population). Left-handed people (10 percent of the population) face a lot of difficulties in their lives. In fact, it seems like society has forgotten about them altogether. Just consider all of the right-handed gadgets, awkwardly designed desks, scissors, and cooking tools that fit comfortably only in your right hand. Shall we require all manufacturers of hand-operated gadgets to manufacture a certain number of left-handed devices?

And do you have *any* idea how hard it is for lefties to handwrite? Shall we make laws normalizing the notion of writing from right to left? Just imagine how left out they feel (no pun intended). At the very least, give them twice the amount of time to write their essays on tests.

Try living in a color-blind world (8 percent of men and 0.5 percent of women). Problems can arise in even the simplest of tasks, including choosing and preparing food, gardening, sports, driving a car, and selecting which clothes to wear. Sometimes a color-blind parent won't notice his child getting sunburnt. Color blindness can even affect one's access to education, grades, and career choice.[6]

Shall we make special traffic lights with symbols instead of colors? Shall we require anyone who makes a PowerPoint presentation to make his graphs with stripes and solids instead of color? And what happens during each American election cycle? All those blues and reds—they mean nothing to many color-blind people. How are they to meaningfully participate in the election-night festivities?

Somehow it's all about the transgenders. *They* get all the attention. It's all about *their* feelings, and *only* their feelings seem to matter. And it's all particularly about how they feel when entering into a bathroom or locker room.

And the media and the progressive left could not genuflect and bow more to their every wish. Claims of transgenders suffering bullying in the bathroom abound as the basis to allow them access to the opposite sex's bathroom.

Never mind that there were virtually no meaningful reports of such bullying, at least not in this century.[7] Just assume it; it must be happening. And the only solution? Allow them to go to the bathrooms and locker rooms designated for the opposite sex. *That* will sure make everyone feel comfortable once and for all.

So, problem solved. Well, at least for the transgendered guy. For the women with whom he's sharing the bathrooms and locker rooms? Not so much. But that's okay, because *their* feelings don't matter. They should just deal with it.

But don't get distracted with all that. Please just repeat with me: Problem solved.

So why is it that we care so much about the transgendered and their feelings and inconveniences, while all the other minority groups I just mentioned matter apparently not a whit?

To twist the slogan among the campaign staff in the 1992 Bill Clinton presidential bid: why, it's the sexuality, stupid.

Do you see it now? We've come to identify ourselves primarily *through our sexuality*, so all those other things don't matter. And transgenderism is the sexuality jackpot. What could invoke more sexuality than your sexual identity? Plus it helps blow up one of civilization's fundamental value distinctions: the distinction between man and woman. Get rid of that, and everything else collapses much easier—like taking out the load-bearing wall in a building.

While we were all not paying attention, the progressives in the print, television, and social media got us to speak a new language, tripping over ourselves about assumptions we were making about who is a man or woman. Suddenly, the wild exceptions (a man who thinks of himself as a woman and vice-versa) started swallowing the rule: the fact that some people with penises considered themselves female meant that we couldn't assume that *anyone* was a "man" or a "woman." And the fact that we did so in the past is a great stain on us all. It's like slavery, when you think about it.

But we generally *don't* allow exceptions to swallow the rule. Seat belts save lives, the saying goes. But not always: sometimes the use of a seat belt prevents someone from getting out of a burning car, or can strangle or fatally wound a passenger in an accident.

Love is good, but love can be too intense or abused. Money is great, but money can do great harm. Hammers are for hammering nails in walls, but people have used them to kill. Airplanes are a great for travel, but some people have used them to fly into buildings.

The point is we would never reclassify any of these things to conflate its extremely-out-of-the-ordinary use *as equal to its primary purpose*. We would never, for example, assume that a hammer has fifty-one purposes all gloriously equal to one another, one of which is to kill people. (And if you did, you'd start looking at hammers quite differently. Is it good? Is it evil? What do hammers want from me? Just what *is* a hammer, anyway?)

But somehow when it comes to sexual identity, exceptions can walk in the room, proclaim equal status with everyone else in the room, and change everyone's name and identity in the process. In fact, they don't just swallow the rule; they'll gobble it up and reclassify you as only a different version of *them*.

So why do we allow this swallowing to happen when it comes to transgenderism and gender identity?

Don't you remember? It's the sexuality, stupid.

Boys Will Be Girls

The gay liberation and gay marriage movement caused many of us to think of ourselves as part of a sexual preference "spectrum" (We can be anywhere on this spectrum, which defines *how* gay we are. It's not just binary, you see. It's more like a combination of a thermometer and a barometer, with endless possible combinations of temperature and barometric pressures. It's ever so complex). And now the transgender movement has gotten us to think that *we* are the ones who might be confused as to our very own identities—that perhaps in a sad way, we've been lying to ourselves. To paraphrase the title of a great Beatles' song, it's like they want us to proclaim we're *all* transgendered now. You know—at least a bit.

Suddenly, seemingly overnight, we learn that we are each but one of fifty-one genders,[8] and the number seems to keep growing like the number of cable channels (oh wait, by the time I finished this sentence there were twenty more genders[9]). It's dizzying; you yourself may have no idea which gender you are.

It's OK to be confused, even very confused. The important thing to remember is that society is to blame for your confusion, so we should destroy it and then rebuild it. Think of it like an art project that you felt just wasn't centered very well. Toss it and start again.

But then they foisted the new transgender world order on the kids, teaching them that they themselves may not be the boys or girls as they may have thought they were. Not only was it fine to have two daddies or two mommies, which was "just as normal" as having a daddy and a mommy, but it was OK to implant in their minds something that they never have thought was a possibility: that their sex was somehow "fluid." They can even be a boy one day and a girl the next.[10]

It's all about whether the transgendered child might feel "distressed" because the rest of his class or the school administration might actually treat him as the sex he or she appears to be. Most of the articles about "what to do" in such situations focus on not using triggering and distressing phrases like "boys and girls," not separating them as such, and not using pronouns that the child has not yet agreed for anyone to call him.[11]

Remember: we're talking about .3 to .6 percent of the population, even under the most liberal and expansive interpretation of what it means to be "transgender." They would have all schools change their rules of addressing one another, communication, and general language (to say nothing of school plumbing) on account of this extraordinarily small group of children.

Never mind for the moment that boys and girls—starting anywhere from the age of three to five years old—predominantly identify themselves as . . . wait for it, wait for it . . . boys and girls.[12] That virtually every adult reading this does not remember this from his or her own childhood memories would astonish me. But our expert betters would have you believe otherwise, as if you have no memory of your own childhood.

But wait, what's this? We as a society have recognized this primary identification over and over again: girls and boys have had different dress codes for millennia. There are many schools *just* for boys and schools *just* for girls. The schools do not divide themselves, say, based on children's blood types.

Let's acknowledge the realities: virtually all young children primarily identify themselves by what's between their legs. One doesn't have to like that. They can even consider that a sad fact if they like, but it's reality.

And it never dawns upon progressives, who constantly yearn to change everything, that maybe it's a *good* thing. Maybe there is a reason why boys and girls schools (and sleepaway camps, sports teams, and church retreats, among many other things) separate along lines of sex. Maybe that's *because it's a primary form of identity for the majority of mainstream kids too* — the ones who were born biologically male or female and who think of themselves consistent with that biology. You know—those children who are *not* transgenders. You don't hear much about them, but it turns out there are a lot of them. (Seriously, Google it).

And yet the LGBTQ *et al.* movement would take that primary identity away from you because approximately .45 percent of the population is uncomfortable with, or confused about, his or her gender. They would have you change core words of your language (your pronouns and possessive pronouns), to say nothing of core institutions (the Boy Scouts, for example) and building infrastructure.

It's called the "Tyranny of the Minority." For a minority for whom *their* issue is *all* that animates them, they will push for legislation to disrupt the majority and the status quo. For example, some people will push to take down crosses and references to the Ten Commandments from public monuments and courthouses. Lest you think it refers to only religious issues, it also applies to the American flags in schools or even taking down statues of historical figures.

Why? Because one person raised a stink and said that the cross, the flag, the statue—or whatever—made him feel uncomfortable. It doesn't matter that the vast majority of the rest of the population feels quite comfortable with such things, or even gets value out of them.

There perhaps is no better example of this tyranny of the minority dynamic at play than the issue of transgenders' demands for access to the opposite sex's bathroom or locker rooms. Everything turns on the feelings of the transgendered person. While his/her feelings of alienation may indeed be real, no one seems to consider the feelings of the majority (particularly girls and women in their bathrooms and locker rooms) who may wish to use the bathroom or locker room without fear of someone with a penis coming in. It's unsettling and intimidating to most women. But because going to the "correct" restroom animates the transgendered as a key and intense component of *his* life, *his* agenda prevails.

And this minority group puts *all* its energy into the cause. It consumes them, day in and day out. But the majority, who does not deal with that certain issue on a day-to-day level, remains passive. It's not "their" issue.

Alternatively, many among the majority adopt a "live and let live" approach: it doesn't affect them, so why would they care what someone wears, with whom anyone has sex or marries, or how he self-identifies?

It doesn't affect them . . . until it does. One day they come to find that the minority has thrust their version of reality upon the majority. Then the majority finds itself on the defensive, trying to preserve what they thought was an obvious foundation of their society. By then, however, it's often too late.

This is what happened in the gay marriage debate, in three different ways. First, homosexual relationships became "main-streamed." That in and of itself was not an issue until it entered the realm of marriage—which is the second issue. That altered what marriage was and what it was for in the first place. Marriage was not only supposed to be about love but about the bonding between man and woman and encouraging the development of a family—the two greatest advancers of what we call civilization.

Third, once the United States Supreme Court claimed same-sex marriage to be a constitutional right, the gay community and their supporters demanded that everyone celebrate with them. If they didn't, that would mean the noncelebrator was violating their constitutional rights. Churches and synagogues were suddenly in the crosshairs because clergy wouldn't marry gay couples. Anyone who didn't *assist* in such celebrations—in whatever way—also found themselves in similar crosshairs.

See how that works?

And despite the Supreme Court ruling that someone *could* refuse to cooperate in the performance or celebration of a gay wedding on religious grounds, as in the *Masterpiece Cakeshop v. Colorado Civil Rights Commission* case, the issue kept cropping up: prosecutors in numerous states didn't care what the court said in favor of those religious nuts. They will hound those righteous, bigoted, racist, and homophobic Christian bastards until they bankrupt themselves defending their backward values. This happened to Jack Phillips, the owner of Masterpiece Cakeshop, who was hit with another civil rights discrimination lawsuit in mid-2017 even after winning in the Supreme Court on the same issue. This time the lawsuit came from a transgendered woman who wanted him to bake a cake to celebrate her "transition anniversary."

So now it's happening in the transgender world. God help you if you refer to someone transgendered as a "he" or "sir," when he wants you to refer to him as a "she" or "ma'am."[13] God help you if you don't agree to fully support your child as young as six years old if he thinks he's a girl, lest your ex-spouse try to take away your custody rights on the grounds that you're an unfit parent.[14] She'll have the support of the LGBTQ community for sure, and there's a decent chance a politically correct-minded judge will take the politically correct path and award her full custody. What a hero everyone would consider his Honor. Thank you, Judge, for your integrity to do what's right, they'd say. How *brave* he was to rule like that.

And in this context, it's not even civil laws or threats of criminal penalties (as already discussed), it's from the culture of entitlement that's slapping at you incessantly, chiding you to bow to the latest trendy orthodoxy *du jour*. (That *should* be an oxymoronic phrase, but sadly it's not—the orthodoxy keeps changing).

So you see a transgendered man in a convenience store, and you realize you have no idea what to do with him/her/them or how to speak to him/her/them. Better to just not say anything. In fact, maybe just run away.

Or more likely you won't have such an encounter (they are only about .45 percent of the population, after all), but perhaps a relevant story will have recently trended in the news (say for example, about two married transgenders who want to raise their kid as a transgender). You might talk about it in a social setting, perhaps at the company summer barbecue. You'll exercise extreme discretion in your words. You don't know who's around you, judging you. But you can't go wrong supporting the new orthodoxy. So you quickly calculate you should throw out supportive words. Or just say nothing.

What is responsible for this new Big Brother 2.0? It's not quite clear. Maybe it's because it's easier to push for something new than it is to push for the status quo and values of old. Maybe it's because no one teaches how the male/female distinction and marriage were essential to the development of civilization; or because the church plays less and less of a role in our lives, and fewer people are out there to advocate against such ideas. Maybe it was the Tyranny of the Minority. Either way, the end result is that we never spoke up to protect our most basic values.

And now here we are. We let the exception swallow the rule.

As the Radiohead song goes, "You do it to yourself. You and no one else."

Blowing Up Johnny and Sally

In addition, it became important to blow up all the stereotypes between Johnny and Janie. God forbid that children might see boys as stronger, bigger, more mischievous and rambunctious, more interested in power and respect, and perhaps better in the sciences. God forbid that children might view girls as interested in dance, unicorns, princesses and makeup, quality relationships, reading and the arts. In a CNN article, an author encourages parents to point to pictures of soft-looking, made-up women in magazines and make clear to their children that "this is not what a real woman looks like," and to ask them "can you believe that?" disapprovingly.[15]

And it seems they never wonder: *maybe there's a reason my girl likes traditionally feminine things*. Maybe there's something inherent in her biology, and it's not necessarily the result of some conspiracy to socialize her.

While they're at it, they might want to ask: maybe there's a reason for these annoying yet stubborn differences. Maybe there's a reason there is *masculine* and *feminine* in the first place. ·

Could it be that men are actually there to protect and build, and women are there to nurture and civilize—all of which are equal and necessary to the advance of civilization? In other words, can it be that the differences between men and women go beyond their obvious physical differences? Can those differences actually explain why civilization has developed as it has? We seem to have no problem saying that a vagina is not a penis, but we seem to have trouble saying that a woman is not a man.

These are things that don't enter the minds of many progressives, who instead imagine a world they'd *like* to see and then try to get human nature to conform to it. It's like jamming together two or more pieces of a huge puzzle that are not supposed to fit. Sure you've gotten them together for the moment—again, *for the moment*.

Sooner or later, though, you'll realize that you won't be able to finish the puzzle.

Gaslighting and the "Spectrum"

The 1938 stage play *Gaslight*, later adapted into a movie in 1944 with Ingrid Bergman, tells a harrowingly devious story. Someone has strangled a famous opera singer in her home and stolen some of her jewels. The singer's niece, Paula, goes to study in Italy to also become an opera singer. While there, she falls in love with the charming Gregory Anton. The two return to London and move back to the aunt's house. But it's all a ruse: Gregory is in fact the murderer of Paula's aunt and just wants to get back into the house to continue searching for the aunt's jewels.

As Gregory searches the attic every evening in secret, Paula begins to notice strange goings-on: missing pictures, strange footsteps in the night, and gaslights that dim without being touched. Gregory is doing this in an elaborate scheme to make her question her own reality. When Paula points these things out to Gregory, he convinces her that she's remembering things incorrectly or that she's even delusional.

It's a gripping psychological thriller, and since the movie, people have used the term *gaslighting* to describe anyone's attempt to manipulate someone else's perception of reality. Sociopaths and narcissists use gaslighting tactics often. Sociopaths consistently transgress social mores, break laws, and exploit others but often also are convincing liars, sometimes even charming ones. They not only deny wrongdoing; they turn the tables on the victims so that they may doubt their own perceptions.[16]

And when it comes to the transgender discussion of today? That's right: you're being gaslighted.

Our national discussion of the supposed plight of transgenders has consumed us, and it's now spreading throughout the modern world. But as they often say about great movies, they're not always what they appear to be about. *Lawrence of Arabia* is not really about a man's exploits for England during World War I. It's about the dangers of narcissism and the intoxication of power. *Star Wars* is not just about fighting battles in space. It was about the use and abuse of God (the "Force." C'mon guys, whom are we kidding?).

And likewise, the story of transgenderism is *not* only about honoring people who feel like they are the opposite sex. It's actually the quest to destroy the basic distinctions that have built Western civilization. And they'll call you primitive, uninformed, or even delusional if you don't agree with the agenda.[17]

How can I say this? Because the agenda push is *not* just to advocate for particular embattled individuals who are struggling with their sexual biology. The push is to claim that *all of us* somehow identify outside of our "inherited" biology. You're not male if you were born with a penis and you call yourself a boy or man; you're "cisgender." Likewise, "gender" is not your sex anymore but "[w]here you feel that you personally fall on the spectrum between male and female." You see, people commonly identify as male or female, but in reality, they all "fall in the middle or move throughout the spectrum."[18]

Ah, there's that word again: *spectrum.* And *you* belong somewhere on it. You're not just a boy or girl anymore. That's too simplistic. Now go and figure out where you are on that spectrum. Go on, now. Explore away. Maybe you'll find other people there on the spectrum who are just as confused and repressed as you are.

You *still* think you're just a boy or girl? Sure you are, buddy. You keep telling that to yourself, you self-denying, self-blinding, and repressed Neanderthal. (Did you know Neanderthals also had their share of transgenders, by the way? It's true).

They make you think you're crazy, or at least backward, for not joining their team. It's become "unscientific" and even cruel—that's right, *cruel*—to assert that one can claim sex by biology alone.[19]

They want you to think that perhaps you're one of them, or much closer to being one of them than you think. If not that, they'd have you believe a whole lot more of them are out there— among your friends, schoolmates, and colleagues. And most of those guys are on the spectrum. You just never knew it, you see. Nor did they.

Still, that doesn't matter. There's an agenda here to push: blur all distinctions between male and female. Please don't get in the way.

Meanwhile, they're plundering your civilization, up there in the attic.

In the end, with robots, you'll never have to worry about your place on any spectrum, whether it involves your sexual preference or your identity. There are no labels when you're in your room with a robot. Come to think about it, there are no identities at all.

The world won't have to conform to you, and you won't have to conform to it. You won't have to think about male and female differences. You won't have to worry about anyone judging you or threatening you with criminal conduct. In fact, no one will ever need to discuss their sexual needs ever again, anymore than they might need to discuss their need for aspirin. You've got a headache? Why are you bothering me about it? Go to the drugstore and deal with it.

Robots fulfill all your needs. Everyone can just leave everyone else alone now. We can end the whole sex discussion, once and for all.

Problem solved.

Chapter 8

Masculinity?
No Thank You!

Transgenderism ultimately invites the demolition of the distinction between male and female. If everyone's on the spectrum and can move up and down it at any time, well then is anyone really "male" or "female"? If you don't know if your boyfriend is going to "stay" male for the next few decades, might that undermine your hopes for a stable long-term relationship?

But something else is going on, beyond the transgender issue.

In the schools, entertainment, media, and even the workplace, there is an attempt to destroy any sense that there is such a thing as masculinity at all. After all, masculinity is inherently "toxic," so we should roundly reject it for the failed enterprise it is—like fascism, communism, the Atkins diet, and the "You've Got Mail" announcement when you used to open your old AOL email account.

And reject it they have, in spades. While girls receive a non-stop diet of "Girl Power," and there's a bucket full of movies where—brace for this—the action hero who saves the day? It's a *girl*. That's right, you read that right: a *girl*. I know; shocking, right? It's enough to turn your whole world upside down.

Not only that, but there's "Social Emotional Learning" now and a general focus on feelings as the most paramount issue of the day. There's little interest in the classic particular attributes of men; only of women. Those predominantly include nurturing, sensitivity to feelings, and caring for one another. That's all good, mind you, but they ignore masculinity. At best, they attempt to "redefine" it.

Why does masculinity need redefining? That much is unclear, but redefine we must. In a "lesson plan" from the *New York Times*, it tries hard: It seeks to "suggest ways to deconstruct definitions of masculinity as they manifest in our society and our lives." The lesson plans promise "suggestions for several projects students might take on to expand and reimagine what 'being a man' might mean in their own lives and in our society at large."[1] Many other articles, symposiums, and genders studies classes aspire to this same "reimagination" mission.

Note how they put quotes around the phrase "being a man," as if it's an antiquated worn-out phrase from a backward past, one that needs a total makeover (reference to makeup intended). To be sure, "being a man" won't mean what you'd think it should mean, at least not as they thought about it way back in the primordial days when men fought the American Revolution, the Civil War, World War II, the Cold War, and all the wars in between. It won't evoke memories of the hard work men did to tame the Wild West, explore space, or the day-to-day actions of the average man to provide for his family, fight off would-be intruders in his home, or to protect women from would-be assaults.

No, no: whenever they want to discuss what "being a man" means—especially when they use those quotes—they mean only one thing: *men should act more like women.* It's always that way. As soon as someone wants to "explore" new ways of defining masculinity, you can rest assured there's a quest to indoctrinate toward a new orthodoxy. There will be suggestions that true masculine men need to "share feelings" and "open up and cry sometimes." It should mean listening, and *active* listening at that (whatever that means). It should mean not just offering up constant "fix it" solutions, either. And—oh yes—being emotionally available (whatever that means too).

In other words, the new masculinity will mean being more . . . I don't know . . . *feminine*. Yes, there it is: *that's* the word I was looking for.

Interestingly, in this very same *New York Times* article, it seems to acknowledge the actual plight of today's boys. It quotes author Michael Ian Black, who bemoaned how boys are getting lost and "left behind":

> The past 50 years have redefined what it means to be female in America. Girls today are told that they can do anything, be anyone. They've absorbed the message: They're outperforming boys in school at every level. But it isn't just about performance. To be a girl today is to be the beneficiary of decades of conversation about the complexities of womanhood, its many forms and expressions.
>
> Boys, though, have been left behind. No commensurate movement has emerged to help them navigate toward a full expression of their gender. It's no longer enough to "be a man"—we no longer even know what that means.[2]

The *New York Times* "lesson plan" seems to understand that we need to pull boys out of their "lost" state. But how will we do so? By making the boys more like the girls, of course.[3] Instead of giving the boys their own direction, they recommend we just direct them toward the girls.

Once again, problem solved. Phew. Just do what the girls do, and you'll have the same success they're having. Turns out the answer was right there all along, everyone. Thanks for coming. Glad it all worked out.

Mr. Lurie: Women have had to live in a man's world for thousands of years. Maybe it's the girls' turn. And maybe men can learn a lot from femininity.

You're missing the point here. No one is saying that femininity is bad. No one is saying that one can't *appreciate* femininity and masculinity, or their differences for that matter. But there's a difference between appreciating the differences and striving to be more like the other sex.

As if walking right into this, TED talk speaker and actor Justin Baldoni presented his speech, "Why I'm done trying to be 'man enough.'" He explains that the tough-guy roles that he played never felt real to him. He discovered in his own personal life that he had just been pretending to be a man that he was not. "It's exhausting trying to be a man all my life," he explained.[4]

But what is it "to be a man," according to Baldoni? It's all about machismo, power, suffering in silence, "grabbing ass" and being violent, pretending to be the toughest man with the biggest . . . assets, and of course objectifying women. You can see the feministas in the crowd nodding along as he speaks. But he's just fed into what the progressives and feminists have proclaimed masculinity is. Interestingly, this particular TED Talk fell under a subcategory called "TEDWomen." Why exploring manhood would fall under a feminine category is not clear. Perhaps here is a clue: the "about the author" section of the website describes Baldoni as "an outspoken feminist, [who] has been doubling down on his efforts to start a dialogue with men to redefine masculinity."[5]

The mantras are all a vague heap of platitudinal garbage. Boys need to learn how to be *men*, and being masculine means being quite *different* from being feminine. Some might even say it should mean the *opposite* of feminine. But schools, entertainment, and news media, and even the churches are failing to teach actual affirmative masculine values: leadership, courage, risk taking, protection, sharing "big picture" concepts, and providing. These are the tenets which should be core to every young man. These are the things that resonate with and animate boys, and which will ultimately make them men. There is no boy who ever dreamed of one day growing up to become a woman or even a nice young man. Boys dream of growing up to do great things, mostly involving saving the world from bad guys.

Instead, through one program after another, schools teach about the worst things men do (violent aggression, rape, and assault) and teach boys not to do that.[6] Then they boast that they are teaching boys to be men. The program is working!

The University of Texas hopes young men can "break the cycle" of masculinity, or at least "develop a healthy model of masculinity." Its program, cutely titled "MasculinUT," builds upon a critique of "restrictive masculinity." The program even has a "Healthy Masculinities Coordinator" to spearhead this important mission. The theory is that men suffer when they feel they must "act like a man" or fulfill traditional gender roles, such as being "successful" or "the breadwinner."[7] Damn straight: women *hate* such things in men. Women say it all the time.

The program actually treats masculinity as a *mental health issue*.[8] That's right: if you're "masculine," there's something wrong with you, buddy. However, if you think you're a woman when you're biologically a man, that's fine. *That* doesn't need fixing.

All they are teaching is how *not* to be a man, and how a man can, nay *must*, "escape" his masculinity. These programs do little to celebrate and channel masculinity's natural attributes (including aggression) toward building or leadership. All these programs seek to accomplish is to make boys into girls.

The American Psychological Association (APA) goes even further: it found that "traditional masculinity" is not only individually harmful but could also lead to homophobia and sexual harassment. What masculine traits are we talking about? Stoicism, competitiveness, dominance, and aggression. "Such traditional masculine traits are, on the whole, harmful."[9] The report claims that "traditional masculinity ideology has been shown to limit males' psychological development, constrain their behavior, result in gender role strain and gender role conflict and negatively influence mental health and physical health."[10]

So the message is clear: stay away from masculinity, people. It just leads to such horrible stuff—vague as that stuff might be. And please—watch out for that *gender role strain*!

Here are two problems with the report: it cannot possibly provide meaningfully objective causal connections between traditional masculinity and all the horrible things it claims flow from it—at least not with a serious face. Also, it defines "traditional masculinity" in an essentially destructive and even criminal light. Then it proceeds to claim that traditional masculinity leads to destruction and criminality. It's compelling at first, but the reasoning is self-referencing and circular . . . like Ponzi schemes.

The second problem is that it ignores that this same traditional masculinity led to the greatest advancements of civilization, gave us freedom and democracy, and stemmed horrific evil such as slavery, fascism, and communism. It also built infrastructure, innovated all our modern conveniences, and eradicated stubborn horrific diseases that had heretofore decimated the population time and time again. Oh, it also put a man on the moon and stuff.

But other than all that, traditional masculinity is downright destructive and primitive. We must expunge it from our midst, posthaste.

The failure of the report even to consider the *good* that masculinity has brought us (yes, even the "traditional" kind) undermines the study from the get-go. And lo and behold, femininity is just the opposite: its qualities have brought us only understanding, judgment-free problem-solving, nurturing and cooperation. There's *nothing* negative about the feminine.

So who can blame our boys when they reject traditional masculinity? As one "millennial" man stated in a survey, he learns his masculine values from men around him who "want to be both caring and strong, both open to others and self-sufficient, and they see no contradiction in these values." Researchers believe that millennial men "are widening their value structure and questioning what it truly means to be masculine."[11] Of course, there's never an answer to the question of what masculinity *is*. Or more accurately, there are no wrong answers. Anything goes, and everything is masculine. And feminine, too.

More odd is that activists trying to change masculinity often don't even include males at all. Two high-ranking University of California women administrators urged women's centers across the nation to take up the task of "deconstructing masculinities." Why women's centers? Because "women's centers play an *essential* role in helping to understand, identify, and deconstruct masculinities" (emphasis added).[12]

What makes a women's center "essential" to define masculinity is unclear, but that's not important right now. One of the administrators explained that, for her, "deconstructing masculinities" includes educating students that "masculinity is not attached to gender." That's why women's centers are at the forefront of this deconstruction, you see, with no men involved. Her reasoning is that "[w]omen can also embody masculinity, masculine of center people don't always identify as men, and some might not identify with masculinity at all." Her theory is that masculinity is not inherently male but socially constructed.

Truly hers is a dizzying intellect. But she's not done: "By analyzing gender, masculinity in particular as a noun, adjective, and verb, women's centers can *interrupt the ways in which masculinity is discussed* and offer alternative ways to think about it"[13] (emphasis added). It's like making an interception at a football game you see.

They boast that their approach to "tackling masculinity" is nearly unprecedented. Did you read that? *Tackling masculinity.* It's as if masculinity has become a pervasive problem that we need to root out collectively, like world hunger, overpopulation, or foot fungus. Masculinity is backward and needs fixing. (Ironic, in a way: aren't women the ones who often complain that men always want to "fix" a problem?) Masculinity pushes harmful "breadwinner" stereotypes and encourages bystander intervention.[14] I'm confused: are those *bad* things?

They seek to include everyone *except* for cisgender men, which, if I whip out and use my *Star Trek* universal translator, apparently means something akin to "straight men" in Earth language.

God forbid straight men should help you define masculinity. Wait: isn't that like a bunch of men getting together and deciding what being feminine means but without any women? Isn't that like studying what Judaism means but without Jews? Maybe we should study science without scientists, and how to fight fires without actual firefighters? OK, you get the idea.

Going forward, the administrators hope that women's centers will begin opening up to the idea that masculinity is something *all* students of any gender can enjoy—except for, you know, straight guys. They argue this is especially important for transgender and "nonbinary" students.[15]

Wait, I thought masculinity was toxic. *A bad thing. Now they do want it for everybody? I'm lost. Can you just tell me what to write on the exam already and let me go home?*

You know, I gotta tell you; I'm kind of confused too.

Where have we heard all this before? It's as if in one gender studies class after another, there's some collective effort to question what it means to be masculine—and then to root it out, or at least dilute it to the oblivion of a thousand vague possible definitions.

But there's good news: both the question and the answer seem to be in harmony throughout the West, and certainly in America:

Question: What does it mean to be masculine?

Answer: Anything that is *not* masculine. In fact, the more feminine something is, the more masculine it should also be.

Got it?

You can almost see the aliens in some sci-fi movie from the fifties, puzzling over these creatures called humans as they study them from their orbit far above the Earth—or better yet, the space aliens Kodos and Kang from *The Simpsons*.

"Foolish earthlings," they'd say. "Why all this self-torment and confusion? Why don't they just let sex robots solve all their problems, like *we* did on Rigel-7?"

Chapter 9

Nobody Needs
Anybody Else Anyway

According to our progressive betters, we're all now some blur of sexual identities—perhaps some mixture of man and woman that is unique to each of us. There may be as many as seventy or more of such genders (yes, it's grown in numbers since about twenty pages ago). We can choose whichever one suits us. It's like we can order our sexual identities at Burger King: "Have it *your* way."

But if there are so many kinds of genders, then do we really *need* an "opposite" sex? Isn't that fair to ask? In a world of that many genders, can there be such a thing as an "opposite" sex? What is the opposite of "pangender?" What is the opposite of someone who considers himself a woman but doesn't have a vagina? Do straight men really have to specify that they like a woman without a penis and a woman who never *previously* had a penis? Or will that be considered some form of discrimination that dating apps won't allow?

Plato wrote about the search for our other "halves," coming from the Greek myth where humans were at one time twice the people they are now. They sort of rolled around to get by, is my guess.

Anyway, the gods viewed them as a threat, so Zeus cut each human in half. Since that fateful day, the myth says, humans go about searching for their other half, to become "whole." The man *needed* a woman and a woman *needed* a man. They completed each other, becoming whole. And when they found each other, they each found their "Platonic half" to complete them. And you thought those ancient Greek guys couldn't be romantic.

Anyway, it's sexual polarity—the notion that we need each other precisely because we are opposite of each other in the most basic way: male and female.

In all the transgender talk, redefining-women talk (see feminism chapter above), and redefining-men talk (see the "masculinity, no thank you" chapter above), the idea of romance seems irrelevant. Better yet, romance seems out of place. It's like seeing the *Mona Lisa* hanging in the same museum exhibit room as a collection of McDonald's ad posters from the eighties.

Few talk about this notion of "completion." In fact, most now seem only to talk and think of their being complete in and of themselves. Once they've figured out who they really are, then they're good to go into the world. The world will accept them because they've finally accepted themselves. All will be harmonious. The moon will be in the seventh house, Jupiter will align with Mars, and so on. You know the rest.

Part of any relationship is the sense that we need somebody else. It's also the notion that you need someone *opposite* of you, thus complementing your masculine traits with her feminine traits. Therefore, man *needs* the feminine, and woman *needs* the masculine. (Did I really have to explain that?) But As author Deanna Lorraine puts it, men don't even see the value of a woman anymore. If a woman acts like a man, competes with him, and brings nothing unique to the table that he doesn't do himself, what's the point in having a wife?[1] Why not just get a roommate to share bills and then just outsource his sex?

What happens when you're told over and over again that there are multiple genders and you don't inherently need anybody else—or at least the idea of needing someone else doesn't even come up? What happens when everyone is considered fluid and can go in and out of genders? In a sense, haven't you become your own self-contained unit—man and woman, together in one body? Isn't that just what you would expect when each sex redefines itself to be more and more like the other sex—if there is such a thing as "the other sex" anymore?

Isn't that what you would expect when the transgender movement tells us gender is not "binary" and everyone is "fluid"? Isn't that saying no one has any opposites to complete them?

No wonder then that women have become the "men" in their own lives—if you will. They've become self-sustaining machines: they provide for themselves, fight for their business promotions, and can have kids from the sperm bank if they want a child (p.s. it always seems to be only one child). And if they meet a nice guy with whom to hang out and exchange orgasms on a consistent basis, so much the better.

But counting on him to "complete" her? She doesn't even understand the concept. Complete what, exactly, please? You can practically see her indignant face right now: *Are you saying I'm insufficient somehow?* (In her defense, however, have you met the actual guys she's hooking up with? Other than the obvious body parts differences, she probably can't distinguish most of them from her girlfriends anyway.)

And the men are no different: they don't need women either. They get all the sex they want, without the accompanying annoying "relationship." After all, there are plenty of self-sufficient women who don't need them either, so what's the problem? Everyone is getting what they want.

Remember our Tinder lady friend, who talked about how sex has become "disposable" for her, how there's always more out there and you move on fast to the next person, the next experience. No matter how awesome a companion you might find, the promise exists of the next adventure, the next orgasm. But to many in the young sex world today, a great partner is like spending time watching a movie. It doesn't matter how fantastic the movie is; there are still only so many times you can watch it.

Sex and bonding have become commodities. It's like the way we once regarded clothes as recently as the beginning of the twentieth century. Back then, before the age of mass production, few people had more than three or four main outfits, and they wore a "Sunday best" outfit for church. Their clothes were expensive, and they mended them themselves. They were elegant and designed to last a long time—at least people strived for that. Hand-me-downs were the rule.

Now virtually all Americans have plenty of clothes, and certainly that's a good thing—a function of supply meeting demand, the creation of polyester and other fabrics and automation in the clothing industry making everything less expensive. But are they elegant and designed to last? Do we take pride in them? That's another story.

That is what sex has become. We wear each other and then toss each other out, looking for the next great thing. Why stick to one thing when you can have constant variety in the latest trends at minimal cost?

• • •

The institution of marriage is not the only thing fading. The notion of relationships is making a rather abrupt exit. That's not to say that relationships will end for everyone; there'll always be holdouts for relationships. And as people get older, they'll discover the need for someone else to help take care of them.

But that may be too late. People won't have the training for what a relationship is, what to expect, what is reasonable and what is not. As they get older, people get set in their ways, and may look for an exit whenever there's the slightest annoyance. After all, they remember how easy hookups were to get in the old days.

The destruction of relationships is happening, especially among men and women in their twenties and thirties, and it's a strong trend. They see marriage—and now even committed monogamous relationships—as something earlier generations had to do (because the "social construct" forced men to provide for women and protect them or because the male patriarchy invented marriage as some sort of trap to keep women down— you choose).

Now they're viewing that the same way about any kind of monogamous relationship at all. In fact, it may be antiquated and less true to oneself to seek out a "only one" relationship. There's nothing wrong with seeking out and wanting multiple sexual relationships; it's just a question of being candid about it.[2]

Time magazine even opined that polyamory—having more than one consensual sexual or emotional relationship at once— can have unique strengths that monogamous couples can "learn from."[3] For starters, polyamory encourages safer sex. It also encourages more communication about each other's needs, to manage one's primitive jealousy. It also fosters a greater sense of independence. It discards unhealthy notions of fairy tale hap-pily-ever-afters. Oh, and my favorite? Such people learn about time management—what with having to plan all their romping around from bed to bed.

Do you see how much we can *learn*? But the idea that we should learn from these orgasms-drive-my-life people is odd. Pigs can also teach you how to roll in the mud.

The tone of these articles is fascinating, in a few ways: First, they suggest not only that polyamorous relationships are equally acceptable modes of romance, but people who engage in them are probably more evolved, worldly, and open minded. To them, polyamory allows for a more enriching life. It's a strange sexual elitism.

Second, nowhere do they lay out the pitfalls of such polyamorous relationships, not the least of which is sexually transmitted diseases. They also fail to discuss the challenges of human nature: that having polyamorous relationships requires a maddening juggle of sexual intensities among different people and undermines the personal stability so many find in having only one partner.

Third, the overall argument seems to go like this: if you don't expect much from a relationship, you won't feel so disappointed when things don't work out. These are the same people who say don't get married because you might get divorced. Or, as Homer from *The Simpsons* taught: "Trying is the first step towards failure."

Fourth, nowhere do they deal with the critical role of *intimacy and trust* in monogamy, and the personal, intellectual, and spiritual growth that intimacy brings to both individuals in a couple. You simply cannot have the same level of intensity or trust when you're sexing it up with multiple partners. No one will care for you as much as a wife or husband with whom you've committed to a sustaining life together. No one. You might as well say having many jobs is the same thing as having one career or that ten people can raise a child with the same quality as two dedicated parents.

Fifth, they give no consideration to the reality of jealousy—or why jealousy even exists—and how it can be destructive. The authors of these articles dismiss emotions of jealousy as "highly illogical," as though they are emotion-free Vulcans, like Spock from *Star Trek* fame.

Yet they would have you believe that it's *monogamous* people who can somehow learn from those who sleep around with multiple people.

Silly Vulcans.

Chapter 10

Porn vs.
the Minimum Wage

Miriam Weeks was a young woman who was quite comfortable with her body. She liked sex and pornography. She was also about to go to one of the most prestigious colleges in America. The problem was tuition, as it was for so many young people. While she felt it was necessary to get the best education she could, she learned she was ineligible for government loans. And she couldn't imagine strapping herself or her family to enormous debt through private loans, either.

She had worked as a waitress, but her boss treated her poorly and the work schedule interfered with her studies. After taxes, she took home less than $400 a month. That kind of money would make no serious dent toward her $60,000-per-year tuition.

What's a young woman with a beautiful body and who feels secure in her sexuality to do? Might there be a way she could at once satisfy her sensuality on the one hand *and* pay her stratospheric tuition on the other?

Pornography was the answer. And why not? It offered much better compensation and working hours. Pornography would allow her to control her schedule, and she could make about *$1,300 per scene*.[1] Two or three scenes a week, and (whip out calculator and punch numbers furiously), hey, that's *real* money—Ivy-league-tuition kind of money.

Barely eighteen in 2013, she started flying out to Los Angeles while on school breaks to perform in pornographic films, and she kept on going.

What wasn't to like? From a pure monetary comparison point of view, the porn route was a no-brainer. Take away the stigma aspect of being a "sex worker," and the matter quickly reduces to a matter of economics. A young woman can make anywhere between $10 to $15 an hour selling clothing at Banana Republic or get $800 to $4,000 per sexual romp. You do the math. And when more and more people start viewing sex itself as a "gig" that pays a lot better than most other day jobs, the good news will travel fast.

Not only was Weeks making good money; she was self-sufficient, she enjoyed the sex, and she was her own boss. She also made friends with her co-sex-workers. They didn't judge her. She had a sense of belonging. It was all good.

And the most important aspect of her story? Not once did she express grappling with whether what she was doing was disreputable or degrading. On the contrary, she believed her role in the porn industry was personally empowering and freeing.

And why *wouldn't* she feel that way? Doesn't she live in a time of Tinder and other hookup websites, where everyone is "disposable" and you move on to the next man? Isn't everyone else sleeping around in the same way, satisfying their libidos just like her? What was the difference? What made her situation "degrading," while other women were satisfying themselves sexually with as many strangers as her? Maybe the difference was only that she had a lovely body and could make money— and lots of it—for letting someone film her encounters.

And by monetizing her sex, wasn't Weeks just doing something really smart here? In the early 2000s, an average female porn star made $100,000 or so a year, and "top-flight" female performers could get as much as $200,000 to $350,000 per year.[2]

In today's culture, where sex is just personal to you, a mere quest for a momentary orgasm, I don't see why most everyone who has a halfway decent figure—especially women—hasn't decided to monetize their sexual encounters too.

Oh, wait—that's exactly what *is* happening:

Apparently, it doesn't have to be for much money, either. Many "amateur" porn websites feature numerous videos by couples having intercourse (or singles masturbating in one way or another). Why? For the thrill of it.

And what happens when more and more women realize they can monetize their sex by letting someone film them? Like anything else, the offering price for any sex scene goes down. That's supply and demand. Already, the average yearly take among women in sex films from 2003 to 2013 went down *by half,* from $100,000 to $50,000.[3]

The price per scene will plummet all the more when porn goes even more mainstream, and no one regards a porn star as a person on the margin of society. They're just in business like anyone else—on the same level as any teacher, fireman, lawyer, web designer, or plumber.

Three ladies meet at a charity fundraiser dinner. Let's listen in on their conversation:

And what do you do?

I'm in sales for pharmaceuticals. My company focuses on diabetes inhibitors. And you?

I'm an accountant for real estate development companies. And what about you? (turning to a third lady)

I'm in the sex entertainment industry, focusing predominantly in blow-jobs and anal.

In the seventies during the "Golden Age of Porn," there were fewer than fifty theatrical porn releases, the rest of porn being available in so-called "peep booths." There were only a handful of porn stars. While many people (especially men) watched their films, most still looked down on porn as a marginal, unseemly, and desperate profession.[4] And if you bumped into a porn star in the street, there was a good chance that many people (mostly men) recognized her.

Not so anymore. With videos, then DVDs, and now the internet, the number of girls participating in porn, and the number of videos and access to porn in the internet generally, has skyrocketed exponentially.[5] In addition, "homemade pornography" has ramped up the numbers dramatically, thanks to technological advances in digital video.

And then the web allowed the distribution of homemade pornography in a way that hadn't been possible only a decade earlier. Dannie Ashe, of Dannie's Hard Drive, created a "members only" section of her website in 1995 and in two years went from grossing $600,000 to $2.5 million. Thousands of new porn producers got their start in the same way.[6] Like bookstores, newspapers, publishing houses, and music stores, the porn industry morphed, seemingly overnight.

To add to this cacophony of lust, literally millions of people video themselves sexually for free, or for very little. It's called "Amateur Porn," and it reflects a growing part of the porn field—much like do-it-yourself music publishing through platforms like iTunes or book self-publishing through Amazon.

But free? Really? One would think that traditional work, even at minimum wage, is a better option. They do it because amateur porn gives them an exhibitionist thrill, or a boost to the ego when they can constantly check to see how many more "views" they got for their video today. The money is secondary.

And it's all so easy; they can use their smartphone and upload their video to a porn website in twenty minutes.[7]

And unlike in the seventies, you can film a scene between you and your boyfriend, upload it, and no one would recognize you in the street, ever. How would they? You'd be literally one of tens of millions of videos out there, constantly refreshing every day with new batches of titillation. So the chances that someone might actually recognize you from such a video? About one in tens of millions.

And if they did recognize you, would it really be all that bad?

And guess what? It's not the faces that consumers of porn are looking at anyway. It's all in the act, the woman's curves, her enthusiasm, and what she's willing to do with her body. Who has time to notice a face?

Amateur porn is cutting into traditional, professional porn. By October 2017 searches for "porn" and "tube" returned 23 million results on Google, up from 8 million less than ten years earlier. Video hosting service "tube" websites feature free user-uploaded amateur pornography, which users now visit more than any other pornography website.[8]

Because the content of these websites is entirely free, of reasonably high quality, and often full length, these websites have sharply cut into the profits of porn paysites and other traditional pornography sources. To add trouble to their woes, the profits of even these tube-site owners continue to dissipate in an increasingly crowded market, with the number of such sites always growing.[9]

Everyone wants in on the "action." But just what is the "action"? It's the realization that the showcasing of vivid sexual activity is for everybody, that few feel any shame about it (they're prudes if they do). It's like a new Gold Rush of some kind, only this time there are no scarce precious metals to dig up. In fact, there's nothing scarce or precious at all. It's something quite different: it's one thing we all have—our instincts and the basest parts of our physical nature, the bodies we were all born with.

People seem to forget that what made pornography successful was the notion that you were getting a glimpse of something "forbidden." It was the socially created scarcity that both tantalized consumers of porn and made them happy to pay for it. But what happens when porn becomes so accessible, so commoditized, and mainstreamed? Doesn't it lose that "forbidden" quality?

What the porn world is experiencing now, with ever-decreasing margins of profitability, is the closing of that window of time between any remaining sense of the taboo of sex and the profiting from that taboo. Everyone is at the trough now, each having a tougher and tougher time finding morsels for himself.

And so the sex-for-profit world will soon turn its sights to the one last most promising lucrative area: sex robots. The focus will be on making them ever more realistic-looking and feeling, ever more responsive, and ever more reasonably priced. It is the inevitable result of our race to the bottom to profit from man's most prurient instinct.

But race to the bottom we will. It's as sure a thing as wondering whether people will claw over each other if they were to see cash flying out of the back door of an armored bank truck.

Except that we won't realize we're the ones giving it away.

Remember that now.

Chapter 11

All for One, and One for One

"What's wrong with masturbation?" Woody Allen famously wondered. "I'm doing it with someone I love." Funny as that is, that may be exactly the problem.

I was going to refer to this chapter as "Masturbation Nation," but I felt uneasy with the word *masturbation* in the title. I grew up in a time where sexual self-gratification was something boys and girls might do, but which parents suggested they avoid, if they discussed it at all. And adolescents felt guilty if they did masturbate. There was a religious element to it, yes, but also a societal one. I'd guess the societal one stemmed from the religious one.

I venture to say that a lot of the "ick" factor of masturbation was the narcissistic element that you were taking care only of your own needs. It was the sense that you were vain and self-absorbed, even shameful.

Philosopher C. S. Lewis put it this way, particularly with regard to men:

> [Masturbation] takes an appetite which . . . leads the individual out of himself to complete (and correct) his own personality in that of another (and finally in children and even grandchildren) and turns it back: sending

the man back into the prison of himself, there to keep a harem of imaginary brides.

And this harem, once admitted, works against his *ever* getting out and really uniting with a real woman. For the harem is always accessible, always subservi-ent, calls for no sacrifice or adjustments, and can be endowed with erotic and psychological attractions which no real woman can rival.

Among these shadowy brides he is always adored, always the perfect lover: no demand is made on his unselfishness, no mortification is ever imposed on his vanity. In the end, they become merely the medium through which he increasingly adores himself. . . .

Masturbation involves [an] abuse of imagination in erotic matters (which I think bad in itself) and thereby encourages a similar abuse of it in all spheres.

After all, almost the *main* work of life is to *come out* of our selves, out of the little, dark prison we are all born in. Masturbation is to be avoided as *all* things are to be avoided which retard this process. The danger is that of coming to *love* the prison[1] (emphasis in original).

C. S. Lewis here was speaking about masturbation on an individual level. He died before he could see how an orgasm culture would lead to worse issues than he imagined—on a broader *societal* level. In his time, I think the understanding was, that if you masturbated too often (or people suspected you did), then you weren't doing your part to advance civilization. It was a sense that you should be instead pursuing a relationship. That was something people took for granted back then, implicitly expecting you to do your part and get yourself into a healthy relationship, marry, and have kids of your own. It was some-thing so entrenched that society never thought it would one day have to teach it, such as teaching someone the value of breathing or drinking water.

Having a family assisted in the advancement for the world. That was hard work, but it's what you directed your life toward. By contrast, masturbation was considered the opposite: somewhat selfish and indulgent, vain, and even lazy. As Lewis said, the goal is to come out of ourselves, not to retreat back in.

If we are to believe old tales, church doctrine so wished to restrict masturbation that clergy insisted you'd go to hell, or at least that you'd go blind. From a social point of view, it wasn't that (it couldn't really be; the blind consequence alone was too absurd—one could easily dismiss the threat after one foray into self-pleasure). The taboo came from a sense that you weren't doing what you needed to do "for the team." You were cheating the rest of us. You were like a guy in a six-man rowboat who decided he didn't need to row. Others would do the work, but not you!

Fast forward a few decades, and it's all changed. Far from demonizing masturbation, we've come to *celebrate* it and tout its extraordinary virtues. In fact, did you know May is now Masturbation Month? Now you know what to do next May.

Wife: Hey, honey, I'm feeling a little . . . well, YOU know. Do you want to make sweet love?

Husband: No can do, sweetie. It's Masturbation Month. Check back with me in June.

That, along with "masturbate-athon" celebrations aim to "remove the taboo and shame associated with masturbation." The first of these self-pleasuring events was held in London in August 2006. And to answer the question in your head right now, the world's greatest masturbator was Masanobu Sato, who broke the world record at this event in 2009 in San Francisco. He masturbated for nine hours and thirty-three minutes. He would later go on to beat that record.[2] His mother was not immediately available to comment about how proud she was.

It's not just self-pleasuring introverts who are singing the praises of masturbation. The web is full of seemingly legitimate resources (*Psychology Today, Huffington Post*) touting the benefits of taking a firm hold of one's needs, and doing so often at that. Self-pleasure advocates claim masturbation can boost immunity, prevent cervical infections, and reduce the risk of prostate cancer and even diabetes. It reduces insomnia and stress and somehow increases better performance when the real deal comes along.[3] Virtually every major nonreligious source discussing the matter seems to promote masturbation as not only perfectly normal but something to encourage. "Go for it, bud," and "You go, girl!" seem to be the major themes.

Is this really a surprise? It's quite consistent with our culture. So many things have become more and more of a have-it-your-way mantra: in television, news, music, business, social media, food, employment, and even hookup I mean dating apps.

You can tailor all of these things to your exact specifications. There's less and less sharing of a common set of stories. Even advertising is just about the individual now. Your eyes won't *ever* have to see an irrelevant ad again (that's what they promise, anyway).

All of this reflects a new social trend toward flying solo. No one's looking at the jumbo screen at the airports; everyone's looking at their smartphone. Airplanes allow you to see what-ever show or play any game you want, on your own private screen in front of you. There's no more announcement on the PA that "today's feature film on this flight will be *Mrs. Doubtfire*," which you would watch with everyone else.

Even the kids in the backseat of your car have their own headsets, lost in their own smartphones, watching or listening to their favorite show or song, tuning out the ride they're supposedly sharing as a family.

And lest you think the family dinner might still remain unscathed, you'd be wrong. That's long gone. Not only does it seem families have no time to coordinate the sharing or cooking of a simple meal; it's all the more easy to get your own food, when you want it—and of course exactly to your liking—what with all the food delivery apps.

Don't forget video games. They enable you to lose yourself in a fantasy world of sorcerers, soldiers, and aliens but where you're often alone. It's a total retreat from reality. The next thing you know, hours and days have slipped away. But in the video, you get to create your settings—and your entire world—just as you please.

There's little sense even of a shared history. Colleges have long ago abandoned a Western civilization curricula, instead favoring the study of whatever history and culture *you* feel is important to *you*. Many colleges today even allow you to propose your own major.[4] Two students can graduate on the same day from the same college and literally not have studied a single thing in common with each other.

We discussed before that many women wear tight leggings, showing as much of their bodies as possible. Do they think for a moment about the propriety of dressing as they do in front of young children and adolescent boys, that it might awaken sexual impulses? Not as much.

Separately, do such women think about the message they're conveying—that they're *promoting* the objectification of women? Instead, it's only about what that particular woman feels and wants, and her rights to walk around as she pleases—because it's comfortable, you see. No thought crosses her mind about the impact of her attire on the outside world, let alone any sense of duty to it.

In fact, to suggest any discretion in women's attire is cause enough for civil unrest. It happened at Notre Dame, where one Catholic mother wrote an opinion piece asking for greater modesty in attire, after she noticed four young women in front of her in the pews at a mass service, wearing leggings so sheer that she wondered whether the girls had painted them on. Her sons and she couldn't help but stare at their buttocks. "I'm fretting both because of unsavory guys who are looking at you creepily and nice guys who are doing everything to avoid looking at you," she wrote. The next day, a thousand students attended a protest to support wearing leggings.

Three generations of women in a family meet.

Grandma: In the sixties, we had the March on Washington. We also busted the first barriers for women. So important.

Mother: In the eighties we had the anti-apartheid movement and saw females in power everywhere, even in the Supreme Court. We were so proud.

Daughter: We showed our butts.

Biological males who claim the "right" to visit a female locker room are also only thinking of themselves. The media has not discussed one whit about the effect a transgendered woman's presence may have upon anyone else—say, for example, the nontransgendered girls and women in that same locker room. It's entirely and only about the feelings of the *transgenders* during their moment.

All for one, and one for one.

Even America is up for interpretation grabs. The main question that seems to matter is, what does "America" mean to *you*? We'll show it through whatever lens you want—gay, Black, female, Hispanic, or oppressive white man. If any of those are too broad, don't worry. America can mean anything: a country of opportunity and liberty; of sexism and suppression; of white privilege and racism; of guns and violence, of religious values or of unbridled greed. What matters is that *you* choose the theme.

Call it self-absorption or narcissism. I consider it a form of masturbation. And our culture pushes it in virtually every manner imaginable.

Even sexual identity and sexual preference seem to fall into the have-it-your-way rubric. Every day it seems like someone is adding another letter to the LGBTQ acronym. It's like how they keep adding digits to the number Pi. And good news: you can be any one of the fifty-plus genders out there. In fact, you may be the *only* one within a particular gender subgroup. And you know what? That's *OK*.

All of these things constitute some form of self-pleasure, indulgence, or self-infatuation. It's more and more of the "inward retreat." Worse, we seem to have trained ourselves not only to think about *ourselves* and our *own* immediate needs but to think this is even a *positive* and *healthy* thing.

But masturbation keeps us away from the pursuit of relationships. You have sexual urges? Take care of yourself, pleasure yourself, and then go on your merry way. All the food here is for take-out or pick-up. There's no need to sit down at the restaurant. Who has time for that?

Into this not-so-brave new world come the robots. The timing could not be more ideal. Wouldn't robots be the *perfect* solution to cater to each of our individual sexual fancies? If our self-pleasuring "all for one, and one for one" attitude pervades almost everything else in our daily lives, why should sex be different?

Or would you rather be stuck in one relationship, all your life? Isn't that like saying you want to watch *Mrs. Doubtfire* for the whole flight?

Hmmm. Maybe I should have called this chapter "Masturbation Nation," after all.

Chapter 12

Sex and Candy

In a *Twilight Zone* episode from the early sixties, thieves successfully rob a train full of gold bullion bars. But they know that if they start trading the bars in for money, they'll be caught. So they come up with a clever plan: their lead guy, a scientist, finds a way for them to hibernate in a desert cave for one hundred years. By the time they wake up, the gold will no longer be "hot," and they can spend it freely.

Or so was the plan. They go into their hibernation tubes and, as planned, wake up after a century. But soon enough, they start distrusting each other. One kills another by running him over with the gang's truck, and in the process, the truck goes over a cliff. The remaining two must now walk across the desert to the nearest town.

One of them (Farwell) loses his canteen of water, and the other (De Cruz) sells him a sip of water from his canteen—for the price of one gold bar. When the water is nearly gone and the fee goes up to two bars, Farwell strikes De Cruz with a gold brick, killing him. Farwell continues, dumping more and more of the heavy gold bars to the ground as he tries to lighten his load. Finally, he collapses from exhaustion and thirst.

Farwell awakes to find a man standing over him. Farwell offers him his last gold bar for water and a ride to the nearest town. But he dies before the man responds.

The man returns to his futuristic car and tells his wife that the man is dead. He remarks to his wife about how odd it was that Farwell had offered him a gold bar—as if it was a valuable thing.

"Wasn't it worth something once, George?" his wife asks.

Sure, the husband says, but that was a long time ago, before they found a way to manufacture it. Before it became cheap.

Such is the history of goods. Clothes used to be expensive. Now they're not. Food used to be expensive. Now it's not. Bikes, cell phones, computers, long-distance phone calls, cars, airplane travel, ride-hailing services, and televisions all used to be far more expensive. But because of innovations and mass production, now they're not.

Sex used to be valuable too. Not "expensive," mind you, but valuable. Few would disagree that sex meant much more one hundred years ago. People referred to sex as one's "virtue." If you wrongly even suggested a woman was of "unchaste character," that woman could sue you for millions for slander per se. The word *slut* or *whore* for a woman was one of the most vile things you could say. Likewise, a man who slept around was a "womanizer" or a "player."

In short, sex *meant* something, at least more than the act of pleasure itself. It wasn't like the fun of eating cotton candy or watching a great sci-fi action movie. It was something beyond only the thrill of sex itself. It was inchoate, intangible, yet we always knew sex was more than just "sex."

It was something a man very much wanted from a woman but which she guarded with the power of "no."[1] Sex was something a man pursued but often could not get before marriage—at least without paying for it. There were rules against adultery, too, even when you did finally marry.

It was all so very frustrating. What was a guy who didn't want to work hard for his sex to do?

Well, good news was around the corner, and it was called the Sixties. Two new paradigm shifts in our culture gave guys (yes, mostly guys) the answer. First, minimize the religious ideal that one shouldn't have sex before marriage. That became old-fashioned and backward thinking. Only a fool would buy a car without test driving it first, right? And while you're at it, test drive *lots* of other cars. Lots. Make sure whatever car you get in the end is *perfect* for *you*. After all, once you're married, then that's *it* for Charlie-boy.

Maybe not, though—not if you go to step two: minimize marriage itself. Say it's just a piece of paper. Say it's just a construct from the bad old days when men used marriage to control women, or at least something professorial like that. And you'll say that if two people want to be exclusive with each other, great. But if not, then not.

And you'll insist that adultery should be legal. We should never call it "immoral," either; that's too *judgey*. Who knows what's right for any one person and his/her situation? And if you want to try polyamory or to move around sexually from a man to a woman to a trans and then back again, so much the better for you.

And no longer is there such a thing as a one-night stand. That would imply that the proper sexual understanding is that once you have sex, you should stay with that person, at least for a couple of weeks. But that would suggest some sort of obligation, and that feels very confining, thank you.

The welcoming of premarital sex while at the same time diluting marriage happened practically overnight, and it's now so in the mother's milk of the culture that we forget what the purpose of sexual restrictions and marriage was in the first place.

In the process, sex became everything. As I showed earlier, it's become the first way many people now identify themselves (gay, bisexual, lesbian, trans, cisgender, and so on). And that's the way they want all of the rest of us to refer to ourselves too. We have to use *their* terminology and pronouns (grammatically correct or not). It's like a linguistic *coup d'etat* has happened. There shall be no more references to pronouns and other sexual identity characterizations of the past.

In the end, we've come to regard sex like the way we regard housing: many people are concluding it's better to rent than to buy. You won't have to pay for maintenance, insurance or property taxes. And there won't be any of those nasty tax consequences when you sell. And if someone gets hurt on your property? It's the owner's problem.

What if someone *is* foolish enough to get married? Well, not all hope is lost. We made sure that divorce is available to anybody who wants it (so-called "no-fault" divorce laws guarantee exactly that). Forty to fifty percent of marriages end in divorce,[2] so you will certainly not be alone. And there hasn't been any stigma about divorce for many decades. Divorce is now not much different than a dissolution of a partnership or corporation. Sure, there might be alimony and child support, but people treat it more like a "breakup fee," like when you used to have to pay to get out of your long-term cable-TV contract. It's annoying, sure, but you do what you gotta do to get better channels with another provider.

Worse yet: where sexuality was once merely a *part* of the institution of marriage, sexuality itself has taken the primal lead. It has become *the* cause, in and of itself. The means has become the end. It is no longer something that belongs to a couple, or something that belongs to the community at large. Sex now belongs only to the individual. It's easy to access, cost free, and emotion free. And it's everywhere.

So once again, problem solved.

And you're welcome, boys.

Sex . . . and Pearls to Swine

It used to be that when a woman had nothing left, she would prostitute herself as a last resort. That's still commonplace among many women in third-world countries, like Venezuela. There, in their desperate quest to leave their miserable Maduro socialist "utopia," women resorted to selling their hair, breast milk, and their bodies—the latter for which they got only seven dollars "per service." (Strangely, they got much more for their hair, ten to thirty dollars per woman). Teachers, police officers, and newspaper carriers were among those turning to the sex trade in Colombia, just so they could provide for their families back home in Venezuela.[3]

Imagine the suffering of such a woman, giving up her body to the highest bidder multiple times a day, so she can get by. She hears about a wonderful country up north, a land of great wealth—where its version of "poor" would be profusely wealthy in her horrid home country.

She aspires one day to escape from her squalid life. She dreams of America's vast opportunities and protections, where she might pursue her wish to be a fashion designer and become rich, and where the horrid things she has had to do multiple times a day are virtually nonexistent.

But for now, her body is all she has to give. She saves whatever money she can in a small hole in the wall, hoping no one will discover it. One day, she hopes to cross into America, where she will have to pay a "coyote" (someone who will help her find passage through Mexico and eventually sneak her across the border). In all likelihood, the coyote will expect sex from her, or just rape her.[4] As many as 70 percent of women crossing the border without husbands or families become victims of some form of sexual violence. And given their illegal journey and fear of reprisals, the rapists know their targets won't talk to any authorities.[5] Many women and even young girls attempting to cross the border will take birth control pills—some at the insistence of their mothers and other loved ones, because they know they will almost certainly suffer at least one rape along their journey.[6]

Even so, the reward is somehow worth the risk. And one glorious day, she makes it. She crosses the border into Texas and continues on to Indiana, where she becomes a nanny to a young family. After some time, she picks up the language and learns more and more about the culture. She learns about the women of America.

What does she find? That the women give up their bodies like it's nothing, like it's candy. They have no sense of the sacred nature of their sexuality, their "virtue."

As the expression goes: it's like throwing pearls to swine.

We went over how the hookup culture in colleges and beyond has made sex less significant, less "scarce," and therefore cheaper. In fact, it's free. It has become trivial, about the pleasure itself and little more. But that opens the door to everything sexual, doesn't it? People will push for and try to normalize polygamy and polyamory (already happening, see previous discussion), incest, bestiality, and even sex with minors. You'll see all those things happen within the next twenty years.

Many progressives will argue that it's "just sex." And if it's just sex and it doesn't mean anything and it's consensual, people will ask why would we think to criminalize or even frown upon such things? That would be like criminalizing someone for enjoying candy or for going on a roller coaster thrill ride. What's the harm in *everyone* enjoying sex?

Here's the conundrum: if it's just sex in one area, then why wouldn't it be just sex *all* the time, in *every* area? Isn't eating ice cream always just eating ice cream? Isn't enjoying a comedy just enjoying a comedy? It shouldn't make any difference that you're doing any of those things with a friend, with your sister, or with many friends. So why should it be any different when it comes to the pleasures of sex?

Ah, but Mr. Lurie, sex is different than ice cream, roller coasters, and comedies.

How so? I thought we all agreed that sex is "just sex." Now you're telling me that sex *isn't* just sex under certain circumstances? I don't get it. Is a classic 1977 Bentley T2 series car expensive and classic on Mondays and Wednesdays but not every other day of the week? Will you find that same Bentley at a monster truck rally on the other days of the week? An ice cream cone is generally cheap; does it sometimes become as expensive as gold?

It doesn't stop there: to be consistent with the "it's just sex" program in feminism, rape should be no greater a crime than, say, being robbed or being punched in the face. That is, if it's just sex.

Yet we know that would never fly. We know that rape is a *far* worse violation than robbery or a punch in the face. Every feminist today would argue that rape is one of the greatest scourges of our time.

So even the ardent feminist can't proclaim that sex is just sex, at least if she's being intellectually honest. At the same time, she'll loudly encourage a woman's promiscuity and runaway sexuality as some form of self-expression (however they connect the dots on that one is a mystery).

So is sex something deeply and meaningfully valuable, or is it something so cheap you give it away to virtually any male passerby who looks passably cute? We're still awaiting your response, Bueller.

The classic feminist wants the world to see her sexuality with great value, yet she herself treats her own body as if it's Halloween candy to give out to whoever knocks on her door. She would never treat anything else she owns like that. She might own pearls and secure them in her home safe, but she doesn't play marbles in the street with them the next day.

Nothing we own—nothing—is both expensive and cheap at the same time.

Yet many women will have no problem going about their sexual lives with this internal schizophrenia. On the one hand, they will have casual sex with multiple men because they should be free to do so and that's proving something for feminism. Or maybe they just want orgasms.

Or maybe it's for some other reason. Frankly, it doesn't really matter. Sex with multiple partners renders sex cheap, degrading and meaningless.

But once they get married, well that's another thing entirely. You see, *then* sex will be special, a meaningful and intimate bond that unites them as one, perhaps even in a spiritual sense, exclusive of all others. Should a woman's husband go outside of that bond for sex, it would be a devastating breach of trust. And that would be very, very bad.

A little confusing, no? In fact, it's downright dizzying. It's like saying that to become an air force pilot you can train by flying in a kiddie plane ride at the carnival. To become an expert marksman, you need only to play a lot of violent video games. To become an erudite rabbi, you can train by watching the movie *Yentl*.

None of these things make sense because we know that to train for any of these things means doing *that thing as early on as possible and for as many years as possible*. If you do so, then one glorious day you might become a fighter pilot, a certified sniper, a rabbi, and so on.

Sexual intimacy and the deep commitment that comes with it requires a tremendous amount of advance training too. Ideally, your parents and church will teach you at an early age of the precious nature of your body, that one day you'll "meet someone very special," and that you and this other person will be united with God through your marriage—and the sexual relations in that marriage. While you'll learn the basic biology of your impulses, you also learn about how to restrain those impulses—much like a martial arts candidate for black belt learns to restrain his desires to sleep in and to forego the "boring" daily routines. Virtually every great skill or accomplishment requires this kind of exceptional patience and restraint to achieve it.

When it comes to relationships, though—especially marriage—somehow the notion of any "training" all goes out the window. According to many, you should pursue one quick relationship after another, testing how things fit with this or that potential partner, before you commit to one person. He doesn't do it for you? He's outta there. Next!

Until that day when you meet, and it "just feels right." All feels as if was meant to be. You just "get" each other. You two will be bonded, intimate, and forever connected in a sort of ethereal, magical way. It'll be quite beautiful, really.

Except when you realize that you have no idea of what it takes to be bonded, intimate, and forever connected. No one trained you for what that might look like. You never even used that muscle, not even once. In fact, the only "muscle" you trained was exactly its opposite: the one that went on total impulse, *without* restraint.

But suddenly, now that you're married, you expect yourself to know exactly how to be intimate, totally loyal, and bonded. That's like showing up at the Olympic stadium and expecting to participate in the marathon because you've been taking walks with your dog on the beach. That's good enough, right?

Sex just isn't what people think it is. It's both an acquired skill and a reward, best left to the experts who've earned it. It is for those who've come to understand the dangers that sex brings in the form of disease, out-of-wedlock unwanted pregnancy, and intense jealousy. In other words, it is highly potent, highly unstable, and highly destructive, but it sure *looks* cool. We should treat it like uranium, radium, or plutonium—to be handled only by those best equipped to handle it. It should be awesome and daunting, all at once. And that means it should be only for those who understand, after many years of restraint and patience, about the deep love of God and His gift of sex.

Let's make it simpler: Sex is like fire: easy to get, incredibly useful, but also easy to get out of control, to run wild in destruction—even with just a few errant embers. With fire, we know to contain it in the fireplace, in the lantern, in the cooking stove, in the campfire. We take all the right precautions.

Why do we do so? Because we have a profound respect for what fire can do.

* * *

How might we explain the "schizophrenia?" I think the answer lies in the question: we don't *want* the schizophrenia. I think most people actually *want* sex to be meaningful; they just don't conduct their lives that way. They may sleep around, but somewhere within them they hope to find a connection with someone who will magically fit with them, like the prince trying out the glass slipper on all the ladies in town until he connects with his Cinderella.

And they know that when they are engaging in "great sex" it's more than just an orgasm. It's a connection, a oneness. They know they are receiving a gift of some kind but that they're misusing it. They also don't really want to live for the perpetual orgasm, consuming one orgasm to the next as if sex is popcorn. I know few people—men or women—who lead such lives and can truly say they're happy with that existence. Women especially seek out that "forever" monogamous connection—even if they might not achieve it in the end. It's still the aspiration. But while they have that aspiration, they rarely seem to ask themselves *why* they have it.

I think it's because we are each infinitely valuable in the eyes of God, and we know everyone with whom we engage in the sexual act is similarly infinitely valuable. And if sex is indeed an act of creation, then sex is wildly potent and, above all, meaningful.

In short, sex is never "just sex." When it is right, it is beyond extraordinary, bringing both men and women to an ecstasy like nothing else. And as we discussed earlier, there really is nothing "better" than sex. Whatever humankind has ever come up with, nothing seems to depose sex from the top rung of things to do on the planet. Nothing else is a close second.

And it doesn't stop there. Through the study of medicine, biology, psychology, and sociology, we've come to learn that there may be nothing more meaningful, nothing safer, nothing healthier, and nothing more satisfying than the act of loving, sexual bonding between a man and woman who are married and truly committed to each other. It seems we all intuitively want that too.

The irony is, we all know it; we always have. As Glinda the Good Witch of the North tells Dorothy in the *Wizard of Oz*, we've had the answer within us all along.

Sex is scary. Sex is hard work. Sex is unique, wildly pleasurable and spiritually ecstatic. But everything that we've learned about it—from the devastating effects of faceless and mindless sex (STDs, unwanted pregnancies, physical and emotional abuse, and turmoil, jealousy, and loneliness), while at the same time the glorious consequences of sex within a loving marriage (improvement to both spouses' immunities, the creation of wanted children who are loved and raised by a father and mother, and spiritual and personal growth)—points us all clearly to what sex is truly for.

In the classic *Spiderman* comic book stories and subsequent movies, Peter Parker learns time and time again that "with great power comes great responsibility." You can see the parents in the audience nod along to these words of wisdom. On the car ride home, they may even remind their kids of this wisdom, along with a couple of things Yoda said in *Star Wars*.

With its awesome attributes (love, intense pleasure, and creation) comes great responsibility. It is for grownups, who are ready to be *responsible* for it and ready to explain it to the next generation. It is for creation itself. It is God's work.

For everyone else, they might as well wear a fireman's hat and buy fire equipment and gear and proclaim they're experts in putting out fires.

And so it is with sex: you may have the equipment for sex. That doesn't mean you know what you're doing.

Chapter 13

Wait, They're
Teaching *What* Now?

Our society has been steadily and repeatedly eroding the notion of sex as a holy enterprise since the 1950s. For better or for worse, many developments occurred:

- the normalizing of premarital sex
- the acceptance of homosexuality as a normal sexual relationship
- the minimizing of the need for marriage, even when planning to have children
- the incredible growth in the percentage of women in the workplace, and the concomitant sense that women do not *need* men, financially or otherwise
- the Pill
- "no-fault" divorce
- the dramatic ease of access to abortion (in some states allowing abortion up to the time of birth)
- the extraordinary advance and mainstreaming (or at least greater acceptance) of pornography
- the recognition of same-sex marriage as a constitutional right;
- women pursuing men for sex

- the push to mainstream transgenderism (and the language changes that go with it)
- the push for everyone to think of themselves in sexual terms as a core part of their identity (you're on a spectrum; choose where you fit)
- the leggings (yoga pants) culture, which appeals to a woman's new liberated sense of sexuality, and encourages her to show as much of her body as possible
- the advent of Tinder and other hookup matching sites.

All of these events have helped chip away at the way we look at sex. In fact, they have completely altered our view: we view sex as something that belongs to the *individual*, something we engage in on an *individual* basis. I know this sounds counter-intuitive; after all, we think (or should think) of sex as something we undertake with *another* person. Somebody, say, other than ourselves.

But it's a reality. There are single guys who chase skirts through their middle-aged years, and there are women who get their orgasms on the go on Tinder or otherwise. Then there is polyamory (having sexual relationships with multiple partners at a time) and the rise of orgies, such as the "Burning Man" event in Nevada every year. (They have something called an "Orgy Dome" there, where people gather to get quick sex I mean share their love).

These are people acting as individuals. Yes, technically they're having sex with someone else, but they're getting sex *for themselves*. This alone may be the most powerful legacy of the past few decades.

Yet none of these would be sufficient to reach our new sexual mosaic had we not first drastically altered the sexual education of our youth.

Just at the moment kids start experiencing their massive hormonal changes; just as the boys start to have erections and girls' breasts begin to develop; just as they're both growing hair where there hadn't been any before; and just as boys and girls are first experiencing deep crushes on each other, *that's* the moment when the sex educators descend upon our children.

The timing itself is not necessarily bad. In previous decades, fifth and sixth graders and beyond learned about the clinical differences between the sexes: how the strongest male sperm gets to fertilize an egg, menstruation and erections, and the like. They might even have discussed the feelings that sex elicits and the dangers of unwanted pregnancy and sexually transmitted diseases.

But over the years, the discussion kept morphing from educating kids about the mechanics of sex and consequences that can flow from sex to a primer about how to get the most sensual benefit out of sex. Throughout the country, school districts are requiring the teaching of oral sex, anal sex, homosexuality, and transgender issues. Much of the teaching focuses on toys, fetishes, and the all-important notion that one should always just do "what feels right." Naturally, everything is fine as long as everyone knows the consequences and does their business with another consenting person (or several consenting persons).

Oh, and as far as "abstinence" goes? That's for the backward religious morons, but do what you like, if that's what suits you.[1] *We're* not going to suggest you curb your sexual enthusiasm. That would be repressive.

In California, parents are upset about the California Healthy Youth Act, the "groundbreaking" state law passed in 2015 requiring that schools teach "medically accurate" and "age appropriate" comprehensive sex education. Those phrases are *not* vague at all, and no one will interpret them too broadly, so don't worry. Your children are in good hands.

Among other things, the law delves into the health and development of LGBTQ students and addresses HIV prevention, relationship abuse, and sex trafficking. According to local reports, there is good news: counties are quickly complying with the new law to update their sex ed curriculum, despite "resistance" from backward people. Turns out many districts were still using books as ancient as 2003, when sex was apparently something different.[2]

On April 23, 2019, Minnesota House Democrats voted in favor of including pornography, as well as oral, homosexual and anal sex as part of the state's Comprehensive Sex Education (CSE). Planned Parenthood will provide the CSE curriculum for Minnesota public schools and had lobbied hard for the legislation.

At the center of the CSE curriculum is "It's Perfectly Normal," a book which Planned Parenthood has aggressively promoted. The book contains explicit drawings of the male and female anatomy and covers such topics as vaginal, oral and anal sex, homosexuality and abortion. Simply put, CSE is pornographic and promotes perversion—a word most people now seem to sidestep, and which is alien and unmentioned in the CSE. The CSE language instead seems unequivocal in its *promotion* of abortion, explicit and graphic sexual activities, white privilege ideology, gender identity and LGBT issues—to children from kindergarten to 12th grade.[3]

It's creepy. It not only promotes abortion but provides step by step instructions on how to engage in vaginal, oral and anal sex with never a hint of disapproval or caution. It includes detailed language and illustrations of homosexual acts, masturbation, pornography and abortion, all of which the book discusses in a lighthearted and positive tone. There are even for-color textbooks now, with entire chapters dedicated to exploratory self-pleasure and same-sex options.

According to CPL, the ultimate goal of CSE is "to change the sexual and gender norms of society." CSE is a "rights-based" approach to sex education and promotes "sexual rights" for children.

Sexual rights for children. Watch for that phrase in that future. You're going to hear it more often.

And the schools are implementing the CSE with a sort of indignantly reckless vigor. The curriculum literally *instructs* teachers to "make it a fun game."[4] So, 10- and 11-year-old boys and girls now participate in "condom relay races," where they practice putting condoms on a model with an erect adult male penis. If they get it right, they race back in line and high-five the next student, who then herself must accomplish this same task critical for all 10 and 11-year olds. If a child doesn't get it right, he or she must repeat the process until he does.[5] (You see? Schools *are* teaching discipline and achievement).

Don't believe this is happening? See for yourself on YouTube; you'll find ample videos of young children in classrooms participating in exactly that. Example: https://twitter.com/Sexetc/status/987770002328686593.

As author and commentator Tess Mullins put it: "Far from teaching children the mere biology of human reproduction, classroom sex-ed is now an Alfred Kinsey fantasyland. . . . It's the sort of X-rated stuff that used to land people in jail and had Kinsey himself hiding in his attic to conduct his "research.'"[6]

Some parents complain about such changes in sex education on the grounds that the new sex ed curriculum goes too far, is emotionally and sexually charged, and puts ideas into kids' heads at too early an age. As one parent put it, are we teaching to inform or to perform?[7] At the least, kids suffer through sex talk and graphic images which tend to stir up ugly and disturbing thoughts.[8]

Ah, but such is language one expects from those who fear progress, *n'est-ce pas?* After all, only a handful really complains, and they can have their children opt-out anytime. See? No cause to complain. Also, the suggestion that fourth and fifth graders are learning graphic accounts of "safe anal sex" is ludicrous, groundless, and has been debunked resoundly. Just look at Snopes.com![9]

But this is too dismissive: First, to say "it's just a handful of protesting parents" is like saying a dictatorship is fine because only a handful of protesters ever make a fuss. It doesn't consider parents who object but who don't want to cause waves with the school district, lest the school lash back at them. Then of course there are the parents who simply don't have the time nor inclination to protest.

Shall districts be able to do with such children whatever they want because so many of these parents do not or cannot actively engage with the school? Isn't that like receiving a form mailer in your mailbox stating that unless you check off a box and mail it back to them within two days, they will assume you approve of whatever they want?

And what about recent immigrant parents from other countries who barely know how to speak English, let alone to confront an educational infrastructure they know virtually nothing about?

Is this a standard we should tolerate? That a school can teach your child however it sees fit, unless you actively complain about it?

Second, the fact that they're *not* teaching anal sex and similar content to fourth and fifth graders is hardly a meaningful pushback. In fact, it's a grand sidestep: It doesn't deal with the fact they *are* teaching exactly that *to sixth graders and older*. So their argument is a bit like the Bob Marley song, where the guy in the song admits that, yes, he *did* shoot the sheriff, but he did *not* shoot the deputy. That makes it all better.

In any event, it is sixth through eighth graders who are the ones to worry about. Fourth and fifth graders think the idea of sex—*any* kind of sex, mind you—is disgusting. (Want proof of that? Ask your fourth or fifth grader.) They have little of the same new raging curiosity that their older counterparts do. Teaching sex is irrelevant to them: you might as well teach Eskimos what to do in case they're attacked by lions.

Ultimately, yes, there are parents who complain about what schools teach, but they're fighting an uphill battle. Parents also want to trust the educational system, and words like *age-appropriate* seem comforting and responsible for the time being. Most of the complaining takes place after the damage is done.

And there is only so much resistance you can put up. There is a cloud of inevitability, and eventually fewer and fewer parents show up. They don't like it, but they figure they'll just push back on the school dogma when the kids come home that day.

But the day is long for everyone. You just don't have the energy. It's not like you're one of the French peasants in *Les Miserables,* who have no choice but to spend all his day in revolution mode. Life is tolerable from one day to the next, and you don't see any perceptible changes in *your* child. So bottom line: Protesting is meaningful and such, but seriously you can't do it every day.

Soon you convince yourself that they can only do so much damage to your child in the sexual propaganda game. And your kid has a good head on his shoulders, so he'll figure out what's what on his own. Right?

Not quite. Friends and teachers become more and more influential in his life. Your house becomes more of a base for him to sleep, eat, and get his laundry done. What with all the crazy scheduling and stuff, you rarely have a meal together.

Then one day, your daughter starts talking about a friend of hers who's proclaimed she's now a boy. She says that you and the rest of the family need to reorient your language, especially in your use of pronouns and how you should introduce yourself. You're not allowed to "deadname" anyone. Every sexual act is fine and equal to all other acts. All the previous understandings of roles are antiquated. And surely you're not one of those who thinks that marriage should only be between a man and a woman, are you, Dad?

Suddenly you realize that your child's school might as well be some sort of Orwellian cult, and it was all happening when you were busy at work, making a living to provide for these very same kids who now look at you as if you're part of some pervasive societal problem that needs fixing.

It's a little sad when you think about it.

You think about letting them know about the sanctity of sex, and that it'd be best if people generally delay it until marriage. You also think about teaching them about the meaning of a woman's virtue and a man's responsibility to a woman. You think of telling them of the emotional, physical, and health risks that go along with casual sex, and that God has a plan for each of us in His own way.

Still, you know that the train for that discussion left the station long ago. It'll all sound so old-fashioned to your kids, who will laugh at your "Victorian" values (assuming they understand that word from the European history class they never took). You don't want to alienate your kids further, so you don't push it.

And then you wonder what you could have done to stop the breaking of the sexual dam upon your kids. After all, your kids have bathed in a hookup world at school, in their entertainment, and in their social media. It was relentless.

It dawns on you that maybe those parents who home schooled their children were on to something there. You make a mental note to remember that when you have kids in your next life.

In the meantime, however, you ain't changing nothin'. The world has taken sex and commoditized it to a sort of universality in their lives, where everything everywhere is sexual. It's not just the billboards on the street; it's also the content of music, art, movies and television, and social media. You can't stop your kids from all that. Hell, you yourself can't escape it.

And now they're pushing it in the schools. It's a *transformation* in the way we view sex and what sex *is*. They've gotten the children all to think of themselves first and foremost *as sexual beings*. Then they've gotten them to think of sex as mostly for pleasure—just avoid those unwanted pregnancies and those nasty STDs. Don't worry: they'll show you how.

But advancing the notion that sex might be for the intimacy of married people, and might be a wondrous and maybe even holy gift from some higher power? Or advancing the teaching that sex has extraordinary potency? That's anathema to us all. Please, my friend: we're well into the 21st century. Catch up already.

What is the school system doing here? Whether they realize it or not, they're pushing the *trivialization of sex*. By de-intensifying and mainstreaming the concepts of oral sex, anal sex, homosexuality, celebrating the do-whatever-makes-you-feel-good-and-don't-repress-yourself and "penile-to-vaginal" sex (seriously, they call it that), the schools treat sex as just one of the many pleasures of life at any time in one's life, like bowling, watching the game, a great meal, or enjoying a pleasant sunset.

Don't buy it? Take a look at any of the literature in today's sex education. Rarely is there discussion of the unique intensity of sex. Rarely is there even a discussion of the *purpose* of sex. The only complications are pregnancy and STDs, both of which are easily surmountable. The tone is light and encouraging. It's as if they want to get you to some idyllic island, the kind where there is only fun. Leave all your worries behind.

So once again, they've paved the way for a world of rampant, meaningless sex. Or better yet—a world where sex itself is meaningless.

The literature out there presents little about limiting your sexual activity, restraining your prurient impulses, or considering that God might be a factor in sex. And don't expect *that* anytime soon.

That would take away all the fun. Like when the good doctor tells you that you just can't do all those drugs anymore.

And then they'll be surprised that so many of these young people will grow up looking to satisfy their sexual lusts primarily, if not exclusively, with a robot.

Chapter 14

Sex Doesn't Belong to You

When did you last hear a young woman refer to another as a slut, or claims that she sleeps around? How about the phrase "one-night stand"? For better or for worse, fewer and fewer people seem to speak in those terms. Even the women who use Tinder and similar hookup matching sites to get their sexual satisfaction don't hide what they do. They don't view themselves as sluts—at least not in the classic derogatory sense of the word.[*] They don't seem to worry much about a reputation. They're just going out and taking charge of their sexual needs, and what's wrong with that?

Interestingly, the same applies for men: no man is really a "player" anymore because he doesn't have to *act the part* of a player. He doesn't have to promise romance or commitment to anyone. So he's not really "playing" anyone, is he? He's just having a lot of sex with a lot of different woman, each of whom in turn don't mind that fact one bit. They're doing the same with him, aren't they? He's not anymore of a player than they are.

---

[*] Some of the more affluent in the younger generation of women now refer to each other as sluts as a *cool* thing (there's even a restaurant chain called "Eggslut"). However, they use that word, along with *bitch* and *dawg*, more as kitchy ghetto language to differentiate themselves from the *real* sluts. They themselves engage in all sorts of loose sexual conduct, but *they* still remain "classy." See Carmen Chia, "Study Examines Why Girls Call Each Other Sluts—It's not about Sex," https://globalnews.ca/news/1373537/study-examines-why-girls-call-each-other-sluts-its-not-about-sex/, June 4, 2014.

I don't know. Maybe it was a good thing that we once worried about such things. Maybe there was some collective sense that you were participating in the building of civilization, that you had a positive role in it. You had a role as a man, as a woman, and as a family. Sex was always there but in the background. You were refraining from sex because you knew it was highly potent, to be used sparingly and for special purposes, like nuclear weapons. (OK, maybe I'm exaggerating a bit there, but not by much.)

The value of sex, in a sense, was collective. It belonged to civilization; it wasn't just your own thing. It was like the way most of us regard highways today: the road doesn't belong only to you. If you want to get from your house to the baseball game, that's fine, but there are rules of the road, and you have an obligation to others to signal, to stop, to be cautious during lane changes, to not drive under the influence of any substances, and to drive at a safe speed. You're even expected to be patient and courteous. The road belongs to us all, and we're all in this together. So do your part so we can all get from our Point A's to our Point B's.

It used to be the same about sex. But today, we proudly proclaim that whatever people do behind closed doors is their business. Everyone needs to be true to themselves. No one should lead a life of repression. And so on.

We all talk about sex as though it's amazingly intimate and personal, and the sole domain of the two (or even multiple) consenting people. But is it? Sex is all very private behind those closed doors, for sure, but the consequences of what happens behind those doors can be very *un*-private, very fast.

Take the example of little Susie. She gets knocked up. Grandma now has to get a job to help out the new toddler on the way. The plans for Susie to go to college must be delayed, but who are we kidding? That ain't happening, ever. It turns out those closed doors opened real quick, and it turns out no one needed a detective to figure out what had happened behind those closed doors.

And that's just example number one. Here's another: Bobby gets a sexually transmitted disease and gives it to his sexual partner. She pays it forward during her own next "closed door" session with someone else, and the gift keeps giving behind the many closed doors after that. What was "none of your business" has suddenly become the business of a whole lot of people.

Then there was HIV and AIDS, all of which people contracted during numerous closed door sessions. But the doors to the hospitals soon had to open wide when the men and women who contracted the disease sought treatment, and for the unfortunate many others who received their blood transfusions and contracted the disease that way. You know what else had to open? Many people's wallets.

A woman and her friend from high school are having fun behind closed doors. She secretly wants to get pregnant and raise a kid on her own. She believes the mantra that fathers aren't really necessary. She doesn't expect him to provide for her or for the baby anyway. As planned, she gets pregnant and has the baby. It's a boy!

But without a father in the boy's life, he soon lacks purpose, gets into trouble at school, drops out, and pursues drugs and crime. He becomes a burden on society. Oh, and Mama had to cut back her hours at work, what with all the troubles she never saw coming. Funny when she looks back on it now, she had never really seen herself with a baby older than two or so. It's a shame she doesn't see her old friends anymore, either.

And then there's the anger and jealousy that sometimes pays a visit to us after sex, like in the movie *Fatal Attraction*. In that movie, a married man meets a woman during a business trip. She asks him if he knows how to be "discreet." Soon they're going at it, hot-and-heavy in an elevator, in an ecstasy-driven session. It was all "closed door." The man had just wanted fun (and thought that's what she had wanted too). But it turns out the woman felt she was going to have one of those "forever" relationships. When he leaves her to go back to his wife, the jilted woman conveys to him she is . . . dissatisfied. As she indignantly threatens him later, "I'm not going to be *ignored*!"

All sorts of horrible things befall the man and his family, including the woman pouring acid over the man's car, kidnapping his daughter, and boiling the family rabbit. Did those *consequences* happen behind closed doors? No, they did not.

Oh, here's another closed-door-but-not-really scenario: A young woman and man have a thing. They find out she's pregnant, but they're in college, see, and they've got big plans—such big plans—for the future. A baby won't be convenient. So off to the abortion clinic they go. And rest assured: the doors there will be very open.

And then there's your run-of-the-mill adultery. Cheating Man and Cheating Woman fool around behind closed doors. (Oh look—there's that phrase again.) Man and Woman get sloppy, and Soon-to-be-man's-ex-wife finds out and tells everyone, including the husband of cheating wife. Families on both sides hear about it, and the affair rips those families apart. The two formerly married couples find themselves in divorce court for years, fighting about custody and alimony.

So much for closed doors.

The Sex Highway

So it turns out sex was guaranteed to be private only for about as long as the sexual act itself. That's about the only reasonable amount of private time you should expect. After that, who knows?

The fact that it becomes so public so quickly—especially when it's outside the bounds of marriage—surely says something about the "highway" aspect of sex. On the Sex Highway, expectations exist that you'll follow some rules: That you'll marry. That you'll wait until after you're married to have children. That you'll be one of two married parents who will raise your children, hopefully a mother and a father. That you'll stay faithful to one another. And we hope that that mother and father will pass along their values of marriage, family, respect for community, manners, and restrained sexuality to the next generation. You know, for continuity of the civilization and such.

We also expect people not to make false promises or play with others' emotions. And we expect people to guard against STDs, and if they've winded up with an STD, to do whatever they can to not spread it further. We do that for the safety of civilization.

It turns out we *do* have rules of the road when it comes to sex, and very public ones at that. Sex *doesn't* really belong to you, no more than "driving" belongs to you. You may think driving "belongs" to you because you own a car, but everything you do with that car involves roads where there are other people—people for whom you are responsible and who are responsible for you. If we're all going to make this system work, we've all got to observe the rules. And we correctly get upset when we see someone violating those rules.

You *think* driving belongs to you. You may even see yourself with your window open, singing along loudly to your favorite song on the amazing sound system you bought with it, with some beautiful babe standing up through your sunroof with a tequila in her hand.

Still, reality is much different: It's about reading traffic and parking signs, waiting at red lights, knowing that pedestrians have the right of way, turning on your blinkers to indicate your directional intentions, knowing the speed limit and when you can pass someone and knowing you should never drive while under the influence of alcohol or drugs. And so on. And every time you drive, you always remember that you have, on average, a two-ton-plus vehicle that can easily kill someone if you don't pay attention.

It's the same with sex. During the act of sex, we *think* we're all alone, discovering each other's sensual bodies, and the rest of the world somehow disappears for the moment. It even feels as if no one else in the world is doing this, like it's your own little secret while everyone else goes about their mundane lives. We *think* we're in our own little space that belongs to just the two of us—the one behind closed doors.

But really, we aren't. Sex actually belongs to *everyone*. In some ways, sex is *everyone's* business, just like the highway. Sex connects each of us. After all, it's the one thing we all have in common, one way or the other.

And like with our driving, we are responsible to everyone else when it comes to our sexual acts. That is, if we want to get anywhere as a civilization.

You've said a lot of wild things in this book, Mr. Lurie, but this one I just ain't buyin'.

Really? An example then: a man has repeated sexual partners, all of whom he failed to tell that he had genital herpes. Now most of those partners have it and are likely to spread it exponentially. One day it may reach you. So it was also with HIV and AIDS in the eighties and early nineties (and still today): many careless people who thought only of their own pleasures ended up affecting the lives of millions of others.

So you better start buying it, my friend. Your sexual behavior and choices *do* affect everyone else.

Sex *is* a highway, we just don't see the cars as easily. And just like on the highway, we have as many people enforcing the rules, whether we see them or not and whether we realize that we, too, are enforcers. We see it among our neighbors and friends who (like it or not) talk about that man who decided he was gay after all and left his wife, about the couple who just divorced, about the couple whose husband cheated on his wife, or that lady who decided to go to the sperm bank and get pregnant on her own. We talk about that man or woman who seems to be with someone new every week.

The neighborhood—or whatever your community might be—is noticing. They're commenting among themselves. They're judging.

Or more accurately: they're *enforcing*, and it's almost exclusively about your sexual lives. It's not like your community will start gossiping about how you smoke; about how you eat too much ice cream late at night; how you have a slight gambling issue, or can't hold down a job. None of those issues seem to awaken the scorn of your community, or at least its attention, no matter how irresponsible you may be.

Sex is a different story. You don't have to like it, but that's the way it is and has always been—no matter how much you'd like to undo that. Maybe the judging won't be out in the open, but it *is* always happening, no matter how hard you try to make your sexual issue (transgenderism, gay marriage, polyamory, swinging, etc.) normal.

And just where are they doing all this gossip and judgment, you ask? That's right, you guessed it. You can't see it. It's all happening behind closed doors.

Irony.

But that shouldn't be the way, you might say. Who are they to judge? In the end, we want our sexuality private, but it's never *really* private. And here I'm not even talking about the consequences of sex as I mentioned above, although they are certainly a part. I'm saying it plays out even in our ordinary daily interactions.

When a woman is at a dinner party and introduces her boyfriend, isn't she in effect really saying: "Look, everybody, this is the man I have sex with on a regular basis"? Sure, she's not actually describing the sex, but she *is* letting the world know just from the word *boyfriend* that sex is going on between her and this person.

That's OK, though, because the people hearing such words will not look askance at such a couple, despite their knowing there's sex going on between them. Why? Because it fits within the norm of community expectations, and because we see that these people are doing their part to participate in the continuation and betterment of civilization. It's why parents are happy to see their kids marry—to a good person.

But those who wish to violate the community's sexual expectations on the sex highway are different. They are not going to introduce a woman at a party as their mistress; or to introduce these, say, four people as part of a polyamorous or "swing" arrangement they've got going on; or that this guy goes back and forth between men and women. They'll always keep such things to themselves, and even pretend they're regular couples, just like you and me. And if you did bring it up somehow, they'll indignantly jab their finger at you and say it's no one's business but their own.

In reality, they want to have it both ways (if you will). They want you and everyone else to honor their different sexuality or sexual identity, while at the same time demanding that no one talk about it and no one judge it—even behind closed doors. In other words, only *they* get be the ones who do anything behind closed doors.

This is no different than the guy on the highway who speeds, drives drunk, or ignores traffic signs all around him. He's going to get to point B *his* way, thank you, without a concern in the world for his obligations to others on the highway.

They never think to ask themselves a simple question: what if everyone did the same thing I'm doing right now?

What if everyone who lusted after someone other than his / her spouse pursued that lust? What if everyone pursued multiple partners regardless of marriage? What if everyone went bisexual? What if no one practiced safe sex? What if every woman who wanted a baby did so only by going to a sperm bank?

What if no one committed to anyone else?

We know, deep within us, when what we are doing is wrong. We're even thankful that there are laws against what we are doing, even if we would prefer that those laws not apply to us. The thief who robs the bank understands that we need laws against robbery. He just hopes no one catches *him*.

We all appreciate and insist on the rules of the road for cars. No one complains that we have such rules, and we expect everyone else to abide by rights of way, age restrictions, speed limits, and traffic lights.

But somehow when it comes to the sex highway, we want to wish away the rules. We resent them. We even pound on the table that there should be no rules in such private matters.

Yet the sex highway and the automobile highway are pretty much the same. The difference is only that we don't easily or immediately see the impact of our ignoring the rules of the sex highway. On the regular highway, running a red light will often lead to *immediate* harmful consequences, even death. That's why everyone readily supports the rules of the road.

On the sex highway, violations also have impacts. But they're not like some multi-car pile-up that everyone can see as they drive by, right after the accident, where we can figure out the cause and effect pretty easily. The impacts of sex free violations are *not* immediate at all. In fact, they often take decades for us to see them. By then we might never realize what the original cause was.

It's best to see sex violations as causing extremely slow-moving crashes in our civilization, ones which you can't see unfolding on a day by day level. In fact, you're barely even able to perceive them at all. Timewise they're probably somewhere between watching a banana rotting and the erosion of that mural on the old city hall building. But it *is* happening all around us: the sexual equivalent of people driving on the left side of the road, running the red lights and driving under the influence— all on a massive scale, and all happening very slowly.

But like I said: few will see it. Why so? Because those kinds of violations all happen behind closed doors.

For many, that will be the beauty of sex robots. They won't have to worry about the rules of the sex highway. Such rules only matter when there's more than one person on the highway. With a robot, everyone's on his own little highway. It's a highway where no one else can get hurt, where there are no consequences to driving any way you like. In a sense, you're completely off the proverbial grid, where no one else can hurt you, and you can't hurt anyone else. And best of all, you never have to worry about any closed doors opening.

So tear it up on the open road, big fella. Push the virtual peddle to the metal, open up the top on that virtual convertible and let the virtual wind flow through your virtual thick and wavy hair.

Because no one's stopping you on *this* highway.

Chapter 15

Fertile Lives Don't Matter

Ricky and Janie loved each other. They had met at a minia-ture golf course, through mutual friends. They soon dated, and found they connected on many different levels. They both loved Radiohead, were both from the Midwest, and they had both played lacrosse for their colleges. Both of them were raised Catholic and were both now the "recovering" kind.

They didn't get married, but they didn't really want to see anyone else. Soon they moved into an apartment together. They each got promotions in their careers and bought a house, a big one with more room than they needed.

One day, Janie hinted how fun it might be to fill the house with the sound of little children.

That's when the discussion began. Everything's been going so well between us. Children are expensive. Children change things. Our lives would never be the same. We won't be able to travel or even go out to restaurants. The boss might see you as a burden once you're pregnant. We wouldn't be able to retire when we want. What would happen if our child is born with some horrible disease or we just don't *like* him?

"Still," Janie said at some point in the conversation. "We'd make such beautiful children together. Wouldn't it be wonderful?"

Ricky's look of disappointment was palpable: "Janie, I didn't think you could be that selfish."

Janie was a bit confused. This was turning out to be one of their first real arguments. Selfish? Did he really say that?

Ricky did not let go: Yes, he said. It was clearly selfish. There were only so many resources on the planet, and it would be irresponsible—from a humanitarian point of view—to have children at all. Each new arrival on the planet would be not only another mouth to feed but another carbon generator, contributing to the ultimate collapse of civilization by way of greenhouse gases and climate change. "I'm not willing to be a party to that," he concluded.

She saw there was no budging him. Ricky meant it. He felt strongly as a "citizen of the world" on this very important issue. And he couldn't believe that she didn't see it the same way. He even said he thought of her differently now.

Janie apologized. "I guess I never quite thought of it like that. I just kind of thought we'd have at least one kid somewhere along the way. But I see now that maybe that's just because of societal dictates knocking on my door, demanding me to comply."

Her pull to have children was there, but Ricky had made good points here. And she didn't want to lose him. Maybe she *had* been selfish.

And there's that word. Watch for it: *selfish*.

It's been a trend for decades now. Population growth is dramatically slowing, even reversing in some countries, particularly in the Western world. And it stems from a new sense, one that first started in the 1970s: the sense that children are not an asset to the world and our future but instead an overall liability. To have them is therefore a selfish act because it's to satisfy the *personal* needs of the couple at the expense of the *global* needs of the planet.

"Animals are disappearing," as a prospective, twenty-nine-year-old mother, Perry Miller, put it: "The oceans are full of plastic. The human population is so numerous, the planet may not be able to support it indefinitely." It therefore didn't seem right to her to bring home a brand-new baby into the world.[1]

And then there's global warming. Many people believe the earth is teetering on the edge of doom because of man's excessive emissions of carbon (via cars, smokestacks, cow emissions, and so forth). They estimate the planet will more or less end by 2030.[2] At the very least, it really won't be as much fun.

So, the way they see it, having a child means that they would be *speeding up* the world's collapse. They think of having children as if you're dealing with a major termite problem in your house. And you want to add *more* termites to it?

Such people won't allow themselves to become hypocrites. No sir—they are taking *action*. Many women have even called for a "birth strike" to avoid an "eco-armageddon."[3] It's an actual movement that originated in Britain—aptly named "Birth-Strike"—and it's gained momentum. As one member expressed it, they've never been so afraid: "We're too scared to have kids, because of climate change."[4]

So having children is like taking a lengthy shower during a drought, cutting in line on the highway, or not taking the time to separate your recyclables. Actually, it's worse than that: it's like throwing all your family's fast-food garbage out the window from your car. Such things reflect thoughtless, "me-first" actions that fail to consider the needs of the community. Having children is just like that. So don't do it.

It's not only that it's selfish vis-à-vis the planet. Even *wanting* children is inherently selfish: you're only looking to pass on your legacy or DNA. And that's just silly, right? It's even cruel to the child you're considering having. As one woman marine conservationist put it: "I don't want to give birth to a kid wondering if it's going to live in some kind of 'Mad Max' dystopia."[5]

In all the discussion about the selfishness of having kids, few ask themselves why anyone has kids at all, let alone why so many people yearn instinctively to have kids. The need to reproduce and give and sacrifice to one's offspring seems to be part of most people's biological makeup.

That's all changing now. Paul Ehrlich's *The Population Bomb* in 1968 sounded an alarm that our population growth needed to stop *immediately*, lest we all perish from lack of food. The world began inculcating the notion that having children—at least having more children than necessary to replace ourselves (i.e., two per couple)—was a millstone around the Earth's neck.

Future decades debunked the book's prediction as unsound. The prediction relied on static, Malthusian-type thinking that didn't take into account the basic creativity of humans to surmount obstacles.

And surmounting obstacles is exactly what happened. Thanks to innovations responding to demand and more countries becoming democracies and embracing open markets, we now have more food worldwide than ever.

Starvation throughout the planet continues to plummet. Whatever starvation remains stems largely from mismanagement and diversion of supplies by some countries' dictators to a privileged ruling class and their corrupt allies who have smartly curried favor with that class.[6]

Still the demonizing of having children as "selfish" echoes among us all, despite history showing that population growth will *not* make life worse for us. In fact, the *more* young people one has in an economy, the more vibrant, creative, and dynamic that economy becomes. That's just Economics 101.

But that's the "macro" need for children. It doesn't answer why any one person might *want* children.

Ask most parents why they had a child—even parents as they're holding their brand new infant in their cute Baby Bjorn carrier—and most of them won't be able to articulate a meaningful answer. Odd, isn't that? Shouldn't they know *why* they had a kid? It's as if they felt they should have children and went about it because they were on some decades-long automatic pilot, a mantra that said: *you must have kids; you must have kids.*

You can see the wife turning to her husband, bobbing her baby in the Baby Bjorn now: "Yeah, honey. Why *did* we have this child?"

They had kids because everyone else does. It's like why men wear ties. But ask men why ties are necessary in the first place, and they won't be able to tell you. And once they think about it even a little bit, they realize there's no real need to wear such things. Now most men wear jeans to work, with a collared shirt.

So it is with having children: couples are beginning to ask why they should have children. It's a legitimate question, which *should* generate answers. But what happens when a couple comes up with no answer that satisfies them?

They have fewer children, or stop having them at all.

The statistics bear it out: the average fertility rate in America in the early 1900s was approximately 3.4 children per woman. Today, it's approximately 1.9.[7] That number will continue to decline as people continue to view having children as a mere cost/benefit proposition. Indeed, since the 1960s, the attitude toward having children—along with marriage—has plummeted.[8] It's as if some ground has suddenly fallen out beneath us, and we're all falling down a bottomless hole.

After all, what will the parents get out of having kids? Children keep you up at night, especially the first two years. They go through horrific periods of hating you. Even when they don't, you still spend much of your time disciplining, listening to irrational fears about monsters in the closet, dealing with social awkwardness and fitting in with peers, arguing with other parents and teachers about whose kid wronged who, and driving them around to chess club, swimming, and dance recitals, to say nothing of driving them back and forth to school. Many have exasperating temper tantrums. They interrupt your conversations incessantly and distract you from work or that good trashy novel you never get to.

And then you worry about them. From the moment they're born to the moment you die, you worry. That's your new profession: worrier.

You give up your fantasies of travel, except maybe when it coincides with school vacations. And making time for exercise or for relaxing with a glass of wine at home in front of a fireplace and making sweet love to your wife when you and she please? Fantasize all you want about that, buddy; it ain't gonna happen.

And that's before you realize how crazy expensive kids are. I mean like, *really* crazy. The Department of Agriculture estimates that a middle-income, married couple with two children will spend $233,610 to raise a child born in 2015. And that number only covers costs for a child from birth through age 17. It *doesn't* include college and also assumes you'll matriculate your child in free public school education until then.[9]

So retirement? Kiss that good-bye, at least for a long time. Maybe you can enjoy your sunset years when you're ninety.

Yet many among the young adults of the new millennium still think having children is "selfish." They're wrong: deciding to have children is not only a self*less* act, but—other than throwing yourself on a hand grenade to save your buddies in battle or donating both your kidneys—it's probably the *most* self*less* thing a couple can do. They sacrifice huge amounts of time and money. They delay gratification for the sake of the new generation. They do it out of a sense of obligation to bring forth good people to the planet, and to continue the positive values they believe in.

Hopefully, the parents achieve some degree of satisfaction, even joy, in the process.

But the hard work of having a kid doesn't fully explain why adults are not having children, or at least so few of them. It may come as a surprise to some, but it was *always* hard work to have kids, and couples *still* had many more kids.

One could explain it by pointing to the rising costs of having a child, but children have always been expensive to raise, feed, and educate. And there has been massive cost *reduction* in electronics, foods, clothing, and toys, which allows for *more* leisure time and *less* cost per child for the basics of life. So that would suggest that parent would want *more* children, not fewer.

One could argue that parents don't "need" children as much anymore because—you know—they don't help with the family farm anymore, what with us no longer being an agrarian society. This argument views children of the past as having served like slaves for their parents' business operations. Regardless, that wouldn't explain the great number of families who had nothing to do with farming but had many children. Also, some of these families were extremely poor and had no business of their own to speak of, yet they still had many children.

But they'd help around with the chores of the house, one might say. Really? You have that many chores to do that you need five children to manage them all? You'd be better off not feeding, clothing, and educating these kids and instead hiring a good handyman. Trust me: it's a lot less expensive, and he'll do the job right. And he won't leave any of those Lego pieces for you to step on.

The next argument is that so many children used to die during late pregnancies, just after birth, or during the first few years of their lives. Therefore, parents would pop out as many kids as possible to hedge their bets, so that they could end up with two or three. As a result, many of them ended up with five or six. This is the "inventory planning" theory; one which views children like goods at the hardware store. Sometimes you just end up with too much stuff in the back room.

It's an absurd argument, of course, and still doesn't explain why parents would want children in the first place.

One could argue that the advent of the Pill and the growing acceptance and accessibility of abortion allowed parents to limit the number of children to only the amount they actually wanted. But this argument suggests that most people, at least in previous generations, were born as a result of some sort of sloppiness on their parents' part, or they were otherwise unwanted. Not only does this defy common experience; it belies all those couples who clearly "chose" to have fewer kids during the ancient days (before, say, 1960). There was always "birth control," long before the pill. They found ways (condoms and otherwise) that helped avoid pregnancy. The pill merely made sex more readily accessible than it had been, a response to the new demand for consequence-free sex, not the cause of it.

To my mind, none of these explanations make sense. On the contrary, technology and more leisure time—as well as the reduction in the chances of a mother dying while giving birth to a child to virtually zero percent— should have instead *increased* parents' desire to have more kids.

So why aren't people having as many children?

Part of the answer is the change in how parents viewed having children. Previously, most parents who were married saw each child as a blessing—as a *good* thing in their lives and a source of pride in the continuation of a family legacy, and perhaps as an obligation to God's commandment to be fruitful and multiply.

That view has changed. Perhaps it was because people lost the centrality of the church or synagogue in their lives. If there is no God, or if God is something you just "kind of" do or you consider yourself merely "spiritual," there's little or none of that sense of obligation to Him, including the obligation to be fruitful and multiply.

Whatever the reason, the end result is that society has stopped talking about why people *should* have kids. Fewer and fewer parents are passing along to their own children this sense of obligation—and joy—of having children. For that matter, they're barely passing along any sense that they should even marry someone one day. So because there is little teaching of values intergenerationally, in batonlike fashion, people have little idea *why* they're having children. As I said: it's like men's ties.

What *are* parents today generally telling their own children about the joy and value of having children? Nothing. Ask most parents today what they tell their own children about having children, and they'll give you a blank stare. It's as if you've asked them what they're teaching their children about the digestive system of bats.

Why *wouldn't* they give you that blank look? Remember: they themselves don't even know why they're having kids. So what great lesson is there for them to pass on to *their* kids about having kids?

If adults don't have a sense of the future, if they don't have a sense of purpose in something greater and beyond themselves, if they don't see themselves as part of a chain of civilization with obligations to generations of the past and to generations of the future, if they believe that children just add burden to the planet, and if they shrug their shoulders at whether civilization is even worth keeping, then why start a family?

Into this pointless void we have thrown our civilization. Now virtually every forecast shows that we find ourselves "on the cusp of a childless, elderly future."[10]

It's fascinating, really: We know we should teach our own children to be thoughtful to others; to value honesty, sacrifice, and hard work; to obey society's general rules; to pursue justice and compassion, to have manners and be responsible to our fellow man. We do so because we know that without imparting those values our kids will not value honesty, responsibility, kindness, and so on.

But imparting the notion that they themselves should have kids? The idea never crosses most people's minds.

Other than a few deeply religious parents, I haven't heard parents talk of such a sense of obligation to their own children. But even the deeply religious don't necessarily talk about it in the schools or churches, let alone directly to their kids. They seem to expect their children to just figure it out on their own.

It's all so strange. You won't get your children to have more kids if you don't show them the value in having more children. It's that simple.

But, as we've discussed, it's worse: if society and schools *are* teaching anything about having children, it's that having them is selfish and harmful to the planet, what with all the carbon they're spewing and precious resources they're depleting. They make it seem like we're in one of those survival movies, where twenty men are trapped in a submarine at the bottom of the sea, and there's only so much air for everyone. They talk about children as if they're a disease, like polio—and scientists are hard at work to eradicate them as we speak.

> *Q: What's worse than volcanoes, wildfires, massive earthquakes, hurricanes, tsunamis, and a nuclear holocaust, all combined?*
> *A: Children.*

People don't seem to ponder *why* people are not having children, let alone consider the societal ramifications of not having enough children. And lest you think this is just an American problem, fear not. The problem is even greater in most of the other modern countries. Japan, Russia, Germany, France, and virtually every other modern country is averaging less than 1.9 children per woman, and many well below 1.5 children per woman (Israel being an exception at almost 3 per woman).[11]

China (1.5 children per woman) has apparently gotten its wish to dramatically curb its population through its horrifically brutal One-Child Policy. It turns out China didn't have to worry: even after the end of the policy (first in 2015, allowing couples to have two children, and then in 2018 abandoning all restrictions), the Chinese didn't have much interest in having children after all. The One-Child policy turned out to be like enforcing a law prohibiting the eating of liver and onions. You got it, buddy. Will comply.

Ironically, China ended the One-Child Policy because . . . wait for it . . . the government came to realize they actually needed more children.[12] Having decimated their population, the great Chinese dictators started getting concerned their dwindling numbers and aging population might undermine their military and economic power.

What a great tragedy it would make. Where's Shakespeare when you need him?

And the world is not just contemptuous of bringing children into the world. A serious school of thought suggests the world would be better off with *no* humans on the planet *at all*.[13] It's called antinatalism and has a significant following. The concept is inherently stupid and counter to every notion of survival of any species, let alone people. But as they say, you can't fix stupid. You can just point it out.

As Nadeem Ali, founder of the Antinatalist Party put it: "The core philosophy of antinatalism is to recognise that being born means to suffer." As he sees it, it's better to forego unnecessary pleasure than to create unnecessary suffering.[14] Don't expect this guy to get married anytime soon.

The way to avoid unnecessary suffering? Stop existing. Just, you know . . . *stop*. This guy must have heard what Buddha said, and now he's taking it *to the max*.

But wait—we're not done. As if the financial cost, sleepless nights, and emotional roller coaster of having children aren't enough, your child might *sue* you for bringing him into the world. Yes, that actually occurred, and it was from an antinatalist.[15] His reasoning? There's no purpose to humanity, which he sees as "totally pointless."

In 2018, the child, now in his late twenties, created a Facebook page, Nihilanand, which featured his many antinatalist messages. Among them were "Isn't forcing a child into this world and forcing it to have a career, [the same as] kidnapping and slavery?" And, "Your parents had you instead of a toy or a dog, you owe them nothing." Your parents had you as a selfish act of entertainment.[16]

And you thought the rebellious teenage years were going to be tough.

It's a natural "I didn't give consent to be born" consequence from antinatalism that before long will soon gain a philosophical hold in the universities. You'll see.

Like I said: you can only point it out. But you *can* take away one thing from it: the growing sense that life is only this "thing" that "descends" upon you. You come and go, just doing stuff while you're here: eating, sleeping, relieving yourself, and trying to survive. Sometimes, just to cope, you even look for dangerous distractions (drugs, alcoholism, satanic cults, Miley Cyrus). And oh yes, you can fornicate. The antinatalists might even use a different word. Surely that's one thing that gets them to stay on the planet.

But I'd guess that marriage, aspirations to a greater good, or any sense of life having purpose are alien concepts to such people. No doubt, in their minds, such things came about only as opiates to numb us to the unnecessary suffering and mean-inglessness in our lives. (Curious: why wouldn't the antinatalists "lead the way" and kill themselves?)

Much of the world *does* recognize the decline in birth rate as a massive existential threat heading our way: too many elderly people to take care of and not enough people to sustain an economy, much less grow it. It requires bringing workers from other countries—many of whom seek to sabotage their new host countries.

Many countries have offered financial incentives to couples in the way of stipends per child and tax deductions for more children. Hungary has even offered any couple who has four or more children never to have to pay income tax *for the rest of their lives*, as well as massive subsidies for seven-seater cars.[17]

But that's only a financial incentive. Few have a sense of the larger picture—that they have an *obligation* to have children, for the simple sake of the continuation of our civilization. No public service announcement proclaims the *good* of having children, its joys, or that it might even be an obligation from God.

Still, governments don't seem interested in the *why* of their empty playgrounds. They never even pose the question. There's no band of teenagers and a dog in a van, à la *Scooby Doo*, trying to figure out the mystery. These countries just want the *result* of more babies. So they literally bribe their people to make them. But you might as well pay a bunch of convicts to be honest. Don't expect too much to change.

That's why these financial incentives won't ever work, at least not on the scale the country hopes for. You see, if your society trains people to think of kids only in a monetary sense, then that's exactly what they'll do.

And so here we are. It turns out that even taking care of *all* of citizens' income tax for the rest of their lives won't be enough to entice them to have kids. That's how much of a burden they think kids are.

It's not because life has gotten worse in any country. Far from that—life has in fact gotten far *better* in most modern countries. So you would expect more kids, not fewer. But to have kids, you need something more than money and free stuff. Much more. You need the *why*.

But where the centrality of God leaves our civilization, there is no *why*. This loss is the only thing that entirely explains the Case of the Disappearing Children.

Too bad no one hired the *Scooby Doo* gang to figure that out.

Like the tie, people are beginning to wonder whether there is a point to having a family at all. And if family is out, then—at least for a lot of men—the concept of a monogamous relationship is pointless.

For many women, likewise, the relationship is all about establishing the ground rules with a man for a potential future with children. (What kind of man is he? Will he be a good father to my children?)

If society makes no real *push* for children and, even worse, views children as blights and the mere products of irresponsible acts, then the notion of a relationship is, to some extent, unnecessary. Sex for sex's sake then rises evermore in status. Sex becomes "just sex."

And so we return to our sex robots. If children are a drain on our resources, it's not hard to see that robots will become all the more appealing—to both men and women. With robots, they get all the pleasure they want while never worrying about having children. Sure, there's no relationship with an actual human, but that's not so important in our new "it's just sex" world.

Think of all the "good" things that would flow from a man directing his sexual needs to a sex robot: less emotional and physical torment to women; perhaps less rape and child molestation; no sexually transmitted diseases, *and* he's saving the planet.

He can feel super good about himself. He's being responsible. In fact, it's better than that. He's being *selfless*.

Chapter 16

How We Learned to Stop Worrying and Love the Automation

Damn the Human Thing, Full Speed Ahead!

I've always loved the world of business. I majored in economics at Stanford, and I earned my MBA with my juris doctorate at UCLA. I learned that one of the inevitabilities in business is that things change. One company makes a better cookie, and that new company displaces the world's previous understanding of what a great cookie is—until the *next* cookie company comes along and improves upon *that* cookie. You get the idea.

I also learned that convenience and cost are major factors in the successful sale of products. It was for that reason the car displaced the horse, the iPod displaced the compact disc, Amazon Kindle displaced paper books, the internet displaced newspapers, and retail is now suffering one of its most massive existential blows ever, in favor of internet-based shopping (oh, who are we kidding? I mean Amazon). These are some obvious "in your face" innovations that we saw change within our own lives within just a few short years.

One other thing that changed was employment regulations, particularly the push for a minimum wage, which caused employers not only to increase prices but to look for ways to reduce costs. Conspiring with that is a growing body of law so labyrinthian that many employers have to hire a full-time "compliance officer," who must know:

- what you can and can't say during an interview;
- when you can claim someone to be an independent contractor;
- what you can require as a dress code;
- what constitutes racist hiring practices;
- whether you can ask someone if he's ever been convicted of a crime (by the way, the answer in California is no[1]);
- how many hours per day—and then per week—you can ask your employees to work without overtime pay;
- about sick days, breaks during the day, vacation days, maternal leave with and without pay, and holiday pay;
- insurance and IRA contribution compliance;
- how a person is allowed to wear their hair (proposed answer in New York City: any way at all—long, uncombed, unwashed, dreadlocks, full afro[2]);
- what you should do if someone announces he's transgender or Muslim and needs accommodations (but not if he announces he's gay, Christian, or Jewish—those don't matter anymore);
- how you may comment on someone's appearance; and, of course,
- what constitutes sexual harassment (answer: you name it).

And that's all *before* the telephone-book-size regulations when it comes to manufacturing, food distribution and restaurants, and OSHA safety regulations.

Ah, America. The land of opportunity.

Good luck navigating all that. Are you still sure you want to start a business? And if you already have a business, maybe you should throw in the towel and let one of your bigger competitors buy you out.

But wait—don't pull that trigger on your temple quite yet. There's good news, an option that can get you out of all this madness. Sure, it's the "nuclear" kind of option, one you never really wanted to use because you're a "people" person and you've always believed that your business is the sum of its people, that intangible *human quality*, if you know what I mean.

But as Bob Dylan crooned, "the times they are a-changin'." And they're changing really fast: more expensive, more burdensome, and more legally ominous. You feel like you might break any moment. Meanwhile you do whatever you must to survive.

Whether it's your child's education, the food you eat, or the surgery your dog needs, we've all got one: a breaking point— that point of cost and hassle beyond which you find yourself saying thank you very much, but it's just too rich for me.

And with all the compliance and taxes and sick days and lawsuits, employees also can cost too much, to say nothing of the productivity you lose dealing with the aggravation, when you could be expanding your business.

So you pull the plug on your employees and replace some of them with . . . automation. Soon the building owner invests in that automated parking lot attendant. The restaurant owner invests in automated kiosks and tablets where customers can order and pay for everything, and machines in the back will process the burgers, fries, or whatever. Soon the business outsources its reception needs to an automated service and asks customers to get all their questions answered via a "search our database" feature or a Frequently Asked Questions (FAQ) section.

You'll only need a fraction of employees to handle the rest. Yes it costs a lot to automate up front, but you'll make it up in a year or so, what with all the new productivity. It may not be what you preferred for your business, but as they say: business is business.

It's like in *The Simpsons*, when a house-alarm salesman pitched Homer a price to install a home security system. The next scene is Homer about to close the door on him. "But surely you can't put a price tag on your family's safety?" the salesman pleads. Homer responds: "You wouldn't think so, but here we are."

Do you see where I'm going with this yet?

No, frankly I DON'T yet see where you're going with this. Just tell me already! And if I read one more Simpsons *reference, I swear . . . .*

I am sorry, dear reader, but we'll get there. And by the way, no one who watches the *Simpsons* would say such a thing.

But here's a hint: The clue is already in what I've written.

After all the minimum wage laws, after all the threatened lawsuits, after all the union demands, the regulations on sick days, maternity leave and so on, the only thing that's surprising is that there is any surprise. Federal, state, and city governments make one law after the other hamstringing employers from making burgers, toenail clippers, or plumbing supplies and making any money, and then they're "shocked, shocked" that employers want to find alternate ways to make money.

You can argue that such innovation is inevitable, what with technology being so advanced, but you'd be wrong. It will surprise many people to read this, but many employers prefer the "human" touch in their business interactions, and prefer it for their customers too.[3] They like the repartee and exchange of ideas; they like socializing with their employees and seeing them grow in the business. Most employers didn't start their businesses just to make money; they wanted to be a part of a team that might do great things.

Many business owners also know that some employees have some degree of flair to their work, a uniquely human ability to cater to someone else's needs. A protocol may suggest one approach, for example, but a person who is good at their job understands when to adjust to the subtleties a situation may require.[4] An obvious example: an automated gate parking lot machine won't let a pregnant lady who's about to give birth just "go through."

The new employment laws, however, keep pushing employers and business owners toward automation. And how tempting it must be: every day technology keeps getting better, more efficient, and promises greater productivity at far less cost.

It must be like the husband who constantly gets attention from that twenty-something hottie at the smartphone accessory kiosk outside his office, when he has to return every night to his ever-aging, ever-complaining, and ever-fattening wife. (*Now* do you see where I'm going? Good).

The temptation is all the more powerful when the employer realizes that, hell, Johnny Robot can operate 24/7 and never get tired. He won't need any holidays or vacation time. The machine won't sue for wage and hour disputes and will never be lazy, claim he's sick when he's really hung over, or lie to him about his department's performance last quarter. The employer won't owe any payroll taxes for the machine, have to pay for maternity leave, or ever have to deal with catty office politics. He also will never have to worry that the machine stole from the company till.

So in the end, he has only one question to ask: *Where do I sign?*

The Weaponizing of Sex and What Did You Expect?

Now we arrive to the automation of sex. In the same way our work force is racing toward automation, the average male is soon going to race toward the automation of his sex. And it will be pretty much for the same reasons.

How so?

We already discussed the Me Too movement, which started in 2017. Hundreds of claims against men in entertainment and media for unwanted attention and harassment took center stage. Women demanded that men not only control themselves but completely reorient the way they view women.

It may have gone too far. Suddenly men have become afraid to make the "first move" in *any* romantic situation, unless the woman gives him an invitation (in which case you probably wouldn't call it a first move.) Even just being taller than a woman and asking her out on a date can be enough to trigger claims of sexual harassment.[5]

It's all become quite confusing. On the one hand, ask almost any woman and she'll state directly that she prefers a man to "take charge," be confident, and make decisions. I've never known any woman to *not* want a man to make the first move romantically. It makes a woman feel wanted, special, and attractive. It also shows her that he can be bold and take risks in life.

On the other hand, if he *does* make the first move and the woman is *not* interested in him, then it's sexual harassment. In other words, it's sexual harassment when a woman doesn't like the man *back*. It's *not* harassment if she does. As a *Saturday Night Live* skit about sexual harassment parodied in a mock fifties-style educational film, *Sexual Harassment and You*, you can avoid charges of sexual harassment by observing these three simple rules: (1) be handsome, (2) be attractive, and (3) don't be unattractive.

Isn't that so simple? Why can't *all* men just do that?

The problem is that the average man can't know if a woman is interested in him, short of her giving him obvious cues, or him awkwardly asking her ahead of time. And asking her ahead of time will instantly deflate the air out of the romance balloon in about 99 percent of women. You know why? 'Cause it's *unmanly*.

It's a circular paradox that's even more confounding than time-travel movies, the ones where the son goes back to save his mom so that she can give birth to him. Or better yet, a man goes back to kill Hitler, but that would mean his Jewish refugee parents would never have met, and he'd never be born. That kind of jazz.

• • •

Colleges and the feminist movement in general now expect men to get actual consent for each new level of physical contact with a woman.[6] They argue it's the only way to ensure that the sexual activity is truly voluntary.

But wait, what's this? Even if it's consensual at first, the woman might regret the sex later and say it wasn't consensual (now there's some time travel for you). A woman can even say, despite having several intimate sexual encounters with a man, that one of them was not consensual, or that it was at first consensual, but then she didn't feel like it in the middle or the end of the sex. It doesn't even seem to matter if the man had no indication from the woman that she was having second thoughts or he believed she was still very much "into it." All that matters is *her* subjective feelings at the moment.

And if it's on a college campus? The new "preponderance of the evidence" standard (as opposed to the criminal "beyond a reasonable doubt" standard) applies.[7] That makes it far easier for a school to "convict" a boy (expel him). All it takes is a college administrative panel to believe the girl more than it believes the boy.

So if a woman has sex with a young man, she suddenly gains an enormous new power over him. Do what I say, or I can claim you raped me. It will be easy for me to file a claim, and I'll get the backing of any number of women support groups.

She can demand that they stay in a relationship. If she's calculating enough, she may even demand money or other special treatment. To upend the famous Pat Benatar song on its head, sex can become a great weapon—for women. That's right: we are weaponizing sex for women, and it's getting more powerful every year.

Why not? Think that wouldn't happen? Girls have done far worse before to men who have scorned or dumped them in the past. Just recall what I listed in an earlier chapter: slashing tires, lying to police to get their ex arrested, wiping out their ex's computer files, and wrecking cars. And don't forget that penis-cutting story.

To give women a far looser standard to accuse a man of *rape*, one of the most vile crimes imaginable, and expecting no abuse or extortion is like eliminating all traffic laws and thinking everyone will drive ever so responsibly.

There are reasons we have certain burdens before we can accuse anyone of a crime, and to change this standard will only cause every man to see each potential female sex partner like a mine in a minefield. It also won't bode well for the health of male-female relationships in the future, what with that Sword of Damocles hanging over your bed.

Despite efforts to change the standard, however, colleges are doubling down on the preponderance-of-the-evidence standard. So Johnny Co-ed is better off just studying, thank you very much. Don't even bother thinking of getting laid, at least with a female human being.

It's f**king terrifying (as it were). What kind of message will this send to even younger male adolescents and boys about sex? When what you thought were clear and obvious lines between consensual sex and rape are no longer clear and obvious; when what you think is a great passionate moment with a woman who is straddling you and enjoying the moment as much as you are (and who may have even initiated the moment herself) suddenly transforms into a moment of *rape* the next day, then sex becomes an absolutely terrifying prospect—one that can forever alter your life.

For a young virgin boy, for whom sex was always a daunting concept but to which young men still looked forward, sex now seems like it has little to offer. As if the dangers of disease and unwanted pregnancy were not already a huge issue, *any* act of sex can be construed as rape. And a virgin boy has no context of sex; all he knows now is that *any* sexual act can ruin him. There's nothing to look forward in that.

A good friend of mine told me of his fourteen-year-old nephew whom he took to a stylish restaurant in Los Angeles. The kid noticed five or six girls from his school walking in, and they were looking his way in recognition.

The uncle saw that the boy noticed the girls, so the uncle said, "Let's get them some pizzas and let them know it's from us." The uncle thought this would be a sweet gesture, one which might impress the young ladies.

The nephew couldn't have shot down the idea faster. "NO, uncle Steve. No way. Please don't do that!" He looked mortified.

The uncle figured this was just his young nephew's natural awkwardness and inability to navigate his way with girls, and he wanted to help. He tried to explain that the girls would think it was so sweet and so cool of him, but the nephew remained adamant and said no.

Next the uncle offered to buy only cookies for the girls. "Cookies should be fine, right? No big deal with cookies, right?"

"Uncle, please STOP!" the nephew said, more adamant than ever, even a little angry. He was hiding his head in his hands now.

The uncle didn't understand and told him so. But he sensed something else was up. Maybe there was some dynamic among those particular girls that he didn't get.

He still wanted to know, so he asked, "What's the problem? We won't get them anything if you insist, but just tell me why."

"Because," the nephew said, his tone still wildly concerned and mortified: "They might say it's sexual harassment."

And there you have it. They're not just terrified of sex but terrified of even *interacting* with the opposite sex, lest someone might construe it as a sexual advance.

Riddle: What do drugs and sex have in common?
Answer: Just say no.

Add to this new dynamic the ever-expanding set of rights of women in the workplace running alongside the ever-growing restrictions on what a man can say to a woman employee. Employers actually worry about saying "that dress looks nice on you," mentoring them, or even about asking a woman employee to lunch. For this reason, sixty percent of men have indicated indicate that they generally feel uncomfortable with women in their workplaces. Specifically: Senior-level men "are twelve times more likely to be hesitant about one-on-one meetings with a junior woman than they are a junior man, nine times more likely to be hesitant to travel with a junior woman for work than a junior man, and six times more likely to be hesitant to have a work dinner with a junior woman than a junior man."[8]

In my days as general counsel to a major basketball franchise owner and real estate mogul, a former woman employee sued the owner because she claimed he had once tucked in his shirt while talking to her. That was it. She sued for millions of dollars. The jury overwhelmingly found against her, but that was only after my boss had spent millions in his defense over two years of litigation.

It's just too powerful a trump card. Like business and restaurant owners who figured it was too much cost and legal exposure to keep employees, men have figured out that sex has become too expensive and presents too much legal exposure. And so, like the business and restaurant owners, men will soon be automating their sex, too. They'll delegate that task to robots.

Remember: everyone has their breaking point. It's finally gotten to that point now for many, many men.

As Homer said: You wouldn't think so. But here we are.

Chapter 17

The End of Discretion

Many movies and stories are about unforeseen consequences. One of my favorites is the movie *The Gods Must Be Crazy* (1980). There, a small remote tribal people in an African desert live a happy and uncomplicated life, until a pilot in a twin-engine plane flying overhead throws an empty Coca-Cola bottle out his window.

The tribal leader Xi (played by N!xau) sees the bottle fall on the ground near his village. He assumes it is a sort of gift from the gods, what with it having come out of the sky. He picks it up. The bottle is so interesting and unique: shiny and transparent. It is also harder than anything he has ever seen before.

Xi shows it to his fellow villagers, and they soon find a myriad of uses for the bottle—kneading and smoothing out bread, making designs, and even playing music by blowing over the top of the bottle. Was there no end to what this strange new object could do?

Soon, however, the villagers start fighting over the bottle, and jealousies and anger develop. It seems to bring out the worst in them—a new sense of possessiveness takes hold, making them do things and have feelings they never thought they were capable of.

Xi tries throwing the bottle back up into the sky—back to the gods—only to have the bottle come right back at him and injure him. No matter what the clan does to get rid of it, the bottle always seems to find its way back and create more mischief.

The tribal leaders decide Xi should take the bottle to the end of the earth and drop it once he's there. It will be a long journey, and that's when the fun and adventure begins.

Sex is like that Coca-Cola bottle. It seems to come to us from nowhere, out of the proverbial sky. It is beautiful and inexplicable in its wonder. It has all sorts of uses, and it brings out all sorts of emotions, too, some that can even surprise us: passion, jealousy, possessiveness, competition, anger, belonging, and intense love and intense hate. For thousands of years, songs and poems have spoken about the pain and wonder of romance and sex, or the sudden need to be with someone he or she just met.

It's a big marvel and wonder, this sex thing, except it's more than just an empty Coca-Cola bottle. It's more like a plutonium rod—bright and shiny, and seemingly so "glowy." But it's not something to hang up as a party gimmick at a wedding or something you can use as a makeshift flashlight in the night. If you were to find such a rod, it would mean death.

But handled and housed properly, with all the right precautions and casings, it can channel and produce energy for cities and even whole countries.

Nature gives us many things, all of which we can abuse. Alcohol? We can abuse that. Eating? We can abuse that too (both eating too much and too little). We can also abuse power, the quest for money, gambling, competition, parenting, compassion, and entertainment. We can work too hard, obsess about diet, grieve too much, be too religious, be too trusting, be too clean, play too many video games, fantasize too much, overdo prescription drugs to addiction levels, and exercise too much. We can even care and love too much.

Any of these human endeavors or attributes can turn destructive. We recognize that they each can reach the point of abuse, and we would rightly encourage anyone engaging in such abuse to seek help. Sometimes close friends and family will force an "intervention" on an individual they deem to have gone too far. Sometimes, Alcoholics Anonymous or other support groups are the answer.

And then there's sex. While it's true there are "sex addiction" support groups, it's nothing compared to drug or alcohol rehab groups. It's rarely broached because we rarely recognize it as some national "problem" that invokes charitable gala fundraisers and public service announcements.

Do you or a loved one have sex with too many partners? Please call. Operators are standing by.

Hardly. If a man "scores" with a different woman every other day, he might well brag about it to his friends. It's a reflection of his animal magnetism, charisma, or whatever. He may even want you to see photos of each of his new conquests.

We all know or have heard of such men. We might admire them, we might pity them, we might think they're shallow. But we rarely think of them as having a problem.

And when it comes to women, they may not show off photos of the various men they're sleeping with, but they won't think twice about satisfying themselves as they please, even if it's with many men. As I've shown before, they have a go-for-it attitude, where "[everyone's] disposable, there's always more, and you move on fast." There is little discussion that one should *limit* one's sexual partners.

There is a national call for *discretion* in alcohol ("drink responsibly"), gambling, drugs, and in virtually everything else. But not sex. And while we are relatively good talking about the consequences of drinking too much, drug abuse, and even cigarette addiction, there is little discussion of the consequences of sex.

Somehow sex is all good. *Any* kind of sex is OK so long as it involves two consenting adults (scratch that—any number of consenting adults): lesbian, anal, gay, threesome, orgy, swinging, bondage, dominatrix, role reversals, and strap-ons. I'm sure there's much more that I haven't even heard of, and which many in our culture consider in the It's-All-Good category. Other than child molestation, rape, and sexual slavery, it seems few things are truly off limits.

Many have no sense of why sex is there in the first place. To them, it just came out of the sky, like the Coca-Cola bottle, and they're enjoying it only for its day-to-day obvious pleasures.

They can't fathom any boundaries within sex. Yet we rightly teach people to *think, dammit, think*: if I drink this tonight and get in the car, bad things might result. If I start smoking cigarettes, I can get addicted and then get lung cancer. If I gamble more than the one hundred dollars I came into the casino with tonight, I could lose everything. If I play too many video games, if I take drugs, and if I don't eat my vegetables, bad things will befall me.

What are you talking about, Mr. Lurie? We encourage people to use condoms and practice "safe sex" all the time. It's in school education and brochures and banners everywhere. Isn't that enough "consequences" for you?

Well, yes—and no. You do hear such admonitions from time to time. But it's the lip-service kind, like how parents agree with their school principal that their children should *not* fight back if another kid punches them. But really, we parents tell our kids to fight back. We don't want *our* kids to be patsies or squealers.

What accounts for the difference? As to alcohol, drugs, gambling, and even smoking and diet and body obsessions, we "tsk, tsk" all the time. We judge such people. Why don't they control themselves? They need help.

It's not so when it comes to sex. Whatever you do in the world of sex is cool. There's no *judgment* when it comes to sex. Johnny is gay; you might be surprised to learn it the first time but, hey, no judgment. Sarah likes multiple partners a week. That's fine; whatever floats her boat.

Part of all this owes to child-development gurus of the latter half of the twentieth century: Dr. Benjamin Spock and Abraham Maslow focused their message not around giving to others, but "self-actualization" and "self-esteem." But to get there, one must eschew discipline, standards and expectations. Because standards were impositions from society, that might interfere with self-esteem. So, please: no "standards."

You see this playing out in our modern lives. For example, you hear rumors that Teddy is bisexual. He also likes to go to orgies. Well, even if it's true, what is it your business? As long as he's not hurting anyone, that shouldn't be a problem. Frank now identifies as a woman and wants gender-reassignment surgery yet plans to still pursue women sexually. Uh . . . good for him!

Jenna and Mickey are swingers, did you know? Yeah, it's true. It's not for me, but it seems to work for them. They seem happy.

There *is* talk of the consequences of extramarital sex, especially anything out of the classic, monogamous, heterosexual vaginal sex norm, but it is only "talk." It's as if they understand that if it goes beyond brief mention, then that might sound too much like you're judging them for their sexual deviations.

And we can't have that. Even when you give blood or undergo a routine physical, your nurse practitioner will likely ask you if you engage in any "risky" sexual behavior (which, let's face it, for the *real* risky stuff, usually means anal sex).

And here's the conundrum: Every doctor will readily acknowledge that there is far greater risk to your health once you take your sex out of the "norm" of monogamous vaginal sexual activity. But will they publish articles and otherwise alert the media to warn about anal sex and multiple partners? Why wouldn't they do that? After all, when there was an outbreak of

Legionnaire's disease in 1976 and several times thereafter, the community rallied to isolate and quarantine anyone afflicted with the disease. We do the same today with many other disease outbreaks: cholera, diphtheria, infectious tuberculosis, plague, smallpox, yellow fever and viral hemorrhagic fevers (like ebola), and severe acute respiratory syndrome (SARS).[1]

But you'll notice no similar alarm when it comes to most *sexually* transmitted diseases, where the incidence among those having many partners and men having sex with men is *wildly* higher.[2] Fascinatingly, while the Center for Disease Control recognizes that multiple partners, male gay sex, and unprotected sex dramatically increases one's chance of acquiring an STD, it's somewhat vague on the specifics (such as the highly dangerous activity of anal sex and "rimming"). Instead, the report refers generally to avoid "risky behavior."[3]

Thanks, guys. That really helps clarify things for me: just don't do risky stuff. You earned your pay this year.

O.k., buddy: here are the car keys. Now, remember: don't do risky stuff.

Here are my words of wisdom about drugs to you, son: Don't do anything risky. Glad we had this talk.

Have fun with your buddies at the gun-shooting range, son. I'll pick you up in an hour. And remember: Nothing risky, okay? Great.

But wait, there's good news: go to middle and high schools, and the administration will be happy to show you exactly what "risky behavior" in sex is (see our discussion above). You won't know that it's actually "risky" *per se* (that would be too judgmental), but what great things you'll discover! And then they'll tell you that you should consider that behavior exactly as normal as heterosexual vaginal sex. By the way, you want to try it? Go for it! Remember: no judgment here. And PS: you can't really judge it until you've tried it, no?

No mixed message there at all.

Chapter 18

Nature's Silent Scream

I remember as a young kid seeing the famous Edvard Munch painting, *The Scream* (1893). What was that man screaming about? I had no idea. But he sure seemed upset.

To this day, every time I hear some shocking news, I think of that man in the painting responding to that news. Maybe if he was around today, it would be because he just learned of how many STDs there are in the world.

There are more than 357 million new cases of sexually transmitted diseases in the world *each year*. These include four STDs alone: chlamydia, gonorrhea, syphilis, and trichomoniasis. These STDs in turn lead to consequences like sterility, infertility, stillbirth, miscarriage, blindness, brain damage, and cancer. Some STDs cause lesions that increase the risk of HIV infection by more than 300 percent.[1] More than 500 million people have genital infection with herpes simplex virus (HSV), and more than 290 million women have a human papillomavirus (HPV) infection.[2]

Despite this massive worldwide issue, the CDC cautions things only thusly:

What activities can put me at risk for both STDs and HIV?
• Having anal, vaginal, or oral sex without a condom;
• Having multiple sex partners;
• Having anonymous sex partners;

• Having sex while under the influence of drugs or alcohol can lower inhibitions and result in greater sexual risk-taking.[3]

Did you read the first great "risk"? *Having anal, vaginal, or oral sex without a condom.* The way the CDC phrases it, there's no distinction among those three kinds of sex. You might conclude that vaginal and oral sex without condoms is just as dangerous as anal sex without a condom.

What's going on here? Political correctness has so intimidated us that *even the Center for Disease Control* can't call out anal sex for the far more dangerous activity that it is. Why? Because advocating the avoidance of anal sexual activity and similar risky behavior might mean sidelining an entire group of people who identify themselves through that sexual activity.

This continues the politically correct agenda of the 1980s and early nineties that AIDS and HIV would spread like wildfire among heterosexuals in America and the West in general. It was a transparent agenda push. Some have said it was a push to control people somehow, to force them into a new (false) morality.[4]

The reality couldn't be farther from that. The real agenda— as I saw it unfolding during my college and law school years— was to avoid shaming and singling out the gay community for fear of some sort of backlash against them. To achieve that, our cultural betters were prepared to embark on a massive campaign to school everyone that AIDS and HIV had nothing whatsoever to do with anal sex (or "risky" behavior). It was something that we *all* had to watch out for, gay *or* straight.

Most people bought it—for a couple of years, at least. And in my freshman year, when the AIDS crisis first hit, it seemed nobody was touching anyone. Guys and girls were afraid even to kiss or hold hands. It was frustrating to me as a young college guy whose teachers had assured me during my high school years that "college will be your wildest, most fun time with girls you'll ever have." Not so much.

But the numbers of AIDS victims among heterosexuals just didn't materialize as everyone had prophesied. Other than intravenous needle sharing and blood transfusions, it was clear that AIDS and HIV stemmed from frequent anal sex. Few bought the agenda anymore, or at least they didn't act as if they were buying it. Soon all was good again, and sex in America resumed its normal reckless pace.

Perhaps the present CDC report refuses to take a strong stand against anal sex for a far simpler reason: to take such a stand would mean *advocating a limitation on sex*. A limitation would suggest something *other* than the notion that sex is "all good." Remember, *all* sexual feelings and activities are valid. All of them are *equal*. The CDC, despite what one might expect, seems to be an advocate *for* sex in all of its glorious forms, and for *lots* of it. Just put on that condom; that's all we're saying.

Sadly, it appears one of the victims of this approach was Freddie Mercury, of the rock group Queen. He acknowledged he engaged in wild rampant sex, engaging stranger after stranger in nightclub after nightclub. He exercised no caution. To a journalist who asked whether the AIDS scare worried him, he said: "Darling, my attitude is 'fuck it,' I'm doing everything with everybody."[5] Then he died from AIDS.

One of his more famous songs ominously went: "Don't stop me now, I'm having such a good time. I'm having a ball." You know something? Maybe someone should have stopped him.

The CDC also dances around the dangers of multiple and anonymous partners. It talks about it in a mere reporting-type way, recognizing the facts that show clearly that those with numerous partners and anonymous hookups are far more likely to acquire sexually transmitted diseases. The CDC shows the numbers, which even a passing glance proves how they *dwarf*

STDs among those who engage in monogamous sex. This is to say nothing of the overall wild "spike" in STDs in the past decades.[6]

To add to the befuddling, the CDC shows virtually nothing of the *positive* health benefits of monogamy, which science has proved time and time again. Those benefits include greater heart health, reduced anxiety, greater longevity, greater happiness and contentment, and reduced chance of depression and bad habits such as smoking and drinking.[7] It's even good for the advancement of civilization: more monogamy means more dedication to one's spouse and family, and more focus on doing productive things such as building, inventing, and discovering. And oh yes, there are virtually no worries about contracting STDs.

You would think, with the CDC's *raison d'être* being to advance the cause of health, it then would certainly push monogamy at the top of its lungs until the cows came home. Alas, it does not do so.[8]

The forces of promiscuity, always relentlessly pursuing good news about their bad habits, are strong. The last thing they would push is for any demand that we limit our sex—in any way. They'll even point to recent research suggesting somehow that *more* promiscuity leads to better resistance and immunity against bacteria—at least in mice and bonobo monkeys.[9] *

---

* It would be nice if they conducted such a study on humans one day. It's not as if it's difficult to find women and men who self-report about their sexual activities, and then the study could evaluate their immunities. Also, this may be one of those areas where it's important to note the difference between humans on the one hand and virtually every animal on the other, vis-à-vis sexuality. With few exceptions [and even those are questionable], female humans are the only mammals that don't go into heat. There is no "mating season" for her, and she can have sex for pleasure anytime. See generally, Jason Goldman, "Do Animals Have Sex For Pleasure?" www.bbc.com/future/story/20140613-do-animals-have-sex-for-fun; June 13, 2014; Luis, Villazon, "Why Don't Humans Have A Mating Season?" www.sciencefocus.com/the-human-body/why-dont-humans-have-a-mating-season/, undated. These articles both attempt to depict human females as *similar* to other mammals, sexually, but rely on examples of one species of apes and some bats. All the while, they cannot deny that human women have sex for pleasure, unlike animals, and that human females can have sex whenever they want (there is no heat, nor mating season).

So again, with the massive tsunami of STDs descending upon Americans in our new culture of open sex, you would expect the CDC to reach some basic conclusions here: Lots of partners: dangerous and bad; don't do it. Anal sex: also dangerous; don't do that, either. Long-term monogamous vaginal sex: good. *Very* good. Do that.

But the report does not offer such conclusions—nothing of the sort. It's like a weatherman who unemotionally describes the weather for the day as "calling for rain, say about twenty inches, with wind gusts of about 140 miles per hour"—without once mentioning that there's a category-4 hurricane about to hit.

Or like this:

Concerned wife: So give it to me straight, Detective. What did your investigation show?

Detective: Well, your husband's body appears to have forty-six machete lacerations, five bullets in the head, signs on his neck of severe asphyxiation just before death. Oh, and his head was severed from the rest of his body. We can't find it.

Concerned wife: Those monsters! What are you going to do now to get those bastards who committed this murder?

Detective: Murder? Please, Ma'am. Let's not jump to conclusions.

Why should anyone be intimidated from pointing out certain kinds of sex are far riskier? Astronauts, firefighters, soldiers off to war, police officers, base jumpers, and other thrill seekers engage in risky behavior all the time, but we certainly wouldn't be insulting them if we pointed out that their activities or professions are risky.

But you can't sound this same alarm when it comes to anal sex, sex with numerous partners, or anything sexual outside of monogamous heterosexual vaginal sex. Somebody might feel excluded or offended.

It's because it's about sex. Sex is different. *All* sex is acceptable, and no sex is worse or better than the other. It's like the mantra they seem to keep drilling into today's kids at school: No one's better than anyone else, and everyone's the best at everything.[10] That's why we may never hear any official announcement admonishing people to limit their sexual activity to "responsible" levels and "responsible" methods. ("Please, enjoy your sex responsibly," said no public service announcement ever).

Yes, they talk about avoiding "risky sex," but they don't actually say don't do it. They just say you should take precautions. You know, like seat belts in cars. But otherwise feel free to floor it and drive as recklessly as you want.

We seem to recognize that there is a right and wrong way to use nuclear power, to use words, to conduct war, to run a business, to drive, to eat, and so on. Oftentimes, these things take hard work and sacrifice, the deferring of gratification, and even a sense of obligation to the community at large.

But somehow that notion of right or wrong, that sense of communal obligation, and the idea of *discretion* all goes out the window when it comes to sex. The sex advocates will tell us that, other than rape, trafficking and child molestation, there can be no right or wrong when it comes to sex. We enable and sometimes even encourage the go-for-it attitude at our own peril, and the peril of civilization itself.

As Robert A. Heinlein once quipped, each generation thinks it invented sex. And each generation is totally mistaken. Whatever it may think is new and wild, beyond the comprehension of our parents' and previous generations, has occurred before. Even today's romance-free, swipe right/swipe left, and insta-sex millennials would cringe at the licentious and often horrific sexual rituals and escapades of the Canaanites, the Sodomites, the Greeks, and the Romans. There was little discretion back then.

Still, there is one thing today's young can and should know better than those who lived in the ancient world: the dangers and consequences of unbridled anything-goes sex. Certainly there is enough information out there. As easy as it is for anyone to use the internet to hookup anonymously with anyone else, so, too, can anyone find tremendous information about the dangers of that hookup.

As we've discussed above, the information we now know and have at our fingertips is screaming one bold warning: sex is nothing to trifle with. Sex is powerful beyond what we can imagine. Sex also has consequences—emotionally, physically, and societally, and it requires enormous discretion before bringing sex into one's life.

But how many people who spend so much time on social or sex hookup sites have ever taken the time to look up the consequences of hooking up? How do they exercise discretion, when they don't even know those consequences? I wonder if they even care.

Sex today has become more than just the pursuit of pleasure. It's become a form of indulgence, an abandonment of the needs of others in favor of the needs only of oneself. Get a woman pregnant? She can handle it—and there's a new "morning after" pill for that. And if the pill doesn't take care of it, there's an abortion clinic nearby. And if you give an STD to someone? It happens. You can easily get rid of most STDs with antibiotics. Sure, herpes is a bummer, but it won't kill you (besides, doesn't everyone have it anyway?)

You see? Problem solved.

That may be the root of the problem itself: we solve these sexual "problems" a bit too easily. Science seems like it's always hard at work to make sex as consequence-free as possible. And that way, we won't ever have to worry about the annoyance of exercising any discretion at all.

But where there are no damages that may flow from an action, people tend to feel less of an obligation to anyone else. Here's a thought experiment: imagine being able to drive as recklessly as you want, and knowing that anyone you might hurt will recover almost instantaneously, and quite cheaply at that. You'd soon drive through red lights all the time and speed full throttle to your heart's delight. You wouldn't care much about anyone you might hit.

That is what consequence-free sex has brought us. You might as well be living in a video game, each participant looking out only for himself, and thinking only for himself. No one really gets hurt. You don't involve yourself in relationships with the other characters in the video game. They can all blow up, as far as you're concerned. Everyone is *disposable*.

And just like when playing a video game, "discretion" in sex today is extraneous. It's all about the player winning, and how many points he scores. There's nothing else.

Conclusion
Planet of the Sex Robots

In the apocalyptic *Terminator III: Rise of the Machines*, humans desperately try to contain a virus that has infected the world's massive artificial intelligent military network. The military leadership gives up control to a new software, Skynet. But it was all a ruse: the Skynet program was just tricking the military to give it total control, so that it could take over the entire military network. And then Skynet commands all existing robots to take over all world, killing most of the humans who created them and enslaving the rest. All in all, it's a pretty bad day.

The process takes years, but ultimately the humans, led by one John Connor, start a resistance. Now there is hope. Sure, millions will die, but the humans are determined to take their world back. So very messy. So inefficient.

It turns out if it really wanted to end civilization, Skynet could have used a much simpler tactic: All it needed to do was unleash millions of sex robots upon the planet. Humans would do the rest for them, satisfying their sex lust with robots, never having kids, and thus imploding their own civilization. It would be like when they killed Zika-carrying mosquitos in 2017 by introducing millions of sterile male mosquitos into the streets of Fresno, letting them pleasure themselves into extinction.

So don't worry, Skynet and all you terminators. You won't need to kill John Connor *or* his mother. In fact, you won't have to do very much to destroy us.

We'll do it to ourselves.

Courtship, chivalry, romance, marriage, love, discretion, having children, and sex itself have all changed wildly since the start of the twenty-first century, if not earlier. One can even say that the first seven have disappeared or are at least fading away. They're things that are no longer a part of who we are. They're not quite like dinosaurs, which we know existed but which no one ever encountered. They're more like the Sony Walkman, video rentals, car phones, pagers, and libraries. Some of us lived during the time of *those* things. We remember them, even with a bit of wistful nostalgia.

Only sex remains. And it's the last of what remains between man and woman. It's the most basic, animalistic part that we pursue in the name of pleasure—and intense pleasure at that. We're all about pleasure, especially the kind that doesn't involve hard work to get it. We're like kids at Christmas: who wants to cut through all the wrappings and ribbons? Just let me get to the video game console so I can start playing already.

It's insta-sex, a world where there is no dancing, flirting, or wondering if someone likes you. There is no more impulse control, and very little discretion, and our culture repeatedly tells us to do whatever feels good for now. There is no judgment anymore: you are not a "slut"; you are not a "player."

And above all else: *tout est bon, et tout va:* It's all good, and anything goes.

Sex is everywhere—to do, to look at, to talk about, to associate with, to market. But why is it so prevalent today? Why do people seek out sex so much, in one form or another? Why do so many now base their identities largely on the direction of their sexual desires?

It's because they have little else in their lives. It's as if our culture stripped away everything from us, as it were, leaving us with nothing but our naked bodies. In a world without God and the traditions of family, commitment, and sense of obligation that go with Him, many people have lost meaning. What else is there?

Having rebuked masculinity, religion, America, and even Western civilization itself as "toxic," they've left themselves little to celebrate. They've only learned to demolish whatever institutions ever served to prop up civilization: chivalry, marriage, truth and justice, the fight against evil, restraint and sacrifice, patriotism and duty to country, religion and faith, and the truly glorious and important differences between man and woman.

It's like the classic Dr. Seuss tale, *The Lorax*, where a mean developer chops down trees for his commercial profiteering purposes until one day he chops down the very last tree. Only then does he start appreciating what he once had.

So what else is there to do but seek the thrills of immediate gratification, whether that means hours-long play of video games, smartphone texts (and "sexts"), streaming of movies . . . and the pursuit of orgasms?

There was an understanding in earlier times that we couldn't have sex all the time. It would interfere with growing as a person, and with progress itself. But today's generation regards Christian and Jewish societies of old as prudish imposers of morality, who demonized sex, strictly confining it to marriage.

They are wrong. It's *not* that Judaism and Christianity were prudish about sex. It's that these institutions of faith understood the awesome *power* of sex. They understood its emotional and societal dangers. They understood that, left unchecked or used without any sense of restraint, sex could be highly destructive. It is part of what the stories of Sodom and Gomorrah, the Canaanites, Herod, and Noah are about: licentiousness and unrestrained sex hurls societies into the oblivion of debauchery and human misery. Always.

Perhaps younger people today feel that, by running from one orgasm to the next, they are "doing" something. Perhaps they feel like this is what engaging in life means. This reasoning is strange. Think of it like jumping off the top of a building: It's true you're moving from point A to point B, but you may not like the destination.

Contrary to what one might think, it's quite easy to pursue orgasms through anonymous hookups—which Tinder and other dating websites have made all the more accessible today. Far more difficult is the exercise of restraint—as anyone dealing with alcoholism, drugs, diabetes, cigarettes, gambling, or weight issues will tell you.

Restraint, ironically, is also what makes life far more meaningful and rich. In a way, the greatest gift Judaism and Christianity gave to the world was this notion of *restraint*. Restraint opened up true freedom of the mind, and freedom of choice. It may seem quite counterintuitive to many that, with all the kosher laws restricting how one can eat and the laws of the Sabbath imposing numerous other restrictions on work in favor of the study of God, Jews can somehow speak of being "free." Judaism even teaches us to restrict what times of the month a husband and a wife can have sexual relations. But it is with these very "restrictions" that we actually exercise our free will.

You know what, Mr. Lurie? That just makes no sense whatsoever.

Well, you're not the first to say that. Let me explain it another way, then. Imagine you love alcohol. In fact, you need and think of alcohol all the time. You go to every bar in town and keep buying drink after drink. You do this day after day, week after week. You're perpetually drunk and can't hold down a job.

Are you really "free"? Or are you, in a sense, just a slave to your alcoholic impulses? The same would apply to any other impulse of choice: not only substances like nicotine or drugs, but your emotions, temper, depressed moods, appetite, and even laziness. Indulging them means that those impulses control you. They "own" you.

But when it comes to sex, we turn the other way. We encourage young people to let their impulses guide them; whatever it is that turns you on, go for it. Almost anything related to sexual activity or sexual identity is just fine.

We see it on a social level: you're a biological male but you *feel* like a woman? We celebrate you as a woman. Why should you (or we) deny who you are?

You're a woman who just wants to enjoy anonymous sex, trying out as many penises as you can? Great! Orgasms are healthy and liberating for you.

You're bisexual? You're even more amazing! Nothing holds *you* back, no sir. You truly go with *whatever* impulse feels right for *you* for the moment. Don't let anyone suggest that you should just stick with the opposite sex.

You want a baby, but there's no boyfriend in sight? Go get that sperm from that bank and you take charge. Good on you, girl!

Like I said: slaves. Giving in to such base impulses is merely the illusion of freedom. Your impulses actually own you. It's the worst kind of slavery—slavery masquerading as freedom. That's how they get you.

Here's a question worth asking: which is more "freeing" to the human soul and humanity at large: sexual *openness* or sexual *restraint?* Sigmund Freud, Alfred Kinsey and most psychologists and sociologists have argued the former. The great religious sages have argued the latter. They can't both be right. If you see sex like air—where there is no such thing as "too much" air, but too little will kill you—you'll fall in the "openness" camp. If you compare sex to drugs, alcohol, gambling, food and so on—where a little is fine, but too much will destroy you—you'll join the "restraint" camp.

It's a simple question. The answer to the question should be simple, too. But you need to think to ask it.

• • •

Karl Marx famously quipped that religion was the opiate of the masses. It was actually an inane and thought-free comment, if you reflect on it. In fact, religious faith involves *constant study, work, and restraint*. Ask any observant Jew or Christian.

Marx missed it. If he had really thought on it, he'd realize the *true* opiate of the masses is—surprise—sex. Society has been pushing it in all its forms. But in the case of *these* opiates, virtually no kind of opiate is too hard or off limits. And everything that might serve to *limit* sex of any kind and sex on demand should itself disappear—whether that's marriage, the family, the church, limitations on abortion or contraception, any judgments regarding sex, and even the notion of having children.

We've gotten rid of all those annoying restrictions. We've thought of them like those jungle thickets we had to cut through with a machete, and now here we are. We've "made it" to some grand valley, where anything seems possible.

Still, something is lacking, despite the newfound judgment-free and easy access to fleshly pleasures. Our happiness remains elusive, somehow unattainable, like in one of those dreams where you're trying to get to a door, but it keeps getting farther away from you.

We don't know why. As Sheryl Crow seems to ponder in her song: "If it makes you happy, then why the hell are you so sad?"

Sex is the opiate, but in a way, the real opiate is more than that. It's living only in the *now*. What feels good at any moment is all that matters.

But we miss so much. Sex is far more profound. Sex should be a means to some greater end, and so many among us confuse the means *for* the end. It's like looking into a telescope and thinking it contains the universe. The telescope is only a *tool* by which to reach out to our universe, to help discover its mysteries.

Maybe, in the same way, sex is a tool for something else, far grander and more meaningful than only sex's orgasmic result. Maybe we've been looking at sex the wrong way. Or better yet: maybe we've *forgotten* how to look at it.

In this book, I have asked a lot of questions: Why are people having fewer children? Why have children at all? Why is sex so intensely pleasurable? Why do we intuitively value monogamy? Why are sex with many partners and certain kinds of sex so rife with disease? Conversely, why does long-term monogamous sex within the confines of marriage lead to such positive health benefits? Why does sex bring about so much emotion and emotional backlash? Why has feminism backfired so spectacularly? Why are people more lonely than ever? Why are there more sexual assaults in America than ever? Where will abandoning marriage, chivalry, courtship, and discretion ultimately lead us as a civilization?

It's difficult to answer these questions meaningfully unless we factor that there might be a *purpose* to sex, that it might have an overall role in some bigger picture. And part of why we don't have answers to these questions is that people don't *want* to consider the questions in the first place.

Maybe they're not quite keen on getting the answers. Maybe it's a willful blindness, like when you don't want to know what all the scurrying noises are in your attic. Or worse yet: like when a mother doesn't want to know why her young daughters are so terrified to be near the neighbor who lives across the street.

Most people *should* know that sex is scary, and that "relation-ship sex" is hard work. They should know that sex has awesome power, and that sex has meaning. Few people want to face these realities. Sex for them is like fatty fast food—they don't want to know what's in it, nor what it might do to their long-term health All they care about for the moment is that it's just fun, cheap, and easy. And P.S.: like fast food, they'd prefer their sex to go.

These questions often don't lead to meaningful answers because people refuse to consider one giant factor that could make sense of it all. it's right there in plain sight. In fact, it's so much so you might call it the eight-hundred-pound gorilla in the room.

It's the spiritual element. It's God.

You really think everything is connected to God, don't you, Mr. Lurie? God is the answer to everything for you. That's so simplistic.

Is it? What's more simplistic: to wonder whether God has a role in sex and to pose these questions I just listed—or to ignore these questions altogether?

Maybe the religious sages of old had some wisdom here. Sex is nothing to be played with, and the role of sex is no different today than it was thousands of years ago. For every aspect of sex we *think* is new, there's been a culture that has tried it before. The quest for many partners and different kinds of sex, the avoid-ance of pregnancy, the jealousies and affairs, sex for sale, rape and incest, and even so-called "friends with benefits." *All* of it has happened before. All that has changed is the technology.

But the sages took the questions head on: it's for joyful pro-creation and for the bonding of one man and one woman in marriage. Maybe the intensity of sex and the feeling of wholeness with another is there to bring us closer to God. When we engage in loving and committed sex, we serve as God's partners in His Creation.

When you see it *this* way, it explains—and resolves—*all* of the questions I have listed above. Every single one.

It is simple, yes. But it's hardly simplistic. It also has the added bonus of being elegant. It explains sex but only after figuring out the environment around sex, its attributes and its consequences—the wake it leaves in our lives. This is what the sages figured out after intense debate and analysis over many centuries. It was no different than when science figured out the earth revolved around the sun, no different than when Einstein developed his theory of relativity, and no different than when the American colonists figured out freedom is the greatest virtue.

They *seem* simple at first blush, if you only look at the end result (examples: $E=Mc^2$ is a simple formula; democracy seems obvious). But they are in fact the product of millennia of piecing together empirical facts and posing questions to explain those facts.

For me, the sages perfectly captured what sex means, what it's for, and how we should handle it. Maybe those observant Jews and Christians, with their seemingly backward ways, were on to something. Maybe it's more than just some old tradition they've been blindly following.

But competing with that age-old wisdom regarding sex is the powerful impulse to satisfy our most basic lusts. That impulse may have won the day, at least in the past few decades. We have so stripped away so many facets of sex and love that it seems as if all that is left is our naked bodies—not even the proverbial shirt on our back.

Think that's only a metaphor? Go to merry ol' England, where in London, naked bars, restaurants, clubs, and rooftops are ever so fashionable. In the restaurant Bunyadi, the first "nude" restaurant, customers could expect a waiting list of 46,000.[1] Their primary offering? That everyone can just walk around and dine naked. (Remember: London is also the proud home of the first Masturbate-a-thon in 2006).

Even when activists protest in Parliament to bemoan how their leaders aren't doing enough for the environment, they do it naked style. As one activist explained: "By undressing in parliament, we . . . highlight the vulnerability that all of us share in the face of environmental and societal breakdown."[2] Ah. The *vulnerability. That's* what the members of parliament are seeing.

There's France, too. France boasts the world's "fastest growing population of nudists." It's the world's top destination for nude tourism, with more than four million people vacationing *au naturel* every year. Paris has theaters where the audience must strip to see the play. The city even hosts naked museum tours.[3] Are visitors coming primarily to see the play and the art? That's unclear. What is clear is that the theaters and museums decided their plays and art weren't enough of a draw.

These restaurants, museums, and theaters are attracting its patrons with literally *nothing*. Everything has boiled down to the sensual, the suggestion of the orgasm. That's the ultimate goal. Everything else is unnecessary fluff.

How's that for simplicity?

It's no wonder that enthusiasm for sex robots is growing at a frenetic pace. Ask most people today (OK, I mean men), and they'll say they just can't wait. *More than two-thirds* of men have indicated they would be happy to try a sex robot.[4] One well-known CrossFit trainer even referred to them as the "promised land."[5]

So why *sex robots*? For that matter, why virtual sex of any kind? No one actually *needs* such things. Men could easily satisfy themselves with hookups and prostitutes—or their hands. But sex robots provide a solution to so much of what many men might need. Society has pushed men *to* the robots, what with the danger and high cost of sex with a real woman. For many, it's like the choice an employer must make between keeping an employee and automating that employee's job: if regulations and the cost of maintaining the employee get too high, an automated attendant will often replace him or her. What choice does he really have?

It's a double whammy: it's gotten to be too much for men on the one hand, and too tempting on the other. And it turns out that, with society elevating the sexual act *uber alles*, and minimizing the "relationship" to virtual oblivion, then the object of your sexual attraction doesn't need to be human at all.

And why should any woman object to robots? At least from the standpoint of a feminist, a woman doesn't need a man, no more than a fish needs a bicycle. That was the message for decades. And guess what? The men have received the message.

For the past few decades, we've been busy downgrading sex from its lofty status somewhere in the sky. Why should sex be special? Nothing else is.

We've come to view the sexual act and its pleasures as mere products of chemical interactions in the brain. We treat each other as mere purveyors and seekers of orgasms, not as humans in God's image. Sex has become how you satisfy yourself, not how you might satisfy someone else. You move fast, and everyone's disposable, remember? We each regard ourselves as nothing special, mere responders to each other's touch: robots, if you will. So why would we expect anyone else to see *us* as special?

What might be the best way to describe all this? Here's a word: *dehumanizing*.

Yet sex—human sex—is one of the central aspects of what *makes* us human. It is about the call of a man and woman to

245

bond, to be kind to each other, to celebrate not only each other but their union. They also celebrate that union through marriage; by which they become an integral and necessary part of the growth of civilization. That is paramount in both Judaism and Christianity.

The demand for robots will not happen among the devout, at least not in any significant way. The very idea is alien to them. They view sex quite differently; sex is wonderful, yes, but it's part of something far greater. So robots? No thank you.

There is little such appreciation of a larger purpose for sex among the secularists. For them, it's all about satisfying an immediate need, but they don't even know why they have the need in the first place. But sex is unlike water or food, which they understand they must have to sustain their physical being. They just know their sexual needs course through their body, wildly. They have no idea why, but it's pretty damn strong and they need to satisfy it. Like, *now*.

So they swing, they use sex toys, they try all sorts of sex and sexual positions, they'll sleep with as many people as possible or at least try to have sex as many times as possible. They even engage in orgies. To twist the famous tagline from *Saving Private Ryan*, the mission *is* the sex.

Dating, relationships, and getting to know someone on a deep level? Marriage with the hopes of raising a family together? For many, such concepts are dead.

So why *not* sex robots? Add into the mix that there won't be any disease, pregnancy, or any claims of sexual harassment or repercussions from a bad breakup, and you've got yourself a pretty damn good proposition there. Don't forget your robot won't get fatter, older, or uglier on you, either. And you can always upgrade.

And there's Ugly Joe or Lonely Brad, who can finally have his pretty girl. The playing field has suddenly leveled. He won't have to compete with that high school quarterback or millionaire entrepreneur. Everyone is a winner now, and everyone gets a trophy. The old adage was that 20 percent of the men were having sex with 80 percent of the women. Well, no longer! Everyone can get laid now.

And let's not forget Plain Jane. She wants to feel wanted; she wants intimacy. Many women will welcome male sex robots as a form of sexual exploration of themselves.[6] Already there are "cuddle professionals" who provide anonymous cuddle services—mostly for women. It's like being with a gigolo but without the sex.

Best of all, robots won't involve any hard work. And it'll all happen in the privacy of your home. Take her with you on vacation or rent one wherever you go. And nobody will ever have to feel the sting of rejection.

Can you hear the clicking of the pens now? They're the ones you're hearing just before they say: *Where do I sign?*

• • •

Where are we headed? Perhaps the answer lies in another question: Why do we yearn not only for sex but for relationships? Why do they both seem so hardwired in us?

Why? Nature could have just infused us with an animalistic sense of reproduction. Just make the males compete for the ladies, and let the ladies go into heat when they're ready, and you're good to go. It's a time-tested model that seems to work with every other species, after all. Why fix something that ain't broke? Why is it that we humans have to be so damn *different*?

But different we are, and so is our apparent programming. What will happen along the way when we ignore that programming? In our quest for orgasms without relationships, or for the "perfect" woman or man, we'll forget that every man and woman—flawed and aging as they may be—is made in the image of God. We won't see them as valuable because we won't see each other as potential partners with whom we can have intimacy on any level. We don't *need* each other. We can just satisfy ourselves.

Think I'm going too far? Then think about your teenagers who engage far more with their cell phones than with you. Which is more important to them? Think about how many times you would rather see an adventure or fantasy movie, play golf, or watch the game, than have a meaningful talk with someone.

Remember: relationships are hard work.

And they're dangerous. It should remind us of the riddle: How do porcupines make love? Very carefully.

Perhaps we should approach sex more like the porcupines. Like scientists who observed the stars and our solar system to figure out Earth's shape and its place in the solar system, we should be making observations. *And nature is screaming the answers to us.* Here it is: all of the faceless, consequence-free sex is not only meaningless; it violates our inherent need for oneness with somebody else.

We weren't meant for such things. And as if the "epidemic" of loneliness were not enough of a message, we face a "hurricane" of STDs compared to the numbers only a couple of decades ago. Yet we ignore nature's message. We do so at our peril—both on an individual and civilizational level.

• • •

Now, to the heart of the matter. In the beginning of this book, I promised you a big surprise. I intend to deliver.

Here it is: this book is *not* actually about sex robots or about virtual reality sex of any kind. Nor is it a warning about such things. It is also not a call, as does the Campaign Against Sex Robots, for their prohibition. It's not even a call to regulate or impose an oversight commission on robots in Washington, DC, or the European Union. In fact, that we can *make* robots should be of little concern. Robots are inevitable, just as guns, drugs, and bad music are inevitable. We have the capacity to split an atom and make nuclear bombs, too, but no reasonable person believes that we can dismantle all nuclear warheads and forever ban them henceforth. They are a fact. So will robots be.

This book is indeed a warning. But it's a warning about *us*. In fact, it's a book entirely *about* us. When we express concern about the rise of robots, we are in fact expressing concern about what's changed within our society, both on an individual and macro level. The robots themselves haven't done anything wrong. Like the antinatalists, they didn't ask to be "born" (and at least they haven't sued us yet).

This book has shown how we've taken the meaning out of sex, displacing it solely with the pursuit of opiate pleasure of the flesh. It's an illicit pleasure: we're not really earning it. We're just stealing it from the bank.

And that pleasure has become so big in proportion. It's crowded everything else out, like leprosy eventually crowds out healthy cells to the point the victim becomes unrecognizable.

If all we do is respond to whatever stimuli comes our way, from our hormones internally to sexual lures externally, then haven't we reduced *ourselves* to automatons—to sex machines? What's the difference? And if so, then why would you care if anyone else used sex machines? Why would you judge them?

Sometimes it feels like we're in the last scene of the original *Planet of the Apes*, where the main character, the astronaut George Taylor, finally stumbles upon the ruins of the Statue of Liberty and realizes he's been on Earth all along. He learns the humans had brought about their own end, thousands of years earlier.

The reality dawned upon Taylor—but upon Taylor *only*. It was a confrontation with reality that only he was privy to.

Neither the ruling apes nor the inferior human "animals" they kept as beasts of burden knew anything of their shared history.

Sex robots may be what sets us in motion toward our own demise. It's like we've decided to surrender ourselves to a new programming. But *this* program isn't very complicated; it involves only one thing.

We tell ourselves that we are no different than the animals, that it's OK to give in to our most base instincts, and that we should always go with what we feel. And when it comes to the sex, there is no discretion or judgment. Everything just is, and it's all good. There is no sense of anything being the better decision for civilization.

It is no different than the sex robot herself: she will have no sense of discretion, judgment, or concern for civilization's growth. And if she did, such attributes would only come about by mimicking such things artificially.

And don't count on that: discretion and judgment would defeat the very reason for the robots' existence in the first place. As our friend Brick Dollbanger asked, "Why in the world would anyone want that?"

And so, we might very well end ourselves. Someday decades from now, maybe someone like the astronaut Taylor will figure it out in a later childless, dystopian future. Maybe he, too, will angrily pound the sands of some beach and call us maniacs. Or something like that. Too bad we won't be there to benefit from his 20/20 hindsight.

But like I said: robots are not the real concern. Not even the creators of the robots are the concern. After all, they're merely responding to a huge new market, just meeting demand.

The concern boils down to one simple thing. We've taken the *humanity* out of sex, not realizing that its central purpose was creation and bonding; not realizing that sex was an exercise of free will.

So from all this, we come to one simple conclusion: *We* have become the robots. *We* are the sex machines we fear.

Ironically, these robots may do one thing for us. In the end, we will know that the virtualization of sex is a meaningless voyage, whether through stories, pornography, sexting, or sex robots. We will ultimately have to compare them to the exquisite beauty of what relationships and sex truly mean, and how they were essential for the growth of our civilization. They will serve, oddly enough, as a foil to reveal how and why the restraining of sex and sexuality has been a part of the fabric of our civilization.

Sex and sexuality are essential to advance civilization, of course (after all, no sex means no future generations), but, taken out of their proper role, they serve only to distract from the work of building civilization. All work and little play may make Jack a dull boy, but all sex and little work makes civilization collapse. You choose.

The problem is, as it was for Hansel and Gretel after the witch had lured them into her house with promises of candy, we may be realizing all this too late. Our godless world of insta-sex and orgasms-to-go will decimate our population and undermine civilization's core sense of purpose. It already has begun, even *without* actual robots. After all, we've been playing the part all this time.

But there is good news. There will be those who will not suffer this fate, those who will not only survive but thrive. They will sidestep all of this madness.

Who are these people? The followers of God among us. They understand what sex has always been actually for: to do God's work, to heal the world and help bring about joy and goodness, to perfect civilization. And to participate in Creation.

Nothing else makes sense. Nothing else but the return to the centrality of God will. Nothing else will bring the humanity and purpose back into sex.

The popular saying goes, *I have seen the enemy, and he is us.* Sex robots are not the enemy. They did not scheme up some diabolical plan over many years to hurt us. They did not invade us. *We* created them. Sex robots merely reveal what we want, how we see ourselves, and what matters most to us.

You see, the truth is, there is no rise of any sex machines.

We have seen the machines. And they are us.

THE END

Acknowledgments

Thanks goes foremost to my good friend and manager Chet Thompson from CT3Media. He made sure I was always on task, and that I took care of important milestones in the publishing of this book. There are many, many such tasks, and it is not easy. He had not started out as a "believer" in what I was warning, but over a weekend where he engaged in a marathon session reading it, he became one indeed.

My friends Ari David and Fini Goodman also spent many hours with me listening to numerous chapters of this book, and who gave exceptional insight into other topics of discussion in the areas of romance and relationships. I cannot thank them enough for their patience and engagement in this process. They were instrumental to the completion and success of this book.

Many thanks to my good friend and author, Robert Hamilton, M.D., a Santa Monica-based pediatrician with a remarkable insight into the blessings of children. His thoughts and comments figured largely throughout the book, especially in the chapter "Fertile Lives Don't Matter."

My brother Rod Lurie again encouraged me as he had with my previous book, *Atheism Kills*. He, too, came to appreciate my warnings of our challenging future—but a future of which we may yet be able to steer clear. David Knight, David Gabor, and my wife, Stacey Lurie, all were kind enough to weigh in on many aspects of the book. I thank them all.

Dennis Prager, Ben Shapiro, Larry Elder, Robert Stearns, Marissa Streit, Ben Lizardi all also showed wonderful support for this book. The topic is a difficult one, even salacious and controversial, but they each saw the daunting reality of the problem. Dennis Prager in particular saw the value of this book immediately when I mentioned I was working on it, and he asked me right away to speak as his guest on his renowned Male-Female hour. I am honored to do so.

Thanks to my parents and to my children—with whom it was a challenge to discuss even the topic of this book. They are the generations of the past and the future, respectively, and they still seemed to understand that the Relationship—not just the Pleasure—is what allows us all to move forward as a civilization. They each supported and even urged me to proceed.

Also, a special thanks to Rabbi Brandon Gaines and Dr. Drorit Gaines, PhD, for their tireless assistance in providing me understanding of the views of the great sages regarding the formation of relationships, and the intense meaning of intimacy. As always, their insights and contributions are priceless. I only wish I could return similar insight and wisdom as they have given me.

Thank you finally to the listeners of my radio show, the Barak Lurie Show, in Los Angeles, California at KRLA AM870. They have chimed in regularly in support of my work, constantly showing up at my speeches and writing correspondence in support.

No man is an island. All great works include input not just from friends, colleagues and family, but from great minds which have preceded them. The author must constantly reach out to his world, and the world before him, if he is to deliver a book that delivers true meaning. This book is no exception, and that is what I have sought to do in writing this book. I am no island.

In a way, this book is all about exactly this. It is the importance of the multitude of relationships beyond our own selves: with friends and family and above all with God and with our spouses. We not only crave these relationships, but we wither into loneliness and despair without them. We know that life is meaningless without them.

And yet somehow, wittingly or not, our civilization is racing to a relationship-free future.

May God help us all.

Endnotes

Chapter 1

1. Tabi Jackson Gee, "Why female sex robots are more dangerous than you think," https://www.telegraph.co.uk/women/life/female-robots-why-this-scarlett-johansson-bot-is-more-dangerous/, July 5, 2017.

2. Gavin Fernando, "How AI sex robots could 'change humanity completely,'" https://www.news.com.au/technology/innovation/inventions/how-ai-sex-robots-could-change-humanity-completely/news-story/4824a52c3c8907351bdf1ea5b49ac3d9, April 15, 2018.

3. Natalie Corner, "She's More than Just a Sex Toy," https://www.dailymail.co.uk/femail/article-5110439/Meet-man-robot-girlfriend-WIFE.html, November 23, 2017.

4. Joshua Nevett, "Sex Robots are Turning the Japanese Into an Endangered Species," https://www.technocracy.news/sex-robots-are-turning-japanese-into-an-endangered-species/, July 25, 2018.

5. Ibid.

6. Lauren Hill-Roger, "DOLL-Y BIRD 'Sex dolls are way better than real women—they don't care what I do to them': Three men reveal why they REALLY use sex robots," https://www.thesun.co.uk/news/7962025/sex-dolls-better-than-real-women/, January 8, 2019.

7. Ibid.

8. Jasper Hamill, "CAERPHILLY DOES IT: Samantha the Sex Robot could be 'mass produced' in WALES, creators claim," https://www.thesun.co.uk/tech/4851058/samantha-the-sex-robot-could-be-mass-produced-in-wales-creators-claim/, November 6, 2017 (supply can't keep up with demand); Andrea Barrica, "How Women Made Sextech The Next Great Frontier For Growth," https://www.forbes.com/sites/andreabarrica/2018/11/01/how-women-made-sextech-the-next-great-frontier-for-growth/#225d5cc7531d, November 1, 2018 ($30-billion market and growing).

9. Ibid.

10. "Sexbots: Love Them or Hate Them—They are Coming," https://www.richardvanhooijdonk.com/en/blog/sexbots-love-them-or-hate-them-they-are-coming/, June 30, 2016.

11. https://en.wikipedia.org/wiki/Virtual_reality_sex

12. Brian Heater, "The Lonely Death of Jibo, the Social Robot," https://abc news.go.com/amp/Technology/wireStory/wary-robot-emotions-simulated -love-love-62647032, February, 2019.

13. Ibid.

14. Ibid.

15. Andrea Morris, "Meet the Man Who Test Drives Sex Robots," https://www.forbes.com/sites/andreamorris/2018/09/27/meet-the-man-who-test-drives-sex-robots/#31aa3f27452d, September 27, 2018.

16. Ibid.

17. Ibid.

18. "Sex robots: Chinese firm sees boom in their artificial intelligent products," https://www.perthnow.com.au/news/offbeat/sex-robots-chinese-firm-sees-boom-in-their-artificial-intelligent-products-ng-b88847574z, May 25, 2018; "Sexbots: Love them or Hate Them—They are Coming," https://www.richardvanhooijdonk.com/en/blog/sexbots-love-them-or-hate-them-they-are-coming/, June 30, 2016.

19. See population stats by age group, generally as found in Richard Fry, "Millennials approach Baby Boomers as America's largest generation in the electorate," https://www.pewresearch.org/fact-tank/2018/04/03/millennials -approach-baby-boomers-as-largest-generation-in-u-s-electorate/, April 3, 2018. I calculate the 8.5 percent figure by combining the millennials (those aged 20–35 in 2016) with the "Generation X" group (those aged 36–51 in 2016). Then dividing 10 million by that sum.

20. Most popular online dating apps in the United States as of December 2017, by audience size (in millions), https://www.statista.com/statistics/826778/most-popular-dating-apps-by-audience-size-usa/.

21. Gwendolyn Seidman, PhD, "Is Tinder Really a Hookup App?" https://www.psychologytoday.com/us/blog/close-encounters/201706/is-tinder-really-hookup-app, June 11, 2017.

22. For a good discussion of the history of iTunes's capture of the digital music industry, see Rosa Golijan, "iTunes turns 10: How Apple music store killed old music industry," https://www.nbcnews.com/technolog/itunes-turns-10-how-apple-music-store-killed-old-music-6C9633923, April 28, 2013.

23. Gearlog, "LimeWire, Napster, The Pirate Bay: A Brief History of File Sharing," https://www.geek.com/gadgets/limewire-napster-the-pirate-bay-a-brief-history-of-file-sharing-1359473/, October 27, 2010.

24. Mike Lockley, "Sex doll rental service launched by mum-of-four who expects business to 'explode,'" https://www.mirror.co.uk/news/uk-news/sex-doll-rental-service-launched-13424028, October 16, 2018.

25. Ian Morris, "Sex Robot Virginity for Sale at Creepy New Brothel—But It Isn't Cheap," https://www.mirror.co.uk/tech/sex-robot-virginity-sale-creepy-13554426, November 8, 2018.

26. Harvey Day, "Scanned Lovers Reveal Outrageous Things They've Done To Get Revenge on Their Former Partners," https://www.dailymail.co.uk/femail/article-4037686/Scorned-lovers-reveal-OUTRAGEOUS-things-ve-revenge-partners.html, December 16, 2016.

27. Associated Press, "Diaper-Wearing Astronaut Jailed In Love Triangle Plot," https://www.denverpost.com/2007/02/05/diaper-wearing-astronaut-jailed-in-love-triangle-plot/, February 5, 2007.

28. Day, *op. cit.*

29. Lili Anolik, "Lorena Bobbitt's American Dream," https://www.vanityfair.com/style/2018/06/lorena-bobbitt-john-wayne-bobbitt-25-years, August, 2018.

30. Mona Charen, "Lorena Bobbitt, America's Feminist Pin-Up," https://www.baltimoresun.com/news/bs-xpm-1993-11-15-1993319151-story.html, November 15, 1993. As this article revealed, Lorena Bobbitt was far from her self-portrayal as domestic abuse victim. Jurists noted key inconsistencies; for example, she told the police on the night of the attack that she had mutilated her husband in a fit of passion because "he always has an orgasm, and he doesn't wait for me. . . . I don't think it's fair, so I pulled back the sheets, and I did it."

31. David Jesse, "Students accused of sexual assault must be allowed to cross-examine accusers, courts say," https://www.usatoday.com/story/news/2018/08/27/sexual-assault-investigation-college-date-rape/1110559002/, August 27, 2018.

32. Callum Adams, "Millennials are turned off sex, study suggests, with one in eight still virgins at 26," https://www.telegraph.co.uk/news/2018/05/06/millennials-turned-sex-study-suggests-one-eight-still-virgins/, May 6, 2018. See also, Janet Burns, "Millennials Are Having Less Sex Than Other Gens, But Experts Say It's (Probably) Fine," https://www.forbes.com/sites/janetwburns/2016/08/16/millennials-are-having-less-sex-than-other-gens-but-experts-say-its-probably-fine/#4f51bf38d958, August 16, 2016. The latter suggests that the online dating sites put too much pressure on physical appearance, and that there is too much discussion about the dangers of sex, instead of the pleasures of it.

33. Kate Julian, "Why Are Young People Having So Little Sex?" https://www.theatlantic.com/magazine/archive/2018/12/the-sex-recession/573949/, December, 2016.

34. "Porn Sites Get More Visitors Each Month Than Netflix, Amazon And Twitter Combined," https://www.huffingtonpost.com/2013/05/03/internet-porn-stats_n_3187682.html, December 6, 2017.

35. Louis Michael, "Hypermasculinity Is A Plague On The Modern Man," https://www.huffingtonpost.co.uk/louis-michael/hyper-masculinity-man_b_13280034.html, November 29, 2017.

36. See generally, Dr. Jonathan Fielding, "Loneliness is an Emerging Public Health Threat," https://thehill.com/opinion/healthcare/410500-loneliness-is-an-emerging-public-health-threat, October 9, 2018.

37. Shannon Lell, "We All Want Good Sex. It's Time for Men to Do Their Part," https://www.washingtonpost.com/news/soloish/wp/2018/02/14/we-all-want-good-sex-its-time-for-men-to-do-their-part/?noredirect=on&utm_term=.8f68f1a77c2b, February 14, 2018. Reader beware: the article has little to do with the title.

38. Ibid.

39. Laura Entis, "Chronic Loneliness is a Modern-Day Epidemic," http://fortune.com/2016/06/22/loneliness-is-a-modern-day-epidemic/, June 22, 2016. The author of this article notes that there could be mathematical reasons it's lower in longitudinal studies (26 percent) than in the referenced cross-sectional studies (about 43 percent).

Chapter 2

1. https://en.wikipedia.org/wiki/Feminism#cite_ref-Beasley_2-0.

2. This is the view of Simone de Beauvoir in her classic *The Second Sex*. She believed that women needed to identify themselves as a group and declare war on men. Women could only gain rights by destroying male superiority and by refusing to succumb to traditions such as marriage. She maintained that "all forms of socialism, wresting woman away from the family, favour her liberation." She also wanted the state to assume responsibility for the maternal functions that burdened women. See generally, Jules Gomes, "How Feminist 'Dambusters' Destroyed the Church of England Beyond Repair," http://anglican.ink/article/how-feminist-"-"dambusters"-destroyed-church-england-beyond-repair, July 25, 2018.

3. Ibid.

4. Pamela Paul, "Are Fathers Necessary?" https://www.theatlantic.com/magazine/archive/2010/07/are-fathers-necessary/308136/, July/August 2010 issue.

5. Jayson Maclean, "Why Are Men Always Idiots in TV Ads?," https://www.cantechletter.com/2017/07/men-always-idiots-tv-ads/, July 20, 2017.

6. *The Incredibles*, quotes; https://www.imdb.com/title/tt0317705/quotes/qt0361943.

7. Danielle Paquette, "The stark difference between millennial men and their dads," https://www.washingtonpost.com/news/wonk/wp/2016/05/26/the-stark-difference-between-millennial-men-and-their-dads/?noredirect=on&utm_term=.2775b78db926, May 26, 2016.

8. See, e.g., Jules Schroder, "7 Reasons Why Millennial Men Are Reinventing Masculinity," https://www.forbes.com/sites/julesschroeder/2017/10/12/the-evolved-man-7-reasons-why-millennial-men-are-reinventing-masculinity/#6ca59865597c, October 12, 2017 (men are "evolving" positively with feminist attributes); Noah Berlatsky, "This Father's Day, Men Are Experiencing a Crisis

in Masculinity. The Solution? More Feminism," https://www.nbcnews.com/think/opinion/father-s-day-men-are-experiencing-crisis-masculinity-solution-more-ncna884051, June 17, 2018 (blaming "toxic" masculinity); Noah Henry, "10 Theories Why Men Have Become Less Manly," https://www.mandatory.com/living/1064340-10-theories-why-men-have-become-less-manly, January 12, 2016 (partly blaming use of a now ever-present chemical, xenoestrogen); Kate Kelland, "Sperm Count Dropping in Western World," https://www.scientificamerican.com/article/sperm-count-dropping-in-western-world/, July 26, 2017 (noting alarming drop in sperm count in the past forty years. Although a study suggested that the *more* "masculine" a man was, the lower his sperm count will likely be: see Christine Dell'Amore, "Deep-Voiced Men Have Lower Sperm Counts, Study Says," https://news.nationalgeographic.com/news/2012/01/120105-deep-voices-sperm-masculine-men-women-science-health-evolution/, January 5, 2012); Paquette, *op. cit.* (suggesting overbearing masculine standards are pushing men away from masculinity).

9. Jarune Uwujaren, "How Women Are Pressured into Being Sexy, But Punished for Being Sexual," https://everydayfeminism.com/2015/01/women-pressured-sexy-punished-sexual/, January 12, 2015. This article describes the whiplash nature of what is expected of women sexually and the price they pay for doing exactly what society expects. The only thing missing in this otherwise excellent article is the *why* it is happening at all. This chapter goes to the heart of that issue.

10. Jené Gutierrez, "The Feminist Argument for Sexting," https://medium.com/the-establishment/the-transformative-power-of-sexting-d35ce9a377fc, October 18, 2016.

11. In some cases, yoga pants are advertised (perhaps more honestly) as "Show Me Your Clit Women's Leggings." See, for example, https://www.lookhuman.com/search/show+me+your+clit+legging?product_type=legging. Notice the "show me" aspect of this.

12. Henry G. Brinton, "False Idols Come in Many Guises," https://www.usatoday.com/story/opinion/2014/09/01/false-idols-come-in-many-guises-column/14750291/, September 1, 2014. It is also fascinating to note how few mainstream websites and periodicals discuss this issue of the uber-glorification of sex. It is as if these outlets agree that sex is paramount and should indeed become our idol.

13. Ibid.

14. Glosswitch, "Chivalry Has Nothing to Do With Respect and Everything to Do With Manipulation," https://www.newstatesman.com/lifestyle/2012/12/chivalry-has-nothing-do-respect-and-everything-do-manipulation, December 14, 2012.

15. Amy S. Kaufman, "Chivalry Isn't Dead. But It Should Be," https://www.washingtonpost.com/outlook/2018/10/08/chivalry-isnt-dead-it-should-be/?utm_term=.f0c5da7002d4, October 7, 2018.

16. Total forcible reported rapes of women in 1960: 17,190, with the total population being 179,323,175. The ratio to the total population would be

.0000958. By contrast, total forcible reported rapes of women in 2017: 135,755, with the total population being 325,719,178. The ratio to the total population would be .000416. That reflects a growth multiple of 4.3423, and a percentage increase of 335 percent during only fifty-seven years. See United States Crime Rates, 1960–2017, http://www.disastercenter.com/crime/uscrime.htm.

Naturally, many factors can account for this, and it is hard to pinpoint any particular trend alone that created this growth in violent crime. Factors such as increased immigration from different cultures (which may have less contempt of and less enforcement against rape), different definitions of "rape," and perhaps the greater confidence women now have in reporting rapes, no doubt play a role. Still, even accounting for all such factors, the rate of rape has grown to staggering proportions. It is also hard to argue that there is no role caused by the rejection of male appreciation of females (what we've loosely called "modern chivalry" as a means of curbing male sexual lust and violence upon women). It is strange indeed that this factor (the end of chivalry norms), which I believe is a far greater factor in destroying the gateway between lust and action on that lust, is almost never factored in as a contributing cause.

There may, at first blush, seem to be pockets of improvement in these numbers. For example, in 2017, the nationwide rate was 30.7 rapes per 100,000 of the population, down from approximately 41 rapes per 100,000 in 1990. See, for example, https://www.statista.com/statistics/191226/reported-forcible-rape-rate-in-the-us-since-1990/. But this may also be on account of greater enforcement against such crimes, especially in New York City during the latter part of the 1990s through 2014. Likewise, it may also be on account of the increase in the average age of Americans, which has shot up approximately ten years (from 28.1 to 38) from 1970 to 2017 alone. See https://www.statista.com/statistics/241494/median-age-of-the-us-population/. Naturally, an older population tends to commit less crime, especially less violent crime.

17. Jon Marcus, "Why Men Are the New College Minority," https://www.theatlantic.com/education/archive/2017/08/why-men-are-the-new-college-minority/536103/, August 8, 2017; Martin Beckford, "More Women than Men in 'High Status Professions, Study Finds," https://www.telegraph.co.uk/news/uknews/6005222/More-British-women-in-high-status-professions-than-men-finds-study.html, August 11, 2009; "Chart: The Percentage of Women and Men in Each Profession," https://www.bostonglobe.com/metro/2017/03/06/chart-the-percentage-women-and-men-each-profession/GBX22YsWl0XaeHgh wXfE4H/story.html, March 6, 2018.

18. "Sexbots: Love them or Hate Them—They are Coming," https://www.richardvanhooijdonk.com/en/blog/sexbots-love-them-or-hate-them-they-are-coming/, June 30, 2016.

19. Ibid.

20. https://en.wikipedia.org/wiki/Feminist_views_on_pornography

Chapter 3

1. "Best Tinder Hookup Stories," https://www.askmen.com/recess/fun_lists/best-tinder-hookup-stories.html, April 11, 2016. See also, Christian Bonnington, "32 Awesome Apps for One-Night Stands," https://www.refinery29.com/en-us/best-apps-for-one-night-stands#slide-2, November 2, 2018.

2. Interview by Anna Moore, "How Tinder Took Me From Serial Monogamy to Casual Sex," https://www.theguardian.com/lifeandstyle/2014/sep/28/tinder-serial-monogamy-casual-sex, 2014.

3. Jake Kivanc, "College Students Tell Us What Their Dorm Sex Lives Are Like," https://www.vice.com/en_us/article/8ge994/students-tell-us-about-their-dorm-sex-lives, May 24, 2016.

4. "University Sex Club Holds Student Orgy," https://www.youtube.com/watch?v=q1Jg1HN1f9U, video first published January 19, 2013. The two hosts, one male and one female, speak approvingly of the university's openness and sexual liberation, while at the same time mocking how such a thing would get immediately lambasted if it occurred in an American college.

5. Kivanc, *op. cit.*

6. Danielle Page, "Rules for Casual Sex," https://www.askmen.com/sex/casual-sex.html.

7. The Blog, "5 Reasons Why More Women Should Make The First Move," https://www.huffingtonpost.ca/bellesa/5-reasons-why-more-women-should-make-the-first-move_a_23348011/ , January 31,2018. The article emphasizes how modern technology (smartphones in particular) have made it ever so easy for women to make the first move. It cites scientist Helen Fisher, author of *Anatomy of Love: A Natural History of Mating, Marriage and Why We Stray*, who looked at online dating data, including statistics from over 25,000 single people. As she writes: "They clearly illustrate that women of every age, ethnicity and background initiate most pickups and, in truth, women have become blatant." She also noted that in 2012, 65 percent of more than 5,000 men she surveyed had reported a woman had asked them out.

Chapter 4

1. Stephen Marche, "The Unexamined Brutality of the Male Libido," https://www.nytimes.com/2017/11/25/opinion/sunday/harassment-men-libido-masculinity.html?_r=0, November 25, 2017.

Chapter 5

1. https://metro.co.uk/2018/05/06/where-have-all-the-rom-coms-gone-the-genre-has-seen-a-significant-decline-in-the-last-two-decades-but-why-7521357/?ito=cbshare

2. Jason Guerassio, "The Big Hollywood Romantic Comedy Is Dead—Here's What Happened to It," https://www.businessinsider.com/why-movie-studios-no-longer-make-romantic-comedies-2017-8, August 8, 2017.

3. Ibid.

4. Ibid.

5. Many women and men are pursuing different kinds of sex, particularly anal. Sixteen percent of women reported engaging in it in 1992, but it has increased to 40 percent as of the second decade of the twenty-first century. Why is this happening? Perhaps because people erroneously perceive that they cannot contract diseases through anal sex. Another reason is that, while they want to enjoy sex and are more "empowered" to do so, anal sex is a mechanism to do so without the risk of getting pregnant. See generally, Jeremy E. Uecker, Nicole Angotti, and Mark D. Regnerus, "Going Most of the Way: 'Technical Virginity' among American Adolescents," https://www .ncbi.nlm.nih.gov/pmc/articles/PMC3153128/, December 1, 2008; and Taffy Brodesser-Akner, "Is Everybody Having Anal Without Me?" https://www .cosmopolitan.com/sex-love/news/a36431/everyone-having-anal-without -me/, March 3, 2015. Or more likely, it is the explosion in sexual activity generally. The more sex one has, the more likely it is that he or she will try additional forms of sex, including anal sex.

6. Ibid.

7. Jason M. Breslow, "What Does Solitary Confinement Do To Your Mind," https://www.pbs.org/wgbh/frontline/article/what-does-solitary-confinement-do-to-your-mind/, April 22, 2014. See also, Terry A. Kupers, "The Harm of Solitary Confinement," https://www.psychologytoday.com/ us/blog/prisons-and-prisms/201707/the-harm-solitary-confinement, July 12, 2017. See also, Brandon Keim, "The Horrible Psychology of Solitary Confinement," https://www.wired.com/2013/07/solitary-confinement-2/, July 10, 2014. It is challenging to find virtually any articles discussing the "why" of the dangers of solitary confinement; there appears to be mostly stories about "what is" and how bad it is.

8. Ibid.

9. Ibid.

10. Aaron Ben-Zeév PhD, https://www.psychologytoday.com/us/blog/ in-the-name-love/201403/why-we-all-need-belong-someone, March 11, 2014, citing R. F. Baumeister and M. R. Leary (1995), "The need to belong: Desire for interpersonal attachments as a fundamental human motivation," *Psychological Bulletin* 117, 497–529; N. Kambert, T. F. Stillman, J. A. Hicks, S. Kamble, R. F. Baumeister, and F. D. Fincham (2013), "Belong is to matter: Sense of belonging enhances meaning in life," *Personality and Social Psychology Bulletin* 39, 1,418–1,427; A. Krebs (2014), *Zwischen Ich und Du. Eine Dialogische Philosophie der Liebe* (Frankfurt: Suhrkamp); and I. L. Reiss (1986), "A sociological journey into sexuality," *Journal of Marriage and the Family*, 48, 233–42.

11. Ibid.

12. Shimona Tzukernik, "Transformation through Intimacy," https:// www.chabad.org/theJewishWoman/article_cdo/aid/1195247/jewish/ Transformation-Through-Intimacy.htm.

13. Steven J. Cole, "Lesson 21: Healthy Relationships (Colossians 3:12–13)," https://bible.org/seriespage/lesson-21-healthy-relationships-colossians-312-13, April 17, 2016.

Chapter 6

1. Tom Stafford, "How Often Do Men Think About Sex?" http://www.bbc.com/future/story/20140617-how-often-do-men-think-about-sex, June 18, 2014. See also, Brian Mustanski, PhD, "How Often Do Men and Women Think Abut Sex?" https://www.psychologytoday.com/us/blog/the-sexual-continuum/201112/how-often-do-men-and-women-think-about-sex, December 6, 2011, which reported similar findings. The report goes on to state that statistical tests indicated that the number of men's thoughts about sex was not statistically greater than the number of their thoughts about food and sleep. Men had more thoughts about all three of those areas than did women.

But there is a difference, I believe: A man will think about food because he is hungry throughout the day. Generally people have three meals a day, so it is not surprising that such a man would think about food while hungry and then think about food while he's eating the food. Likewise, he will think about sleep if he's tired throughout the day (which man people are; I take naps myself), and of course later at night.

By contrast, the thoughts about sex are not based on the imminence of our having sex three times or more a day. They seem to be thoughts that remind us to go seek out sexual activity, regardless of the time of day, or needs of the body for nourishment or sleep.

2. Brian Alexander, "Free Love: Was There a Price to Pay?" http://www.nbcnews.com/id/19053382/ns/health-sexual_health/t/free-love-was-there-price-pay/#.XBg2ERNKjOQ, June 22, 2007.

3. Ibid. The article also points out how although hippies tended to look down on money, women sometimes served as a replacement currency. "Women were used as an inducement to get new members into a commune or crash pad. If you joined, you got to have sex with the girls."

4. By Laura Schwecherl, "Why Monogamy Might Be Good for Your Health," https://www.everydayhealth.com/sexual-health/why-monogamy-might-be-good-for-your-health.aspx.

5. Ibid.

6. Mark Hyman, MD, "How Malnutrition Causes Obesity," https://drhyman.com/blog/2012/02/29/how-malnutrition-causes-obesity/, undated.

Chapter 7

1. Lukas Mikelionis, "Use Wrong Pronoun for Transgender Senior? California May Punish You," https://www.foxnews.com/us/use-wrong-pronoun-for-transgender-senior-california-may-punish-you, September 25,

2017; Joe Tacopino, "Not Using Transgender Pronouns Could Get You Fined," https://nypost.com/2016/05/19/city-issues-new-guidelines-on-transgender-pronouns/, May 19, 2016. (Employers and landlords who intentionally and consistently ignore using pronouns such as "ze/hir" to refer to transgender workers and tenants who request them—may be subject to fines as high as $250,000.)

2. Steve Smith, "Gender Reassignment Surgery Is Now Available To Oregon Minors Without Parental Consent," https://www.medicaldaily.com/gender-reassignment-surgery-now-available-oregon-minors-without-parental-consent-342670, July 13, 2015.

3. Ibid.

4. James Doubek, "Colorado Baker Sues State, After Refusing To Make Cake For Transgender Woman," https://www.npr.org/2018/08/16/639147599/colorado-baker-sues-state-again-after-refusing-to-make-cake-for-transgender-woman, August 16, 2018.

5. Jan Hoffman, "Estimate of U.S. Transgender Population Doubles to 1.4 Million Adults," https://www.nytimes.com/2016/07/01/health/transgender-population.html, June 30, 2016.

6. "Living with Colour Vision Deficiency," http://www.colourblindawareness.org/colour-blindness/living-with-colour-vision-deficiency/, dated only 2018.

7. Paris Lees, "Fears around gender-neutral toilets are all in the mind," https://www.theguardian.com/commentisfree/2016/dec/02/fears-gender-neutral-toilets-women-trans-people-violence, December 2, 2016. This article claims that there is "no evidence" of women having problems in the bathroom with transgenders, while at the same time presenting dubious, if any, evidence that transgenders suffer victimization in the bathroom. The article cites to the horrible beating of a white transgender woman at McDonald's in Maryland, by two black women. From this anecdote the article intuits a wild slew of violence against transgenders in and out of the bathroom. Also, the assumption is that the transgender is attacked because of her being transgender. Why so? There is no discussion of the possibility, for example, that she was being beaten because of her being white. Or maybe the transgender said something racial or snarky to the black girls, or otherwise did something to cause them to explode on the transgender. Nothing is known about what happened to actually start the attack.

Also, the study points to the murder of less than three hundred transgenders during that year, *worldwide*, suggesting this is an astoundingly high number that should shock the conscience. But for comparison purposes, substantially more than this number of people are murdered—570, mostly black—in the city of Chicago alone in the year 2018 (and that was significantly down from the two years prior), https://www.chicagotribune.com/news/local/breaking/ct-chicago-homicides-data-tracker-htmlstory.html.

An additional problem here is the assumption that each of these approximately three hundred murdered transgenders were killed *because of their being transgendered.* The article presents zero evidence to back this up. Jews are murdered every year but not all because they are Jewish. Blacks are murdered but not just because they're black. And so on. The liberties this article takes (and others like it) to advance their point is palpable.

See also, Nico Lang, "New Study: Rates of Anti-LGBTQ School Bullying at 'Unprecedented High,'" https://www.thedailybeast.com/new-study-rates-of-anti-lgbtq-school-bullying-at-unprecedented-high, June 4, 2017. The problem with this seemingly agenda-driven article is that it makes no sense that antitransgender violence would actually increase (nor does the article attempt to explain why it supposedly has). Second, the article makes no reference to violence against transgenders *in the bathroom or locker room,* let alone explain why allowing them access to the opposite sex's bathroom would make any improvement in their safety. The article merely talks about reports of greater feelings of insecurity and assaults, generally. There are literally no statistics, and very little appears elsewhere on the web in the way of police reports or school administrative actions to address violence against transgenders. No doubt such incidences do exist, but they do not seem to rise to the statistically meaningful proportions—let alone "unprecedented" and *rising* levels, as the article implies.

8. Aleta Baldwin, "What Each of Facebook's 51 New Gender Options Means," https://www.thedailybeast.com/what-each-of-facebooks-51-new-gender-options-means, February 15, 2014.

9. Author unknown, "Facebook's 71 gender options come to UK users," https://www.telegraph.co.uk/technology/facebook/10930654/Facebooks-71-gender-options-come-to-UK-users.html, January 2, 2019.

10. Lane Brown, "Gender neutrality: Why teachers won't ask boys and girls to line up in Lincoln, Neb.," https://www.csmonitor.com/The-Culture/Family/Modern-Parenthood/2014/1009/Gender-neutrality-Why-teachers-won-t-ask-boys-and-girls-to-line-up-in-Lincoln-Neb, October 9, 2014.

See also, Jon Brooks, "Boy? Girl? Both? Neither? A New Generation Overthrows Gender," https://www.kqed.org/futureofyou/335790/boy-girl-both-neither-a-new-generation-overthrows-gender, April 24, 2017, describing the 2015 California Healthy Youth Act, requiring comprehensive sex education for grades 7–12 to "teach pupils about gender, gender expression, gender identity, and explore the harm of negative gender stereotypes." A checklist from the California County of Superintendents, designed for school systems to evaluate their compliance with the law, includes this definition of gender identity: "One's internal, deeply-held sense of being male, female, *neither of these, both, or other gender(s).* All people have a gender identity," (emphasis added in website).

11. Ibid. See also, Melinda Mangin, "Supporting Transgender and Gender-Expansive Children in School," https://www.kappanonline.org/mangin-transgender-gender-identity-school-policies-gender-expansive/, September 24, 2018.

12. See Carolyn Pope Edwards, Lisa Knoche, Asiye Kumru, "Play Patterns and Gender," *Encyclopedia of Women and Gender*, the University of Nebraska-Lincoln (2001), 809–11. While the authors here seem to recognize the identification, they attribute it to having shared interests and activities (among the boys), while girls "tend to think about interests also, but in addition, consciously make their friendship selections considering liked and disliked personality characteristics." According to the authors, much of the so-called identification is merely a function of socialization from adults and peer expectations within the same gender.

13. Chris Dyer, "Furious transgender woman rages at store clerk after he calls her 'sir' instead of 'ma'am,'" https://www.dailymail.co.uk/news/article-6536045/Furious-transgender-woman-rages-store-clerk-calls-sir-instead-maam.html, December 28, 2018.

14. Walter Heyer, "Mom Dresses Six-Year-Old Son As Girl, Threatens Dad With Losing His Son For Disagreeing," http://thefederalist.com/2018/11/26/mom-dresses-six-year-old-son-girl-threatens-dad-losing-son-disagreeing/, November 26, 2018.

15. Kelly Wallace, "How to Teach Children about Gender Equality," https://www.cnn.com/2017/09/26/health/gender-equality-teaching-children-parenting/index.html, October 2, 2017,

16. "Gaslighting," https://en.wikipedia.org/wiki/Gaslighting.

17. See, Denise Grady, "Anatomy Does Not Determine Gender, Experts Say," https://www.nytimes.com/2018/10/22/health/transgender-trump-biology.html, October 22, 2018. Oddly, this very article then seems to contradict itself by recounting how, in the 50s and 60s, doctors encouraged parents of boys born with defects in their penises to simply castrate them, build them vaginas instead, and raise them as girls. Their identity would follow, the doctors reasoned. But "[t]he idea was a failure. As they matured, many had a clear sense that they were [actually] male. According to a study of sixteen of them, more than half wound up identifying as male." Oops.

18. "The PBHS Closet," http://thepbhscloset.weebly.com/a-list-of-genders-sexualities-and-their-definitions.html, undated.

19. Neil Munro, "Democrats: 'Cruel and Unscientific' to Define Legal Sex by Biology," https://www.breitbart.com/the-media/2018/11/11/democrats-cruel-and-unscientific-to-define-legal-sex-by-biology/, November 11, 2018.

Chapter 8

1. Caroline Crosson Gilpin and Natalie Proulx, "Boys to Men: Teaching and Learning About Masculinity in an Age of Change," https://www.nytimes.com/2018/04/12/learning/lesson-plans/boys-to-men-teaching-and-learning-about-masculinity-in-an-age-of-change.html, April 12, 2018.

2. Ibid.

3. Ibid.

4. Justin Baldoni, "Why I'm Done Trying to Be "Man Enough," https://www.ted.com/talks/justin_baldoni_why_i_m_done_trying_to_be_man_enough/transcript?language=en, November, 2017.

5. Ibid.

6. Jaclyn Friedman, "Building better men: how we can begin to redefine masculinity,"
https://www.theguardian.com/world/2018/mar/12/masculinity-gender-men-sexual-assault-rape, March 12, 2018.

7. Toni Airaksinen, University of Texas to Treat Masculinity as a 'Mental Health Issue,'" https://pjmedia.com/trending/university-of-texas-to-treat-masculinity-as-a-mental-health-issue/, April 27, 2018.

8. Ibid.

9. Ibid.

10. Ibid.

11. Ben Renner, "Millennial Men Ditching Traditional 'Masculine' Values, More Likely To Embrace 'Emotional Strength,'" https://www.studyfinds.org/millennial-men-ditching-masculine-values-embracing-altruism/, December 1, 2018.

12. Toni Airaksinen, "UC Administrators: Masculinity is Not Attached to a Gender," https://pjmedia.com/trending/uc-administrators-masculinity-is-not-attached-to-a-gender/, November 16, 2018.

13. Ibid.

14. Ibid.

15. Ibid.

Chapter 9

1. Deanna Lorraine, video, "Modern-Day Feminism is Killing Romance," https://www.msn.com/en-us/lifestyle/lifestyle-buzz/relationship-coach-modern-day-feminism-is-killing-romance/vp-BBRIMor, January 2, 2019.

2. Touriq Mousa, "Why You Should (and Shouldn't) be Monogamous," https://bigthink.com/against-the-new-taboo/why-you-shouldnt-and-should-be-monogamous, May 13, 2103. It's like the author has been on the planet for only half an hour. He decries jealousy as irrational, and that everything should be about logic when it comes to sex.

3. Samantha Cooney, "What Monogamous Couples Can Learn from Polyamourous Relationships, According to Experts," http://time.com/5330833/polyamory-monogamous-relationships/, August 27, 2018.

Chapter 10

1. "Belle Knox," https://en.wikipedia.org/wiki/Belle_Knox#cite_note-CNN_name-16. In 2012, a *Hollywood Reporter* article stated that a female porn performer's earnings can range from eight hundred dollars for a sex scene

with another woman, one thousand dollars for a scene with a man, and up to four thousand dollars for more adventurous exploits.

Dan Miller, the executive editor of industry magazine *XBIZ*, told the newspaper that the most popular 250 women can expect to get regular work, filming between 100 and 150 scenes a year.

Agent Mark Spiegler said that the average earnings of female performers have halved from about $100,000 a year to $50,000 in the past decade, though the highest earners can take home $350,000.

2. "Hollywood Salaries Revealed, From Movie Stars to Agents (and Even Their Assistants)," https://www.hollywoodreporter.com/news/holly-wood-salaries-revealed-movie-stars-737321, October 2, 2014. See also footnote below (Helen Lawson article) for other averages reported in the industry, as well as trends.

3. Helen Lawson, "What makes 'pretty, good girls' pursue a career in porn? Director follows 16 actresses and discovers they 'like the power,'" https://www.dailymail.co.uk/news/article-2318212/What-makes-pretty-good-girls-pursue-career-porn-Director-follows-16-actresses-results-VERY-surprising.html, May 2, 2013. This also seems not to jibe with information from the *Hollywood Reporter*, above, which suggests that the average salary has gone down to $50,000. Regardless, the point is that salaries have decreased dramatically with time.

4. See generally, "Golden Age of Porn," https://en.wikipedia.org/wiki/Golden_Age_of_Porn#Films_of_the_period.

5. Mark Ward, "Web Porn—Just How Much Is Out There?" https://www.bbc.com/news/technology-23030090, July 1, 2103. This article underscores what any researcher attempting to quantify numbers no doubt has discovered: It is virtually impossible to even *estimate* the amount of porn sites and videos, let alone provide an actual figure. All we know is what anyone knows already; vastly more porn exist because of the internet, and that growth is accelerating at an exceptional rate.

6. Brian McCullough, "Chapter 6—A History of Porn," http://www.internethistorypodcast.com/2015/01/history-of-internet-porn/, January 4, 2015.

7. See generally, Russell Goldman, "Do It Yourself! Amateur Porn Stars Make Bank," https://abcnews.go.com/Business/SmallBiz/story?id=4151592&page=1.

8. "Amateur Pornography," https://en.wikipedia.org/wiki/Amateur_pornography#User-generated_online_content.

9. Ibid.

Chapter 11

1. C. S. Lewis, *Yours, Jack: Spiritual Direction from C. S. Lewis* (New York: HarperOne, 2008), 292–93.

2. https://en.wikipedia.org/wiki/Masturbate-a-thon

3. https://www.psychologytoday.com/us/blog/stress-and-sex/201401/touchy-subject-the-health-benefits-masturbation; see also, http://yourdost.com/blog/2016/11/masturbation.html?q=/blog/2016/11/masturbation.html&; https://www.health.com/sex/female-masturbation. However, see https://www.psychologytoday.com/us/blog/sex-life-the-american-male/201403/unacknowledged-harm-masturbation (indicating that masturbation leads to the "unacknowledged harm" of "paraphilias," which include pedophilia, sexual activity with a prepubescent child; exhibitionism, exposure of one's genitals to an unsuspecting stranger; frotteurism, touching and rubbing against a nonconsenting person; and transvestic fetishism, sexual arousal to cross-dressing, among many others that can become permanent once "hard-wired" through too much fantasy related to masturbatory activity. Specifically: "Each time a male masturbates to a paraphilic fantasy he further etches it into the hardwiring of his brain and increases the risk of future 'significant distress and impairment,' particularly regarding sexual functioning and satisfaction. Once a paraphilic interest has fully developed, it is almost impossible to ameliorate."

4. Sarah Wright, "Universities that Let Students Study their Own Major," https://study.com/articles/Universities_That_Let_Students_Create_Their_Own_Major.html, undated.

Chapter 12

1. Tammy Bruce, "Feminism 2.0," https://www.prageru.com/videos/feminism-20, February 10, 2014.

2. Centers for Disease Control and Prevention, "Marriage and Divorce," https://www.cdc.gov/nchs/fastats/marriage-divorce.htm, as updated March 17, 2017; see also, "Marriage and Divorce," https://www.apa.org/topics/divorce/, dated 2019, noting that the divorce rate for subsequent marriages is even higher.

3. Author unknown, "Venezuelan women refugees are 'forced to prostitute themselves for just $7 and sell locks of their hair to Colombians,'" https://www.msn.com/en-xl/latinamerica/top-stories/venezuelan-women-refugees-are-forced-to-prostitute-themselves-for-just-dollar7-and-sell-locks-of-their-hair-to-colombians/ar-BBRr5qQ?li=BBKxOg5, December 25, 2018.

4. "Sexual assault of migrants from Latin America to the United States," https://en.wikipedia.org/wiki/Sexual_assault_of_migrants_from_Latin_America_to_the_United_States.

5. Ibid.

6. David Agren, "Fearing Rape, Femal Migrants are Taking Birth Control Before Crossing the Border," https://www.foxnews.com/world/fearing-rape-female-migrants-are-taking-birth-control-before-crossing-the-border, updated January 11, 2017.

Chapter 13

1. Greg Burt, "Concerned parents speak out against graphic, discriminatory sex education curriculum in San Diego," https://californiafamily.org/2018/concerned-parents-speak-out-against-graphic-discriminatory-sex-education-curriculum-in-san-diego/, March 16, 2018.

2. Author unknown, "Parents Protest 'Graphic' Sex Ed Curriculum in California Schools," https://www.cbsnews.com/news/parents-protest-graphic-sex-ed-curriculum-changes-cupertino-california-schools/, March 30, 2017.

3. Tess Mullins, "It's Perfectly Normal: Classroom Sexual Abuse of Minors," https://www.remnantnewspaper.com/web/index.php/headline-news-around-the-world/item/4460-it-s-perfectly-normal-classroom-sexual-abuse-of-minors, May 7, 2019.

4. Rebecca Fredrichs, "SeXXX Ed in California Public Schools," https://www.youtube.com/watch?v=6jN4y44u5g0&feature=youtu.be&t=244&fbclid=IwAR1AlWNkkPvW6GP8HEX41RL0cfaIeVGJKEjuviUXqv5qK0HlZDwhYO56Ax4, May 21, 2019.

5. Ibid. See also Melissa Barnhart, "California Sex Ed Guidelines are 'Shocking,' and 'Medically Risky,' for Kids, Teachers Says," https://www.christianpost.com/news/californias-sex-ed-guidelines-shocking-medically-risky-for-kids-teacher-says.html, May 29, 2019.

6. Mullins, *op cit.*

7. Author unknown, *op cit.*

8. Mullins, *op cit.*

9. "Chicago Schools Are Teaching 'Safe' Anal Sex to Fifth Graders?" https://www.snopes.com/fact-check/binders-full-of-womens-condoms/, November 18, 2014.

Chapter 15

1. Maggie Astor, "No Children Because of Climate Change? Some People Are Considering It," https://www.nytimes.com/2018/02/05/climate/climate-change-children.html, February 5, 2018.

2. Arthur Neslen, "By 2030, We Will Pass The Point Where We Can Stop Runaway Climate Change," https://www.huffingtonpost.com/entry/runaway-climate-change-2030-report_us_5b8ecba3e4b0162f4727a09f, October 5, 2015. One congresswoman, Representative Alexandria Ocasio-Cortez (D-NY), proclaimed that we needed a bold "Green New Deal," which would more or less completely undo the world's economic structure. The cost as estimated by the congressional budget office? About $93 trillion. What it will actually do is unclear.

3. Virginia Hale, "UK Women Promote 'BirthStrike' Baby Ban to Prevent 'Eco-Armageddon,'" https://www.breitbart.com/europe/2019/03/07/uk-birth-ban-eco-armageddon/, March 7, 2019.

4. Ibid.

5. Astor, *op. cit.*

6. See, e.g, Marilyn Berger, "Suharto Dies at 86; Indonesian Dictator Brought Order and Bloodshed," https://www.nytimes.com/2008/01/28/world/asia/28suharto.html, January 28, 2008. See the legions of articles of course regarding Venezuela, a once wealthy nation that ultimately required its citizens under the dictator Maduro to line up for hours for bread and other supplies, and where average weight loss per citizen in one year (2017) was *24 pounds.* See https://www.reuters.com/article/us-venezuela-food/venezuelans-report-big-weight-losses-in-2017-as-hunger-hits-idUSKCN1G52HA. Starvation also happened throughout the Soviet Union and fascist Europe, to say nothing of the horrors in Africa, which, while rich in resources, suffer at the hand of controlling dictators who hoard whatever minor wealth there is. And let's not forget perhaps the most emblematic example, North Korea, especially in comparison to the well-fed families to its south, in South Korea.

7. See Mark Mather, "The Decline in U.S. Fertility," https://www.prb.org/us-fertility/, July 18, 2012; https://www.statista.com/statistics/718084/average-number-of-own-children-per-family/.

8. Zoya Gubernskaya, "Changing Attitudes Toward Marriage and Children in Six Countries," https://www.researchgate.net/publication/249984027_Changing_Attitudes_Toward_Marriage_and_Children_in_Six_Countries, June 2010.

9. Kathryn Vasel, "It costs $233,610 to raise a child," https://money.cnn.com/2017/01/09/pf/cost-of-raising-a-child-2015/index.html, January 9, 2017.

10. "Special report: The aging, childless future," https://apple.news/Ar0WtXXDDQxiEID9QOpQ0lw, December 18, 2018.

11. "Fertility Rate by Country 2019," http://worldpopulationreview.com/countries/total-fertility-rate/.

12. Ben Westcott, "China moves to end two-child limit, finishing decades of family planning," https://www.cnn.com/2018/08/28/asia/china-family-planning-one-child-intl/index.html, August 29, 2018.

13. William Widmer, "Would Human Extinction Be a Tragedy?" https://www.nytimes.com/2018/12/17/opinion/human-extinction-climate-change.html, December 17, 2018. There are ample other similar examples of suicidal approaches to humanity.

14. Kashmira Gander, "Antinatialism: The People who Think the World is Better Off if Humans Didn't Exist," https://www.independent.co.uk/lifestyle/antinatalism-people-think-world-earth-better-off-if-humans-not-exist-humankind-extinct-a7565591.html, February 7, 2017.

15. Geeta Pandey, "Indian man to sue parents for giving birth to him," https://www.bbc.com/news/world-asia-india-47154287, February 7, 2019.

16. Ibid.

17. Griff Witte, "Hungary is so desperate for kids that mothers of four won't need to pay income tax," https://www.washingtonpost.com/world/

europe/hungary-is-so-desperate-for-kids-mothers-of-four-wont-pay-income-tax/2019/02/11/04701764-2e01-11e9-ac6c-14eea99d5e24_story.html?utm_term=.ec7da5b4c148, February 11, 2018.

Chapter 16

1. Dennis Romero, "New Law Says Employers Can't Ask Applicants About Criminal Past," https://www.laweekly.com/news/new-california-prohibits-employers-from-asking-applicants-about-criminal-past-8760230, October 17, 2017.

2. "New York City Aims to Stop Hairstyle Discrimination," https://www.washingtonpost.com/national/new-york-city-aims-to-stop-hairstyle-discrimination/2019/02/18/ff3a464c-339c-11e9-8375-e3dcf6b68558_story.html?utm_term=.571d3b127dc9, February 18, 2019.

3. Ron Miller, "Technology Can't Replace the Human Touch," https://techcrunch.com/2017/01/15/technology-cant-replace-the-human-touch/, undated, circa 2017.

4. Ibid.

5. Author unknown, "Mizzou Official: Tall Man Asking Short Woman Out Could Be Considered 'Sexual Harassment,'" https://abcstlouis.com/news/local/mizzou-official-tall-man-asking-short-woman-out-could-be-considered-sexual-misconduct, December 28, 2018. There, school officials at the University of Missouri suspended a male student for asking a girl out—no threats, no intimidation. Their reasoning? He was guilty of sexual harassment "because his size and gender gave him 'power' over a female he pursued romantically."

6. Nancy Levit, Robert R. M. Verchick, *A Feminist Legal Primer* (New York University Press 2006), 203.

7. This started from the somewhat notorious 2011 "Dear Colleague" letter from the Obama administration, which gave a new directive to universities regarding how to handle sexual harassment on campuses, which campuses widely embraced. For background to the matter and its application, see generally, Emily Yoffe, "The Uncomfortable Truth About Campus Rape Policy," https://www.theatlantic.com/education/archive/2017/09/the-uncomfortable-truth-about-campus-rape-policy/538974/, September 26, 2017.

8. Courtney Connley, "60% of male managers now say they're uncomfortable participating in work activities with women," https://www.cnbc.com/2019/05/17/60percent-of-male-managers-now-say-theyre-uncomfortable-mentoring-women.html, May 17, 2019.

Chapter 17

1. "What diseases are subject to Federal isolation and quarantine law?" https://www.google.com/search?q=diseases+that+need+to+be+quarantined&oq=diseases+that+need+t&aqs=chrome.5.69i57j0l5.6657j0j4&sourceid=chrome&ie=UTF-8, updated September 4, 2009.

2. Sexually Transmitted Disease Surveillance 2017, https://www.cdc
.gov/std/stats17/2017-STD-Surveillance-Report_CDC-clearance-9.10.18
.pdf, pp 28, 57ff. Note that the focus of this study is on "reportable" sexually
transmitted diseases, specifically chlamydia, gonorrhea, syphilis, and chan-
croid. There is reference to HIV but somewhat in the background. Regardless,
the obvious does come out: men who have sex with men are far more likely
to test positive for HIV. Likewise the reason: "The relatively high incidence
of STD infection among MSM may be related to multiple factors, including
individual behaviors and sexual network characteristics. The number of
lifetime or recent sex partners, rate of partner exchange, and frequency of
condomless sex each influence an individual's probability of exposure to
STDs," 28. However, it tries to point to other factors, "such as high prevalence
of STDs, interconnectedness and concurrency of sex partners, and possibly
limited access to healthcare also affect the risk of acquiring an STD. Further-
more, experiences of stigma—verbal harassment, discrimination, or physical
assault based on attraction to men—are associated with increased sexual risk
behavior among MSM," id.

The latter categories' explanations seem a bit far-fetched—a wishful
thinking attempt to blame the exposure to HIV (and other STDs, for that matter) on "society," and less on the sexual activity itself. There is no assignment
of the percentage, for example, of men who acquired HIV because of these social avoidance issues, let alone the causation. The article also fails to articulate
how, even if there were no social stigma (which the report fails to quantify in
any event), greater access to healthcare might have avoided their HIV+ status.

Fascinatingly, this report barely mentions the specific kind of sexual
penetration that most likely leads to acquiring the HIV virus: anal sex. There
is scant mention of the phrase "anal sex" or "anal intercourse." It only refers
elliptically to "men who have sex with men." Why does the report dance
around these words?

3. "STDs and HIV—CDC Fact Sheet," https://www.cdc.gov/std/hiv/
stdfact-std-hiv.htm, last reviewed December 16, 2014.

Chapter 18

1. "Sexually transmitted infections increasing—250 million new
infections annually," https://www.ncbi.nlm.nih.gov/pubmed/12316765,
December, 1990. Note that the 357 million figure was an estimated extrapo-
lation I made from the 250 million new STD cases in the report, which was
published in 1990. Given the approximately thirty years that transpired
since 1990, I added an additional 100 million as a reasonable estimate in
light of a variety of factors, including population growth in the past thirty
years, plus the clearly growing acceptance of sex for sex's sake and the rise
of Tinder and other similar hookup apps. It also was consistent with later
reports, e.g. below.

2. World Health Organization, "Sexually Transmitted Infections (STIs)," https://www.who.int/news-room/fact-sheets/detail/sexually-transmitted-infections-(stis), February 28, 2019.

3. Ibid.

4. Brendan O'Neill, "The Exploitation of Aids," https://www.theguardian.com/commentisfree/2008/jun/12/aids.health, June 12, 2008.

5. Mikal Gilmore, "Queen's Tragic Rhapsody," https://www.rollingstone.com/music/music-news/queens-tragic-rhapsody-234996/, July 7, 2014.

6. Brian Alexander, "Free Love: Was There a Price to Pay?" http://www.nbcnews.com/id/19053382/ns/health-sexual_health/t/free-love-was-there-price-pay/#.XBg2ERNKjOQ, June 22, 2007.

7. Macaela Mackenzie, "Seven Ways Monogamy Makes You Healthier," https://www.shape.com/lifestyle/sex-and-love/7-ways-monogamy-makes-you-healthier, October 14, 2015.

8. At best, the CDC recognizes that "long-term monogamy" will likely *reduce* the chance of contracting STDs, https://www.cdc.gov/std/prevention/default.htm. That is fine but stops short of what it should be doing: actually *advocating* monogamy.

9. "Monogamy and the immune system: Differences in sexual behavior impact bacteria hosted and genes that control immunity," https://www.sciencedaily.com/releases/2012/08/120830141405.htm, August 30, 2012; see also, Marc Winn, "Is Monogamy Bad for Your Health?," http://theviewinside.me/is-monogamy-bad-for-your-health/, April 15, 2015.

10. With kudos and apologies to Principal Seymour Skinner from *The Simpsons*, from the episode "Girls Just Want to Have Sums," first aired April 30, 2006.

Conclusion

1. Barry Neild, "What it's like to eat at Bunyadi, London's naked restaurant," https://www.cnn.com/travel/article/what-its-like-in-naked-restaurant-bunyadi-london-food/index.html, June 15, 2016; see also, Ben Norum, "Naked Rooftop Bar Launches in London . . . Sort of," https://www.standard.co.uk/go/london/bars/naked-rooftop-bar-launches-in-london-sort-of-a3316361.html, August 10, 2016.

2. David Rivers, "Naked Protesters Storm Parliament Ahead of Brexit Vote," https://www.dailystar.co.uk/news/latest-news/769282/naked-protesters-parliament-brexit-news-house-of-commons-mps-vote, April 2, 2019.

3. Cecilia Rodriguez, "Eating Nude: Why Naked Restaurants are not Good Business . . . Yet," https://www.forbes.com/sites/ceciliarodriguez/2019/01/13/eating-nude-why-naked-restaurants-are-not-good-business-yet/#690575531a42, January 13, 2019.

4. "Sexbots: Love Them or Hate Them—They are Coming," https://www.richardvanhooijdonk.com/en/blog/sexbots-love-them-or-hate-them-they-are-coming/, June 30, 2016. When polling people generally (men and women),

four out of ten admit they would want sex with a robot. Allen Pike, "This is How Many People Actually Want to Have Sex with Robots," https://www. menshealth.com.au/four-in-ten-americans-want-to-have-sex-with-a-robot, May 7, 2018. Men are also twenty-one percent more likely to say they would have sex with a robot. Sixteen percent of the 2,000 Americans studied would even prefer to have sex with a robot than a real human. Some would even rather date a robot, with thirteen percent saying they'd prefer a relationship with a robot than a human. Author unknown, April 27, 2018, "40% of Americans Would Have Sex with A Robot, Study Finds," https://www.swnsdigital .com/2018/04/40-of-americans-would-have-sex-with-a-robot-study-finds/

5. See https://me.me/i/crossfit-jesus-rollins-sladeseye-me-waiting-on -my-sex-robot-20356905. Some women might even embrace the arrival of sex robots because they will weed out the men who would go for that sort of thing and leave the good men for the real women. Barbara Ellen, "Female sex robots, feel free to replace us if you want to," https://www.theguardian.com/commentisfree/2017/dec/03/ sex-robots-technology-women-artificial-intelligence.

6. Morgan Reardon, "The Willy is Incredibly Lifelike," https://www .thesun.co.uk/living/2605288/westworld-humans-robots-coming-rise-sex- machine/, January 15, 2017.

Made in the USA
San Bernardino, CA
16 November 2019